WEBS AND WARDROBES

Humanist and Religious
World Views in
Children's Literature

Joseph O'Beirne Milner
Wake Forest University

Lucy Floyd Morcock Milner
North Carolina Governor's School

UNIVERSITY
PRESS OF
AMERICA

Lanham • New York • London

Copyright © 1987 by

University Press of America,® Inc.

4720 Boston Way
Lanham, MD 20706

3 Henrietta Street
London WC2E 8LU England

British Cataloging in Publication Information Available

Library of Congress Cataloging-in-Publication Data

Webs and wardrobes.

Bibliography: p.
Includes index.

1. Children's literature—History and criticism.
2. Humanism in literature. 3. Theism in literature.
I. Milner, Joseph O'Beirne, 1937– . II. Milner,
Lucy Floyd Morcock, 1941– . III. University Press
of America.
PN1009.AlW36   1987   809'.89282   87-14800
ISBN 0-8191-6545-X (alk. paper)
ISBN 0-8191-6546-8 (pbk. : alk. paper)

All University Press of America books are produced on acid-free
paper which exceeds the minimum standards set by the National
Historical Publication and Records Commission.

To our parents -
      teachers -
      children -
      students -
who instilled in us a delight in
and seriousness about literature,
religion, and humanity.

ACKNOWLEDGEMENTS

Such an acknowledgment can only hint at the debt we owe the many individuals who contributed to the completion of this book. Rosa Ann Moore gave her impetus in moving the original ideas to essays. Betty Veach contributed her inestimable gifts of patience, good humor, and uncommon sense to the oversight of every stage of the production. Wake Forest University staff and students assisted her with the many steps by which the manuscript moved through typing, formating, proofing, and indexing to final collection. Particular thanks are due Janet Berry, Danielle Bordeaux, Sherry Buckalew, Audrey Carr, and Diedra Murphy. Xu Di of Peking University lent final assistance to the production with intelligence and indefatigable energy and spirit. To all those named and unnamed, we express our sincerest thanks.

TABLE OF CONTENTS

PART V Beyond and Before Polarities

PREFACE

After reading and rereading two children's classics, *Charlotte's Web* and *The Lion, the Witch and the Wardrobe* to our three children and for our Children's Literature students, we were struck by what fundamentally different perspectives these two equally winsome books posed. A more deliberate stocktaking revealed even sharper differences and led to an essay, the first section of this book, defining those differences. We found that the books expressed the crucial division between a humanistic and a religious world view. That dichotomy represented a difference so basic and significant, we felt it warranted exploring in other children's literature. Recent events in our culture have given strength to that idea.

Edmond Fuller in *Modern Man in Fiction* argues for the importance of recognizing the departure of much late nineteenth and twentieth-century literature from the "vast, centuries-old accretion of our literary heritage . . . based on the premise that there is a God." Man, "seen within this vast, varied, but basically consistent tradition is individual, responsible, guilty, redeemable." Fuller has noted that the modern "canon of critical values" which evaluates and promotes literature and thus influences creators and readers is one that provides a corrupted and debased image of man. That image is not in keeping with Judeo-Christian "tradition, which still primarily influences our moral and ethical thought, and [which] has not become in any way obsolete, though we might be led to think so by dwelling long in the inner worlds of certain of our writers." In response to this trend, Fuller proposes that "at least one part of the critic's task is to appraise the validity and the implications of the image of man projected by the artist's use of his materials."

In contrast, Sheila Schartz has written thoughtfully in acknowledgement and affirmation of a more secular view of man in *Teaching Adolescent Literature: A Humanistic Approach*. A recent Slate newsletter of National Council of Teachers of English (NCTE) offered a brisk rationale for this more secular, humanistic approach:

> Its [humanism's] function has been to provide concerned human beings with an acceptable alternative to the traditional religious imperatives which are rooted in supernaturalism, mysticism, and miraculism. Humanism offers the reasoned view that human beings alone shape their own destinies, leaving to scientific inquiry the probing of nature's unknowns in the endless search for truths, knowledge, and facts.

Although Fuller and others would reject the pejorative suggestion about the roots of religion and humanism's simple reliance on reason, such a clear and dispassionate posing of the polarities is rare. The gap between the two camps is widening, the positions are becoming more rigidified, the arguments more polemic.

The *Pro Family Forum, Moral Majority, Eagle Forum* and others have one-dimensionalized and reduced Fuller's position. The American Library Association, Association for Supervision and Curriculum Development (ASCD), National Council of Teachers of English, and others have mustered their defenses against these strident attacks with antagonism of their own. Newsletters from ASCD, NCTE and others have featured articles on the censorship and "secular humanism" issues to warn their members against the intimidating tactics of the religious dogmatists. The more intense the battle, the more caricatured the perception of the opposing view. Religionists flood parents and educators with pamphlets such as "Is Humanism Molesting Your Child?" and films like "Let Their Eyes Be Opened." Humanists, though perhaps less zealous or dogmatic, often evidence a smug disregard for those who champion ideals and metaphysical propositions which they consider quaint.

A great need, then, arises for one volume to comprehend both views at once, to embrace the opposites rather than further advance the polemics. The essays collected in *Webs and Wardrobes: Humanist and Religious World Views in Children's Literature* attempt to explore the expression of both views in literature written for the young through deliberate scholarship and reflective interpretation. After an introductory and definitive essay, the volume divides into four sections which look at an exclusively humanistic view, an exclusively religious perspective, a polar or split posture, and a supra- or post-categorical view. The editors have written brief statements before each chapter to mark connections between chapters and sections and to introduce the essays.

While, clearly, the editorial intent is to enhance the reader's awareness of the deeper messages in children's books, three other important benefits might accrue from the essays of this volume. We believe the essays also 1) deepen an understanding of individual books and authors, 2) sharpen the perception of the function of literature in the lives of children, and 3) broaden acquaintance with a wide range of children's literature. That range encompasses nineteenth-century as well as contemporary literature, American and British, as well as international, and children's, preadolescent, and adolescent fiction. (A bibiography cross-references book titles with the chapters in which they are discussed.) The treatment of this volume's basic intent, the critical analysis of secular humanistic or religious world views in children's literature, is as varied as the contributing authors. Some offer classic literary scholarship examining connections between the authors' social or familial milieu, literary paradigms, cultural movements, and their fiction; others explore psychological phenomena triggered by the child's encounter with literature; others provide close and sensitive "new critic's" readings of the individual texts. We hope this diversity will lead anyone interested in literature written for and read by and to the young -- parents, teachers, librarians, students of children's literature -- to a quickened awareness of and a heightened tolerance for the deep messages at the heart of children's books.

Joseph O'Beirne Milner
Lucy Floyd Morcock Milner

Winston-Salem, North Carolina
October, 1986

PART I WORLD VIEW IN CHILDREN'S LITERATURE

1

WHEN WORLDS COLLIDE
THE HUMANIST-RELIGIOUS ETHOS IN CHILDREN'S LITERATURE

Joseph O'Beirne Milner

In an editorial supporting the Right To Life movement, James Buckley recently referred to a California medical ethics bulletin whose defense of euthanasia and abortion dramatizes the battle lines which have been drawn between those who follow the old ethic rooted in Judeo-Christian belief and those who ascribe to the new ethic anchored in man-centered humanism. Susan Sontag has pointed to this same split (though for opposing reasons) in *Against Interpretation*, and the schism has been the continuing concern of neo-orthodox theologians, philosophers of science, and popularizers like the secularist Jacob Bronowski. For these and other wide-ranging minds, the struggle between the rational, ethical, man-centered style of the humanist and the mystical, supernatural, faith-centered life of the religious man has occupied center stage.

One might have supposed that such Weltanschauung games would never have been played on the fresh turf of children's literature, but the contest is clearly underway. Sheila Schwartz, in an article in *The Humanist* (January, 1976), shows she has recognized the clash and has entered it in championing the cause of the new ethic in a polemic which celebrates the new adolescent novel for serving the "humanistic function" of making the world "more knowable to young people." And though her salvos have only been vaguely directed at those she refers to as the religious "crazies" from Kanaway County and North Dakota, her consciousness of the fray is apparent. Madelein L'Engle's editors must also be aware of the fracas, for they chose to include on the dust cover of *Circle of Quiet* the fact that she is a "practicing Christian."

If, in looking at the field of children's literature, we take on this humanist-religious mind set, we become aware of the dichotomies that pervade all genres of literature. We have two sorts of mysteries: the puzzle mystery (humanist) like *Encyclopedia Brown*, which always promises us a cognitive solution, and the true mystery (religious) like Boston's *Green Knowe* books with their confounding situations. In nature stories which center on a nostalgia for the land, we find very different world views: celebration of man's cohabiting with nature like Donavan's *Wild In the World* (humanist), and Peck's *A Day No Pigs Would Die*, which speaks of man's stewardship and domination of a divinely created world (religious). These same kinds of dichotomies can be found in fantasy, ethnic, realistic, and science fiction, and other genres.

1

These oppositions are perhaps most clearly revealed in two favorite pieces of children's literature, E.B. White's *Charlotte's Web* and C.S. Lewis' *The Lion, the Witch and the Wardrobe*. They not only clarify the differences between these contending world views, but also heighten our appreciation of these two powerful books. A careful look at them reveals the disparate sources from which their power is drawn. Three points of clear demarcation between two contrasting worlds are apparent: presentation of other worlds, mode of characterization, and sense of death and transformation.

Presentation of Other Worlds

Clear differences emerge readily in White's and Lewis' presentation of other worlds in *Charlotte's Web* and *The Lion, the Witch and the Wardrobe*. The creation of these worlds, the manner in which they are entered, the separateness of the old world and the other world, and the attitude toward the departure and return of the old world are all remarkable and significant.

It is evident that White is clearly interested not only in the notion of separate worlds, but also in their oneness. Spots of time exist in which Fern is wholly in the world of family and friends, even though these times are relatively rare in the course of the book. At other times she is so wholly immersed in the world of Charlotte's web that Wilbur and the barnyard exist with or without Fern's consciousness. Nevertheless, it is apparent that this other world takes shape only in her imagination and, without Fern's imagination, exists only as fat rats, uneven webs, and loud geese.

Thus we see that though the birth of Charlotte's children and Wilbur's stay of execution have made a perpetuation of the story possible, it must end because Fern, like Puff the Magic Dragon's creator, Jackie, has entered the world of Henry Fussy's ferris wheel. Such a barnyard world is sparkling and bright as long as the childlike imagination can nurture it, but it becomes insubstantial without such human generative power. This power, of course, is exactly what White is hoping to kindle or keep alive in his readers, so that they may raise the curtain on more numerous fantasy shows of their own.

Through the wardrobe, Lewis' children enter the land which is a permanent fixture, although it is sometimes open to them and at other moments barred from their vision. Accessibility and existence are clearly different matters. The land of Narnia is neither of Lucy's making nor is it a vision shared solely by the four children. It has, in Lewis' perspective, a substance which endures and which is impervious to time's onslaughts.

Secondly, the matter of entrance is a point of differentiation; although in *Charlotte's Web* the access to this world lies in Fern's hands, this is not true of Lewis' world. Because the transformed barnyard world is the product of Fern's imagination, willing suspension of disbelief is necessarily the result of inner environment. Thus, though Fern has some power over her stay in the world of noble animal gestures, Lewis' children have none. At times the passageway is open and inviting; at other times the firm wooden back of the wardrobe is solid and immovable. The children grope and stumble their way into the magic kingdom when access is permitted. Entrance is not, as it is in Fern's case, a result of the children's attitudes. Although Edmund, skeptical and rational, thinks Lucy's account of Narnia is "all nonsense," while Lucy is more open and accepting, both are given passage to this new world.

The separateness or division between the two worlds is the third significant point of differentiation. Fern and the reader become entangled in the world of Charlotte's terrific web, but the animal talk and the life-saving spinning are always superimposed on the fabric of everyday barnyard smells and sounds. The imagination always transforms the reality to new heights, but the dreams are made of the soft earth. And though Fern can become almost wholly absorbed in that world, she does answer familial calls from the old world. In contrast, the Narnia world is separate and unrecognized in the world on the near side of the wardrobe. Though Lucy is persecuted by Edmund for holding fast to that "nonsense," both of them, for distinctly different reasons, remain believers during their stay at the professor's house with Peter and Susan. Once in that other kingdom for a lengthy period, they forget the world left behind. Only by "chance" do they ever venture out of Narnia; nothing in their own dispositions lead them to the decision to return.

Of final significance is the attitude directly expressed or implied toward the departure from these other worlds. In Fern's case we sense the wisdom of her mother who suggests that some day an end will come to the barnyard reveries. We seem to be told that this is a part of the natural process, that growth and development demand Fern's putting aside childish ways. Henry Fussy has come for her as inevitably as did Emily Dickinson's caller in "Because I Could Not Stop For Death." There is neither wailing nor lament, nor is there prospect for her return to this golden age. Fern has matured in this respect just as Wilbur has changed from self-centeredness to compassion. When the once-royal quartet tumbles out of the wardrobe, they, the wise professor, and the reader know they will be in that realm many times more.

So in all four aspects of this major difference between White's and Lewis' visions, it is clear that a serious philosophical difference separates and distinguishes their dramatizations. The humanist world feels that imagination is the "necessary angel" which has had to hold the ground left by faltering religion in a world of science. From this perspective, the creation of other worlds is wholly human, dependent on nothing outside of man. Lewis' religious perspective is in every respect different. It argues for the solidity of this other world, one which is in no way dependent on man for its existence. It is, moreover, a world that (in orthodox Christian theology) we are bid into rather than one entered into through the sheer force of will. Once entered, this other world becomes *the* world and, even if left for a time, continues to exist in a compelling way for its former visitors.

Mode of Characterization

White's and Lewis' mode of characterization is heavily influenced by their clearly different perspectives on man. White fills Zuckerman's barnyard with a spectrum of characters. Idiosyncrasies and foibles are mixed with virtues and graces so that characters do not give the impression of being on the side of either evil or righteousness. Templeton is a pretty bad sort, worse than the rest, but with the proper incentives, he can work for the good cause. Charlotte seems almost too airy to be mortal, yet she has her officious and pretentious side. All of them are accepted for what they are. If one had to stretch them out from bad to good they would scatter evenly across a spectrum rather than bunching up at one end or the other. (This could be said as well of the "real" people in White's book.) If they did bunch anywhere, it would be at the center.

Lewis' Narnia folk are not so arranged. The goats and sheep are clearly separated. The workers of evil are under full control of the White Witch and cannot help but serve her hellish ends. The good folk are just as clearly good, even under threat of her spiteful power. In the face of the awful power and sacrifice of King Aslan, the evil ones revile him, spring on his helpless, bound form and pummel him to death. The Beavers stand on the side of good, though they are fully aware that their home and their lives are endangered. Even the four children are set apart as good and bad, with Edmund's state being clearly marked by the separation from the other three and the followers of Aslan.

In definition of character clear differences also emerge. For White's characters there is a humanistic sense of growth or development as in Wilbur's movement from an egocentric, whining young shoat to an empathetic, mature pig whose noble gesture gives Charlotte new life in the barnyard. This steady growth is clearly the product of his own striving, the tutoring of his wise mentor Charlotte, and a little help from his friends. Wilbur's plodding slowly toward his pig potential has White's total affirmation. It is a model of what man in community can achieve.

Lewis develops characters fully but does not celebrate gradual change and growth and the power of human change agents as does White. Pauline conversions and superordinate interventions are the rule in the kingdom of Narnia. Though he has been brought into the camp of Aslan, Edmund retains his basic personality when he becomes King Edmund. Most of the other figures do not move at all, but grow older within the character mold already portrayed in the early moments of the tale. They stride the stage much more like morality play figures than members of a contemporary psychological drama.

The lead characters in the two stories offer an exaggerated extension of this same contrast. Appropriately, Wilbur is more like the modern anti-hero in that he is not asked to transcend his personality wholly in his noble gesture at the fair, and he does not grow to enormous heroic proportions in the book. A touch of self-satisfaction is demonstrated in his desire to bring Charlotte's progeny back to the barnyard, for they would perpetuate his beloved friend wherever they spring forth. Aslan and his gift of self are of another magnitude or dimension. He is beyond heroics; he gives all for the needy but undeserving. A measure of the difference is found in the fact that a reader can identify with Wilbur and his care, while he is only able to respond to Aslan in astonishment and awe.

An adjunct of this same point of contrast is the terrible burden of responsibility for self-definition and meaning making which is placed on Wilbur and his friends and which Lewis' four children and their cohorts do not bear. For Wilbur it is a happy burden in which he is daily forestalling death, but there is no essence or overarching construct of which he is conscious or to which he is committed. Lewis' quartet in contrast are, like Moses, not up to the assigned task. They cannot rely on their own maturation or on any help that their friends might give. Though Mr. Tumnus and the Beavers come to the children's aid in a most admirable way, their efforts are wholly futile and would end in utter failure but for the intervention of Aslan. Only his gifts offer the children sufficient strength for the mighty foray with the forces of evil.

In a broad view of the two writers' use of character then, we see in White the humanistic tendency to see life as an array of forces and folk neither wholly malevolent nor beneficent, but spotty mixes of a very mortal kind. Even his heroes are just plain folk, occasionally able to rise to the noble gesture. Lewis presents life as a painful struggle between good and evil. Ironically though, his good folk are not self-sustaining or self-directed, but must look to higher sources for strength to endure against the satanic forces.

The final ground of difference is perhaps the most significant: Death and Transformation. What death represents to the peoples of White's and Lewis' worlds and how that knowledge moves them sets these authors in two distinct camps. Death is a finality with which White's characters must grapple. Charlotte seems to have a good understanding of the cycle of nature and, sensing her death, prepares for it. She constructs her egg sac and even spins one last life-preserving web for Wilbur, knowing that those life-giving acts are depleting her own strength. Wilbur is much less able to cope with the dominion of death through the early months of his existence. He crumples under the withering news from the sheep that his fattening period has an all-too-dreadful purpose. The mechanism which makes the whole tale proceed is, in fact, the desire to forestall Wilbur's fate. Lewis' characters do not have this same consciousness or dread of death. They seem to quail at the evil of the White Witch rather than at the death blow her wand can land. They seem to take comfort that death shall have no dominion because of the assurance that Aslan is coming. The reader, too, admires the courage of Mr. Tumnus and the Beavers but knows that they *must* work for good and so has no real fear for their ultimate fate. Lewis makes the frozen, statuary death of the White Witch's victims seem less than permanent; what is frozen can always be thawed.

Transformations and perpetuations are the stuff of White's world while thaws and reconstitutions are the core of Lewis' way. Here lies the most telling distinction between the two writers. Wilbur and the reader are offered solace in the ongoing essence of Charlotte in the five-hundred-odd newborns that Wilbur awaits so longingly and greets so lovingly. Wilbur himself is a part of Charlotte's eternal life in that he carries her memory and, even more essentially, replicates in his loving gesture, the most basic character of their relationship. This very human perpetuation and the prospect that Charlotte is, in the decay of death, returning to a more fundamental relationship with the eternal quality of Nature, are the best hopes White offers for a life beyond life. Lewis offers something else. Aslan gives himself up to a very real and grisly death and yet, as the essential Aslan, overcomes those bonds of nature. After his reconstitution, the full new life which was hinted at by the thawing snow is given to all of his followers. Life stands against death; evil is sundered. Tumnus lives to fight again and the other unfrozen lion stands by Aslan's side exuberant to be one of "Us Lions."

So the two books stand as mighty opposites in philosophical or theological perspective. Both are truly fine children's books, but each can be made the more powerful when harnessed in tandem with the other. For whether children or any other readers consciously articulate the fundamental differences presented in these two tales or merely intuit them, they will grasp their reality all the more fully when they can perceive them in the way Niels Bohr saw the complementarity of the sub-atomic world which underlies the reality in which both books reside (Walter Heisenberg, *Physics and Philosophy: The Revolution in Modern Science*). Those readers who apprehend reality wholly, as does White, need also to comprehend that reality which Lewis presents so beautifully and those who are clearly satisfied with the transcendence of Aslan's kingdom, need to be pulled back into the sweet smelling dung of Wilbur's world.

Part II THE HUMANIST CASE

2

FROM SALINGER TO CORMIER: DISILLUSIONMENT TO DESPAIR
IN THIRTY YEARS

Rebecca Lukens

Luken's essay opens the exploration of the humanist case, not because of its broad overview, but because it presents the nature of the contemporary secular world of adolescent fiction in such stark terms. Essentially, she contrasts J.D. Salinger's *Catcher in the Rye* with three novels by Robert Cormier. If Holden Caulfield reflects Erik Erickson's definition of the tension of adolescence, he nevertheless finds his identity in a disllusioned world through faith in himself. Cormier's characters do not arrive at any such affirmation; their worlds are evil, even the best motives are questionable and ultimately destructive. The thirty years between Salinger and Cormier have seen humanism's disllusionment with traditional institutions and its subsequent despair.

FROM SALINGER TO CORMIER: DISILLUSIONMENT TO DESPAIR
IN THIRTY YEARS

Some years ago, 1951 to be exact, *The Catcher in the Rye* took reading Americans by surprise. The book said what adolescents were feeling, and what they thought no one knew but themselves: "Surely," adolescents thought, "no adult can put into words our anxiety about our most intimate concerns. Furthermore, my concerns aren't quite like other people's. No one else is as troubled as I." But J.D. Salinger caught them all, all those anxieties and uncertainties. As if he had taken Erik Erikson's *Identity: Youth and Crisis* for his text, Salinger put his finger and his pen upon the conflict between idealism and realism, between hope and disillusionment. Chronicling the quest of Holden Caulfield for people and experience that could verify his most optimistic wishes, Salinger shows Holden's growing disappointment as he finds many of his idols standing upon feet of clay. And yet Salinger's hero, although he writes from a sanitarium, becomes a realist. Many of his idols have fallen, and his quest for perfection has left him with only ten-year-old Phoebe whose innocence is still inviolate. But Holden will work himself out of his depression; by novel's end he is rising from it. His self-told story shows that within himself are the seeds of good. If there are others like him -- and his millions of readers over thirty-five years prove that there are -- the world cannot be all bad.

Robert Cormier, on the other hand, begins from quite another premise. The world is rotten: the honest people flee; those who remain are corrupt; the government is ineffectual but controlling; organized violence is ubiquitous. There is no hope. Between 1951 and 1974 the world-view in popular literature flipped; the realistic *bildungsroman* of 1951 showing youth's awakening awareness of evil has given way to another world view in which the pervasive forces of the unseen and the sinister are in control. Hope is gone; despair remains.

Look first at Holden's story. Incident after incident and character after character come into Holden's three-day account of his dismissal from Pencey Prep and his clandestine return home. The byword for his recounting these incidents is "phony." He decries phoniness wherever he finds it, expressing in his earliest utterances his disappointment in his brother's selling out to Hollywood. Big brother D.B., writer of great stories, admirer of Ring Lardner's tender-tough little tales, is writing for the most depraved of institutions. Holden sees the phoniness in the school principal who talks to parents of rich kids and ignores those with rumpled suits and corny shoes.

Yet Salinger depicts more than Holden's sense of the discrepancy between the genuine and the fraudulent. Holden is also caught in his own contradictions between his critical perception and his instinctive compassion. Although Stradlater "gives girls the time" in the back seats of cars, Holden mixes disappointment and scorn for him with genuine generosity tinged with envy. Holden dislikes pimply neighbor Ackley who disturbs his personal possessions and stinks up the room with unwashed socks. And yet Holden senses Ackley's loneliness and invites him to the movies. Holden admits he's sexy and dreams of girls, but always stops at their "no's." He wants sexual experience in preparation for marriage, but he wants the purity of his admired Jane Gallagher to remain untarnished. He thinks an encounter with a prostitute would be useful, and yet a prostitute no older than himself who wears freshly cleaned frocks and doesn't smoke or drink saddens him. Holden is kind to his teacher, bent and dedicated Old Spencer, visiting him in his illness. When he seeks refuge with Antolini in New York, he fears that Antolini's tender touch is that of a homosexual, but he admires Mr. Antolini for caring about the student who jumped out of the dorm window, and for caring about what happened to Holden. He dislikes the towel flicking kid whose mother he meets on the train, and yet he gives her what he knows she would like to hear, "Your son's great, the best choice for class president." Sally Hayes is a fake, too; she seeks out the theatre-goers from the right schools and turns on a fraudulent charm. And yet Holden suggests that together they get away from the corrupt world and live in the virgin wilderness. He calls the elderly bellboy in the hotel a pimp, which he is, and yet he worries about how he can live on small tips, a bellboy all his life. He sneers at the extravagent mechanical Christmas pageant of the Baby Jesus at Radio City, and yet remembers with tenderness the drummer in the orchestra there as well as the real message of a humble Jesus. Often Holden's contradictions are borne out of the tension between his critical perception and his instinctive compassion. Holden talks at length with the nuns in Grand Central Station, worries about how hard it must be for them to read about seductive Eustacia Vye and the heated passion of Romeo and Juliet, then gives them a donation in case they ever need one. He never speaks ill of his parents, but sees them as loving and bumbling, his mother "nervous" after Allie's death, and his father growing too wealthy by honest work.

It is Phoebe alive, like Allie dead, that gives Holden hope for the world. Phoebe, being young, is as yet uncorrupted. Allie having died young, will never be corrupted. Because he finds the discovery of imperfection so painful and disillusioning, he would keep the young innocent forever. Holden wants to be "the catcher in the rye," catching all of the roller-skating or museum-going children before they fall over the cliff into disillusionment.

Salinger speaks to adolescents in a way that is realistic and yet hopeful. His humor softens the discoveries of one human imperfection after another. His recognition of adolescent temptations and distractions keeps his story believable. Disillusionment, it seems, can coexist with tenderness and concern. Adjustments can be made to reality. Even the wounded can be compassionate and survive.

"They murdered him." So opens Robert Cormier's The Chocolate War (Dell, 1974). The setting is the football field where Jerry, being tested by a vicious coach, endures attacks to knees, stomach and head, a brutal battering without a helmet. We are immediately plunged into a world of physical brutality perpetrated by adults. Psychological brutality is the domain of Brother Leon who not only beats, but humiliates his pupils. He appeals to honest Caroni to become an informer about the chocolate war, then he threatens him. Caroni who wants his legitimate "A," questions, "Were teachers as corrupt as the villains you read about in books or saw in movies and television?"(p. 85). Two pages later, when he gives in to his teacher for the sake of his grades, Caroni becomes the informer. "And he did see--that life was rotten, that there were no heroes, really, and that you couldn't trust anybody, not even yourself" (p. 87). Organized brutality is the domain of The Vigils, fellow students who force Goober to dismantle the classroom so that its furniture crashes to the floor and the shock sends Brother Eugene to a mental hospital. When The Vigils credit Goober with fifty boxes of chocolate he has not sold, he, too, capitulates to peer and teacher pressure knowing he cannot face the punishment of The Vigils. Goober wills himself to feel nothing, not rotten, not traitorous, not small or cowardly; "then why was he crying all the way to his locker?" (p. 150). Brutality opens Cormier's novel, and it escalates to unbelievable heights in the final beating. It envelops adult and adolescent; it shows no one with strength sufficient to withstand evil.

The source of the novel's conflict is, or seems to be, Jerry's wish to hold out against The Vigils, to disturb the universe by resisting evil. The real protagonist in the novel, however, is not Jerry but the villain Archie. By skillful use of omniscient point of view, Cromier makes us see Archie's compulsion to keep, himself on top. To forestall his own defeat and to retain control of The Vigils and thus of the school, Archie must concoct one more, and one more vicious scheme. Archie must create the terror-producing plans, plans that use his club members for evil, then turn back upon them so that no one can win except Archie. "It was good to have people hate you--it kept you sharp" (p. 106). All kinds of brutality keep Archie's control over The Vigils. When Rollo is dissident, challenging The Vigils who can't even keep "a little freshman like Jerry in line," he gets a blow to the jaw: "Rollo's head snapped back--*snap* like a knuckle cracking--and he bellowed in pain" (p. 131). In payment for his obstinate refusal to sell chocolates, Jerry suffers. In scrimmage, when he makes his assigned tackle and gets Carter, he suffers a blinding blow to the kidneys. To the macho society of Trinity School, the ultimate disgrace is to be called a fairy, and this Jerry suffers, too. At Archie's charge, Emile enlists the neighborhood children, a ruthless gang of evil tots. Wanting to kill him, to blind him, they pile into Jerry, kicking him in the groin. Children, too, are corrupt and ruthless; they join the attack as hired assassins. Archie's Vigils will not suffer disobedience or defiance. They make silent phone calls to Jerry all night long. They call out to him, evening phantoms on the street. They destroy and clean out Jerry's locker so that he does not exist. Ignored by students and faculty alike, he is nothing, no one.

The violence and brutality of the chocolate raffle and the rigged fight conclude the bitter novel. What The Vigils have done to the school and to Jerry, "they would do to the world when they left Trinity" (p. 172). Greed and cruelty--the chance to win a hundred dollars and to see a bloody fight--control everyone. That's why it works . . . "because we're all bastards" (p. 175), explains Archie. Finally, even Jerry, the last holdout against evil, strikes out furiously and illegally in the ring at Emile in a "beautiful" blow. He is invaded by a "new sickness . . . of knowing what he had become, another animal, another beast, another violent person in a violent world, inflicting damage, not disturbing the universe, but damaging it. He had allowed Archie to do this to him"(p. 183).

If *The Chocolate War* ended with Jerry's defeat but with the banishment of Brother Leon or The Vigils, or with an uprising that set things at least into a neutral or holding pattern, it would not end in despair. Instead, in the final pages of the novel Jerry wishes he could tell Goober "Don't try to disturb the universe. You can't." Brother Leon, who, to serve himself, manipulates kids and other priests, remains in power. Hope vanishes. Despair wins.

In 1977 Cormier added to this tale of terror a second novel, *I Am the Cheese* (Dell, 1977). With the complexity of three interwoven levels, Cormier weaves the story of a boy's psychological search for his father with his search into his memories of the past. The novel revolves and circles in Adam's continuous and frustrating struggle to remember, mingled with a fear of remembering. His search for his dead father cannot end; the novel opens and closes with the same paragraph: "I am riding the bicycle and I am on Route 31 . . . on my way to Rutterburg, Vermont . . . the wind like a snake slithering up my sleeves . . . But I keep pedaling, I keep pedaling." The circular movement of the novel is like "The Farmer in the Dell," the child's continuous and circular game. Throughout the story, Adam, his father, and his mother sing the song, calling it the Farmer family's own song. The last verse is not sung until the final pages when psychologically damaged Adam, orphaned by the violent gangland murder of both his father and his mother, sings the last lines: "The cheese stands alone . . . I am the cheese."

Early in the fantasy of Adam's search for his father he hears that "it's a terrible world out there. Murder and assassinations" (p. 24). Such fears are only the beginning; they are followed by paranoiac fear of someone's stealing his bike, of homosexual overtures, of careening cars, of his mother's Never Knows, of a bomb on the accelerator, of strange voices that answer Amy Hertz's telephone. Endless fears. Throughout Adam's fantasies and memories run recollections of Amy's mindless mischief as cheerfully unmotivated as the violence of the young thugs and as unpredictable as Mr. Grey's comings, goings, and plans. Not until the final pages do we know that suspicious Mr. Grey is a legitimate government agent whose real task is to relocate prime witnesses.

The enigma of the novel is, how much does Adam Farmer, once Paul Delmonte, know about his past, and more importantly, who needs to find out--Adam or the government? Adam's father, an investigative reporter, has uncovered important evidence of corruption and been given a new identity; the family has been relocated and lives in fear of discovery. Adam learns his parents' secret and must become a stranger to his school world. The normal reticence and isolation of adolescence are exacerbated by fear and puzzlement, then by distrust of Mr. Grey, and by absolute terror of attacking dogs and predatory young loafers. As the story moves back and forth between Adam's bicycle ride through his fantasy and his dialogue with the psychiatrist, we are exposed to the actual events of his life in the present. At the novel's end we discover that Adam is not being pscyhologically healed after all. The interrogation which seems at times humane and therapeutic is merely politically expedient.

The reader's puzzlement carries the novel along; our fears are never allayed. Adam Farmer/Paul Delmonte will never be able to live free of the annual interrogation, or to move ouside the sanitarium walls. The disturbed adolescent who loves Amy Hertz and wants to love her forever is the same dependent child who clutches his stuffed animal, Poley the Pig. The government is vigilant; should Adam remember all and so be healed, he becomes dangerous. In the clinical records we see that Grey, Adam, his father and mother are all merely numbers. No matter how healthy he might become, Adam will never be able to untangle himself from the maze of regulation and red tape. In his fantasy Adam continues his search for his father and keeps pedaling, keeps pedaling. In reality, he is only a series of digits in a government file.

The effect upon the reader is not merely fear, but often sheer terror--terror not only of cars and dogs and secret agents and theft and homosexual invitation, but of the endlessly connected underworld and of uncontrollable impulses to speak the forbidden or to discover what must be left undiscovered. Again, Cormier has written skillfully, with plausible happenings and shocking attacks on the reader's sensibilities. The effect, once again, is that life is filled with sinister elements, government-related ones at that. There is no hope for the honest citizen in today's society. The forces of evil prevail and despair is the winner.

Cormier's third novel, *After the First Death* (Pantheon, 1979), is another skillfully written narrative. This time Cormier poses two father and son combinations against each other, one ostensibly the "good guys" and the other the "bad guys." As this tale unfolds, commitment to patriotism results in the suicide of the good-guy son and the assassination of the bad-guy father. Our sympathies lie with the American general and his victim son, and yet the sacrifice of that son to the good of the state is no more admirable than the comparable sacrifices made by father and son on the other side of the conflict. Subtly, with all his artistry in building plot and portraying character, Cormier once again gives us a sinister world and challenges the possibility of finding comfort in traditional values. This time it is not the microcosm of a school dominated by evil in *The Chocolate War* or of the wider mob-controlled American life in *I Am the Cheese*, but the international macrocosm of terrorism motivated by patriotism.

Briefly, the story opposes Inner Delta, the American secret defense agency administered by General Marchand, and the group of patriotic terrorists led by Artkin. Each of the two patriots has a son; Ben, son of Marchand, and Miro, the "perhaps" son of Artkin. The American Ben is aware only that his father's work is secret, and knows that if he can help, he wants to. Miro knows no more about Artkin's organization than that it too is patriotic; his obedience is mindless and unquestioning. Ben is a human child acting out of love; Miro is an automaton acting out of intensive conditioning and training. Artkin confronts Inner Delta by taking hostage a busload of children and isolating them on a railroad trestle. Ben at his father's request acts as the vulnerable messenger in the negotiations for the hostages. Miro at his father's command earns his manhood by agreeing to murder while guarding the hostages. Ben breaks under torture by Miro's father, Artkin; feeling he has failed, he cannot look his father in the eye and kills himself. Miro, trying to save himself from Inner Delta's attack on the bus, fails to warn Artkin and is responsible for his father's death. The two survivors are the loving father, who for patriotism has knowingly sacrificed his son, and the terror-trained son who for patriotism agrees to murder but brings about his father's death.

Within the novel are several significant statements about values and motives, and questions about commitment and sacrifice. For example, suspicious Artkin, hearing that General Marchand will send his own son on the dangerous assignment of emissary to the bus controlled by the terrorists, asks, "Who knows about Americans? Perhaps they cherish their children more than their agencies?" (p. 204). Who knows? Perhaps. Not so. On the wireless Artkin and his counterpart General Marchand speak of the General's generous offer of his son. Artkin says, "Either you are a great patriot or a great fool." Ben's father thinks that Artkin knows

> exactly what I was. What I am. Just as I knew exactly what he was and to what lengths he would go. We knew each other across the chasm; we had recognized each other across the ravine, although we had never met (p. 193).

The two fathers are the same breed. Their motives and values are the same. Again, reminiscing about World War II, Ben's father speaks silently to Ben.

> We were poorly trained in those days, Ben, but trained superbly in one thing: patriotism. There are all kinds of patriotism; ours was pure and sweet and unquestioning. We were the good guys. Today there is patriotism, of course . . . But this generation looks at itself in a mirror as it performs its duties. And wonders: Who are the good

guys? Is it possible we are the bad guys? They should never ask that question, Ben, or even contemplate it (p. 134).

General Marchand advocates blind obedience to patriotic duty; it kills his son. Similar blind obedience to patriotic duty motivates Artkin as he trains his boy to torture and to murder. Again Cormier turns conventional virtues, here commitment and sacrifice, on their head.

For generations American adolescents have thrilled and chilled to Poe's gruesome, yet fanciful tales of men and women laughing diabolically at their devices for perpetrating a living death. Poe's characters, however, are mad, insane; readers marvel at Poe's ingenuity. George Orwell in *1984* creates another tale of terror, this time of a political stranglehold on people's lives. But in the allegorical style of the novel, the totalitarian state with its language and institutions is unlike our own. By using an unemotional narrator who reports happenings in a country different from our own, where an abstraction called Big Brother represents institutional surveillance, Orwell creates distance and objectivity. As for adolescent protagonists, William Golding's *Lord of the Flies* has Ralph who opposes Jack, reason and humanity opposing impulse and violence. Although Golding does not comment on original sin, readers are struck by their own capacities to relate to both Ralph and Jack, and are thus frightened at the potential for savagery they detect in themselves. But the fantasy island setting in a remote time permits readers at least to hope that in the here-and-now *they* would not behave with savagery.

Poe, Orwell, and Golding permit us to discover and to contemplate the evil sides of society and ourselves, to search within for the source and the placement of our sympathies, and to hope that we can withstand. Cormier, on the other hand, takes another tact because he holds another view. He gives the reader no quarter. The immediacy of Cormier's situations, the feeling of "today," the skillfully portrayed reality of the particular evils in the "now" produce terror in the reader. His terror is unrelieved. The reader can find no distance.

Both Cormier's and Salinger's novels reflect the contemporary challenge to traditional institutions and conventions. Cormier's challenge is more severe; his world is pervasively evil, his characters are more seriously troubled. Neither author suggests that the repository of answers to the dilemmas which vex their characters is external to the efforts of human kind: the adolescents themselves, their parents, their adult role models, their professional helpers, representatives of their governments. Yet within this same secular, anti-theistic humanism, the answers which emerge in the novels are quite different. Holden finds that he is his own best hope for the phoniness of adult life. Cormier's characters come to no such faith. They are left without hope. The world grew darker between 1951 and 1974. Both writers skillfully create a realistic picture of the adolescent world, but unlike Salinger who offers discovery, Cormier offers only despair.

3

SOME WORLD VIEWS FROM ABROAD

Joan S. Nist

Whereas Lukens presented a historical perspective on a tonal shift in realistic adolescent novels written thirty years apart, Nist presents a broad cross-cultural perspective in her discussion of thirteen European books for the young. She uses the touchstone of a humanistic/religious world view to examine the thirteen recipients of the Batchelder Award (given annually for the most outstanding translated children's book published in the United States). She concludes that humanism predominates in these contemporary European books. Embedded in the general humanistic perspective, however, is a diversity of tone, setting, style, characters, and values. A few reflect Europe's post-war despair with religion and secular humanism. The majority are more positive and consistent in their celebration of the individual's reason and will and thus humanity's hope for a good life in the here and now.

SOME WORLD VIEWS FROM ABROAD

American children's literature flourished during the 1960's and 1970's with one continuing exception: books translated from other languages were few. International exchange between the United States and non-English-speaking countries was and remains largely one of American export and sparse foreign import, with most of the latter coming from the German or Scandinavian languages. John Donovan of the Children's Book Council has documented the paucity and inferred that "American children read a body of books that may be more parochial than those read by children anywhere in the developed world."[1]

A number of factors contribute to the small number of translated works in the United States. The great range of children's literature available in English has provided such diversity that little need has been felt to bring books from elsewhere. The monolingual bent in America has been abetted in recent years by the schools' deemphasis of other languages and their cultures. Mary Orvig, secretary of the International Research Society for Children's Literature, writes of the influence of "political constellations, copyright questions, and monetary relationships. Economic laws . . . play a very important part in this context. Nor should one forget the great influence of ancient cultural links on the translation scene."[2] Anne Pellowski, director/librarian of the Information Center on Children's Cultures of UNICEF, points out the practical reality that "ninety percent of current print and audio-visual literature for children is produced in a handful of countries."[3]

European concern for exchange of children's books as a way to international understanding was early expressed by Paul Hazard, the French literary historian, who wrote of "the universal republic of childhood."[4] Jella Lepman devoted herself after World War II to building *A Bridge of Children's Books*,[5] and her efforts, joined with those of others, resulted in the International Board on Books for Young People (IBBY) and its international journal, *Bookbird*. In addition, she worked to found the International Youth Library, long directed by Walter Scherf who has maintained a dedication "to promote deeper understanding of groups which . . . follow different ways of life."[6]

It is true that American children have available to them many books about other nations, with settings in other countries, but few of these are works created in the languages of other peoples, intended primarily for children of that culture, reflecting social customs and beliefs from a foreign point of view. Benjamin Whorf stated that "each language is not merely a reproducing intstrument for voicing ideas but rather is itself the shaper of ideas . . . ."[7] If one accepts the notion that a language system shapes a culture's world view, then providing American young people with translated works which embody different perceptual bases and alternative ways of thinking would have a powerful impact.

To encourage publication of foreign works which attract a small market and therefore present a commercial risk to publishers,[8] the American Library Association (A.L.A.) instituted the Batchelder Award to accompany its better known Newbery and Caldecott recognitions. Given annually for the most outstanding translated children's book published in the United States, the Batchelder citation was first presented in 1968. It honors Mildred Batchelder, who for many years headed A.L.A. children's services and worked to promote international understanding through "interchange of children's books between countries, through translation."[9] A cursory examination of the select group of thirteen foreign books which have received the Batchelder honor provides an

16

insight into some contending world views from abroad, primarily from Europe. Although religious faith and its institutions play a role in many of the books, a secular humanism seems the most pervasive perspective. For most, that humanism is optimistic about the individual's providing his own redemption in the face of personal and societal challenges. In several, the vision is as pessimistic as that found in many of their American counterparts. The "scrimmage of appetites" continues unabated.

Interestingly, the two Batchelder books which present religious belief most overtly and suggest its impact to be most powerful are both set in pre-historic times. One is nonfiction written by the German historical writer Hans Baumann; the other is fiction by A. Linevski, a Russian archaeologist. Baumann's *In the Land of Ur: The Discovery of Ancient Mesopotamia* uses different time frames to reconstruct both the life of ancient Sumeria (Ur) and the exploration of the nineteenth-century archaelogists who uncovered its cities. Baumann's account of the religious life of Ur suggests his own world view. As the ancient civilization developed, a man arose in each settlement to be not only prince but also priest, "the highest servant of the god and his representative as well" (p. 51). Baumann tells us that the temple was the center of the city. "Everything was so thoroughly steeped in the will of the god, that not only men but fields, rivers, winds, and stars were considered members of his community" (p. 52). In his anthropological tone of disinterest, Baumann tells us that a system of religious law dictated the order of society, and that it was an order necessary for survival. For these early citizens, death was seen as a transition from earthly life to the immortality of the gods, and mass graves have been found where attendants voluntarily followed the ruler into death. Baumann gives us a clue to his values when he arrives at a very humanistic conclusion: the *human* achievements were, in fact, Sumeria's great bequest to us. The invention of writing (p. 116) and "the earliest example of great literature known to us" (p. 50), the epic of Gilgamesh, are two examples.

Linevski's fiction suggests even clearer secular assumptions. In *An Old Tale Carved Out of Stone* he portrays the precarious existence of a prehistoric Siberian tribe. The hunt for food to stave off hunger is the people's driving preoccupation. The young shaman of the group, imaginative and innovative, makes carvings on the cliffs which engender fear and cower the already superstitious tribespeople. Their primitive religion is threatened, but finally dominates the challenge to it. The chief hunter warns the boy: "You have disrupted all the old order . . . today you have introduced a new ritual! . . . Remember, if you do not wish to bring harm to yourself, we will live now, the way we lived before" (p. 47). The postscriptive religion of the tribe is harsh and cruel; disobedience incurs human sacrifice. To save his life, the young shaman flees south and becomes a member of another tribe. Significantly, he is accepted by this more advanced group, one which makes traps and domesticates dogs. There, he becomes a toolmaker, utilizing his artistic ability. The tale ends with some hope that the two tribes will unite. Linevski, thus, subtly advances the anthropological belief that the demise of superstitious, otherworldly ritual is necessary for man to advance and progress. The young man could realize his potential only by casting off the religious assumptions of his fathers.

This implicit humanism becomes more obvious in the other eleven books. When religion surfaces it is tangential. The first work to receive the Batchelder Award was *The Little Man,* a fantasy told with gentle humor by the German, Erich Kastner. The setting is a circus where the two-inch tall hero assists his conjurer guardian. While Kastner mildly spoofs pomposity, whether in ringmaster or civic official, he shows the affection between the hero and his guardian to be warm and genuine. Of their act, the Little Man says, "Perhaps it's *not* much . . . But . . . what is 'much'?"(p. 105). The Professor magician replies, "Preventing war . . . Conquering famine . . . Neither of us can do that sort of thing. Pity. We can only do two things. We can astonish people and make them laugh" (p. 106). Yet these modest accomplishments are "much better than nothing" (p. 105). They reflect Kastner's assessment of his own literary contributions and the survival of his faith in humanity despite the fact that Hitler had burned his earlier works. Clearly, for Kastner man's best hope in life resides in *man*, not in any transcendent power or meaning. His is a winsome affirmation of the little efforts of even little men.

Another Batchelder Award book from Germany directly treats the issue of Nazism and the resultant Holocaust. *Friedrich*, by Hans Peter Richter, is an autobiographical novel which focuses on the friendship of two boys, Jewish Friedrich and the unnamed narrator. The beauty of Jewish ceremony is shown in a Sabbath service and at Friedrich's bar mitzvah. Yet observance of his religion leads the boy's father to an acceptance which cannot withstand the growing Nazi horror: "God has given us Jews a task . . . We have always been persecuted . . . Perhaps we'll manage to put an end to our wandering by not seeking flight anymore, by learning to suffer . . . " (p. 73). They suffer only to die. Nor can the narrator's friendly family offer much help for fear of reprisal. The perversion of humanity is vividly depicted in one scene where the narrator himself is caught up with a violent mob and briefly feels himself drunk with the desire to destroy. During the years of the Third Reich, the author implies neither man nor perhaps God could sustain a sense of faith and hope. The terrible and haunting challenge of this time to a belief in the nature of man and the nature and existence of God has formed the basis of much adult fiction and non-fiction. Richter has brought this challenge to a younger reader with all its troubling and unanswered questions.

A second Batchelder novel set in World War II, Alki Zei's *Petros' War*, conveys a spirit not of hopelessness, but of resistance. Zei's setting is Greece. Throughout invasion and occupation, the young hero and his people endure hunger and cold and yet maintain their vision of freedom. The cost is high: many die, including two of Petros' friends. Others are imprisoned, go underground, or join forces in exile. Death and famine make Athens a city of terror where people hunt for garbage and orphans sleep on the winter sidewalk: "Over the iron gratings of the subway station crouched strange forms: children with wizened old men's faces and tattered clothes" (p. 118). Religion offers little solace; rather it is the bravery of the partisans--painting walls with signs to "GIVE US FOOD!," printing defiant leaflets, and sabotaging the enemy--which helps sustain the people. Petros joins the freedom fighters and grows from boyhood notions of glorious heroism to a painful appreciation of the varied acts of sacrifice which liberate his land. The realities of war are stark, as in Richter's book; traditional institutions and values succumb to its onslaught; the young and the old are left without sufficient anchor and with scant hope. Zei's answer to this ravaged world is perhaps more hopeful than Richter's but it too has no religious component: a young man discovers the *human capacity* for sacrifice.

Zei is the only author to have received the Batchelder Award more than once, and another of her novels, *Wildcat Under Glass*, also depicts the unquenchable Greek spirit of liberty. Set in the 1930's on an island, the story shows how one family reacts when a dictator takes over the government. The young heroine assists her cousin who goes into hiding until he can get abroad to fight against the fascists, "the black-shirt bullies who don't believe in democracy and freedom, and want to force everyone else to do as they think!" (p. 65). He sends her messages hidden in the stuffed wildcat under a glass cage in the parlor. Their grandfather has imbued the young people with faith, a belief based on his "Ancients," the classic Greek myths and philosophers. Even though his books are burned as "harmful," the heroine remembers his words: scientists and others who work to benefit people "think about humanity and not just about themselves. Even though they may no longer be alive, their names remain immortal" (p. 8). As in *Petros' War,* Zei suggests that human hope, even for immortality, is not in God's grace, but in man's action.

Zei's third Batchelder book is cross-national, an adaptation of part of a Russian novel of the last century. Zei lived for some years in Russia, but her portrayal of the pre-Revolutionary class struggle is infused with her feelings toward repressive governments she herself has experienced. Throughout the brief narrative, tension is shown between formal religion and human aspirations. The heroine's German governess is dismissed because of her fearsome superstitions; the gypsy girl is taken to church in hopes of a miracle cure before the heroine's doctor father can treat her; and the family cook idolatrously worships her icons: "Holy Virgin, sweet savior of souls, don't let my stew stick!" (p. 52). But hope lies in human hands, those of the doctor who treats both rich and poor and of the new tutor who is a revolutionary and believes that heroism consists of helping others. The rumble of the trains on the nearby tracks, like *The Shadow of the Dragon's Feet* in old legend, portends vast changes in the country. The strength to meet those changes, Zei implies, will come from human, not divine, action.

Two other Batchelder works are also cross-national; in both cases the authors have lived in the developing nations which are their settings. Cecil Bodker of Denmark has written an adventurous novel of the kidnapping of a young Ethiopian herd-boy. The boy goes from his small country compound to a large trading town because of his dangerous knowledge that cattle are being stolen not only by *The Leopard,* but also by a scar-footed thief. The boy seeks aid from The Great Man, the religious leader of a neighboring village: "One bought good advice and charms for protection against threatening diseases from him" (p. 17). Inadvertently he betrays his knowledge to the thief and is kidnapped. Eventually he becomes one of a group who hunts down the criminal. At the climax, the leopard and the thief fight to the death. The boy is given the leopard's ear as a charm. "Now he would never have to go to The Great Man's village, he thought" (p. 185). He leaves happily for home, returning to the simple existence of the compound. Simplicity is celebrated; the complications of a more sophisticated life, of which the thief and the religious man are representative types, are denigrated. The leopard ear charm, won through one's own hard efforts, is sufficient for the good life.

S.R. van Iterson's hero is a boy without parents, hope, or even a proper name. "'Pulga? Flea? That cannot be your real name, can it?' . . . He almost had forgotten his name himself" (p. 46). *Pulga* is one of the spawn of street urchins in Bogota who scrounge, beg, steal, until by accident he becomes the helper of a trucker hauling loads throughout Colombia. In the book -- originally written in Dutch -- there are surface references to religion, but the boy's basic belief is fatalistic: "A person can't swim against the current. If he does, it will only add to his misery. God knows, not much is needed to increase one's burden" (p. 95). As the truck travels on, however, the boy gains a glimpse of another life, one where he not only eats regularly, but also finds that his work and he himself are worth

19

something. The book ends at Christmastime, with hope that the boy will escape from the street life of resigned submission to fate. But ironically the essential Christmas vision of man's redemption by God's gift is only a backdrop. Pulga's vision rests on human salvation.

The Batchelder Award can be given to picture books; consequently, two of the works honored, both German Swiss, are in this format. One is the Grimms' tale of *The Cat and Mouse Who Shared a House,* retold in text and large, humorous illustrations by Ruth Hurlimann. The cat is a lazy, greedy liar, who sneaks off in three trips to eat up their communal winter's store of butter. The mouse is tidy, naive, and talkative, unsuspecting of the cat's perfidy. The tale's framework is mock-religious, for the two hide their pot of butter in a church from which the mouse believes "no one would steal anything." Nor does she see through the cat's three-time excuse of being godmother, though the name of "Half-gone" is not on the calendar of saints (nor are "Top-off" and "All-gone"). Finally when the mouse sees the empty pot, the truth is out and the false friendship up: pounce and gobble. The old folktale champions common sense and the natural scheme (and scheming) of things. More naturalism, some realism, less humanism, least religion.

In contrast, *Rabbit Island* is a stark *modern* allegory. The text by Jorg Steiner is complemented by the detailed, panoramic, realistic pictures of Jorg Muller. The mechanization of modern society is symbolized by the rabbit factory which so distorts life for its animals that when two of them escape, only the new, young rabbit can function in the natural world. His older friend has been conditioned to factory existence, even to creating a mythology: when the fattened rabbits are taken away, they go to "a much better place . . . [where] White Watch Rabbits protect the good rabbits and they skin the bad ones alive." But the younger animal wants the reality of earth to burrow and clover to taste. His friend returns to the factory, for he has forgotten how to fend for himself and cope with danger. He has lost his drive for freedom and retreats into determinism: "That's how life is; you can't change it."

Quite different from this somber tone is the humor of *Konrad,* written by Christine Nostlinger of Austria. Here too a programmed way of life is juxtaposed against a freer lifestyle. The work employs a science fiction device: Konrad is a canned Instant Child, processed by the "Final Preparation Department" to be perfectly behaved. The middle-aged mother to whom he is mistakenly delivered is not a model of maternity in her T-shirts, green polished nails, and cigar-smoking eccentricities. But along with a weirdly balanced diet and flamboyant clothes, she gives him affection and tells him the truth: "'adults like to think they can trick children into believing things . . . the things I'm telling Konrad *are* true! . . . Truth is truth! . . . And that goes for children too!'" (p. 47). When the manufacturer threatens to reclaim Konrad, he is re-educated into mischief. His mother says, "It's ridiculous to say you can't be any different" (p. 107). True enough, he tries and succeeds in being deprogrammed from model child to normal boy. Man has become creator of his own life as well as shaper of his own destiny.

Norwegian Babbis Friis-Baastad has written a serious novel about the extent of human capabilities in *Don't Take Teddy.* The young hero is burdened with guilt because he believes that he has inadequately fulfilled the responsibility of caring for his mentally retarded older brother. When by chance Teddy injures someone, the younger brother runs away with him -- by bus, streetcar, and long painful hike -- to their uncle's mountain cottage. They both become ill with pneumonia before they are found. The crisis evokes a change in the family; his parents relieve the boy of guilt when they tell him that "A youngster like you shouldn't have that big a responsibility. It was wrong of us to ask you to take care of Teddy so much" (p. 214). He himself comes to realize that a special school is the best thing for Teddy and he loses his fear that Teddy will be taken from them: "I'll tell everyone who thinks Teddy should be locked up that he's going to school now" (p. 213). A person's proper understanding and acceptance of his own capabilities is the answer to the dilemma posed in *Don't Take Teddy*.

These thirteen award-winning foreign books clearly present a predominantly humanistic outlook to American readers. The tone of these presentations varies from the fervent championing of man's democratic spirit in Zei's three historical novels to Kastner's mild, almost fantastical, yet steady affirmation of the worth of small accomplishments. The three realistic novels by Bodker, Friis-Baastad, and van Iterson, also show the power of the human spirit: the African boy conquering his own fears as well as overcoming dangerous external obstacles; the Scandinavian youth gaining insight into ways he and others can help his brother beyond just caretaking; and the hopeless Latin American orphan developing self-esteem and a plan to improve his lot. Hurlimann's old-fashioned folktale does not challenge the power of mouse, cat, or human spirit, but rather concludes with a humorous acceptance of the usual state of things. Nostlinger is boisterously modern in her fantasy, exulting in the human power to change and the primacy of free spirit over regimented indoctrination. The two works which do not reflect a positive view of human civilization are Steiner's allegorical depiction of a systematized society which has supplanted natural life, and Richter's autobiographical fiction of the massive trauma which Germany suffered during the years of Hitlerian perversion. So their pessimism extends to human as well as divine salvation. The two books in which religion plays a more prominent part, Linevski's fiction and Baumann's nonfiction, show the strictures of early religions. They both focus on the creative individual achievements which enabled prehistoric groups to progress out of primitive, regressive superstitions.

Edward Fenton, who translated Zei's works into English (and was himself the author of children's books), has written that Americans, like other peoples, "require to be nourished by other cultures."[10] An appropriate way to provide such nourishment for of children the United States is through translated books. Even this cursory examination of the Batchelder books, ones which have been judged outstanding, indicates that they do, indeed, present world views which can greatly enrich young people's reading experiences. Unfortunately, they do not offer a comprehensive representation of world views. All of the works receiving the Batchelder Award are from Europe, almost half of them--six--from the German language alone.[11] They, nevertheless, promote a better understanding of cultures outside our own, and they point out a field for potential growth within children's literature: the presentation through more translations of a greater diversity of the world's peoples and their ways of thought. Our examination of them on the touchstones of religious and humanistic world views has hopefully broadened our knowledge of the diversity of writers of books for the young and deepened our perception of their pervasive, secular humanism.

NOTES

[1]John Donovan. "The Civiliz(s)ed Competition for English-Reading Young People," *School Library Journal* 26. December 1979: 52.

[2]Mary Orvig. "Children's Books in Translation: Facts and Beliefs," in *Issues in Children's Book Selection* . New York: Bowker, 1973, p. 186.

[3]Anne Pellowski. "Internationalism in Children's Literature," in Zena Sutherland and May Hill Arbuthnot, *Children and Books,* 5th ed. Glenview, Ill.: Scott, Foresman, 1977, p. 616.

[4]Paul Hazard. *Books, Children and Men,* Trans. from the French by Marguerite Mitchell . Boston: Horn Book, 1944, 1960, p. 146.

[5]Jella Lepman. *A Bridge of Children's Books,* Trans. from the German by Edith McCormick. Chicago: American Library Association, 1969, p. 142.

[6]Walter Scherf. "Introduction" to *The Best of the Best.* New York: Bowker, 1976, p. 16.

[7]Benjamin Lee Whorf. "Science and Linguistics," in *Language, Thought, and Reality,* ed. by John B. Carroll. Cambridge, Mass.: Technology Press MIT/John Wiley, 1956, p. 212.

[8]See Virginia Haviland. "International Book Awards and Other Celebrations of Distinction," *Bookbird* 14 ,September 1976: 12-13.

[9]Mildred L. Batchelder. "Learning About Children's Books in Translation," *ALA Bulletin,* 60, January 1966: 34.

[10]Edward Fenton. "Blind Idiot: The Problems of Translation," *Horn Book* 53, October 1977: 512.

[11]Joan Stidham Nist. "Cultural Constellations in Translated Children's Literature: Evidence from the Mildred L. Batchelder Award," *Bookbird* 17, June 1979: 3-8.

BATCHELDER AWARD-WINNING BOOKS

Baumann, Hans. *In the Land of Ur: The Discovery of Ancient Mesopotamia.* Trans. from the German by Stella Humphries. New York: Pantheon, 1969.

Bodker, Cecil. *The Leopard.* Trans. from the Danish by Gunnar Poulsen. New York: Atheneum, 1975.

Friis-Baastad, Babbis. *Don't Take Teddy.* Trans. from the Norwegian by Lise Somme McKinnon. New York: Scribner, 1967.

Hurlimann, Ruth. *The Cat and Mouse Who Shared a House.* Trans. from the German by Anthea Bell. New York: Walck, 1973.

Iterson, S.R. van. *Pulga.* Trans. from the Dutch by Alexander and Alison Gode. New York: Morrow, 1971.

Kastner, Erich. *The Little Man.* Trans. from the German by James Kirkup. New York: Knopf, 1966.

Linevski, A. *An Old Tale Carved Out of Stone.* Trans. from the Russian by Maria Polushkin. New York: Crown, 1973.

Nostlinger, Christine. *Konrad.* Trans. from the German by Anthea Bell. New York: Franklin Watts, 1977.

Richter, Hans Peter. *Friedrich.* Trans. from the German by Edite Kroll. New York: Holt, Rinehart and Winston, 1970.

Steiner, Jorg. *Rabbit Island.* Trans. from the German by Ann Conrad Lammers. Pictures by Jorg Muller. New York: Harcourt, Brace, Jovanovich, 1978.

Zei, Alki. *Petros' War.* Trans. from the Greek by Edward Fenton. New York: Dutton, 1972.

Zei, Alki. *The Sound of the Dragon's Feet.* Trans. from the Greek by Edward Fenton. New York: Dutton, 1979.

Zei, Alki. *Wildcat Under Glass.* Trans. from the Greek by Edward Fenton. New York: Holt, Rinehart and Winston, 1968.

4

ALICE AND DOROTHY: REFLECTIONS FROM TWO WORLDS

Ann Donovan

Donovan's essay is less concerned with the *what* of children's literature than with the *how* of literature. The breadth of scope in the first two essays of this section is complemented by Donovan's deep examination of how literature functions in the lives of young readers. Donovan assumes that the fundamental problem of self, the adequacy of the individual, is the subject matter of the most enduring books. She uses two humanistic classics, Lewis Carroll's *Through the Looking Glass/Wonderland* and Frank Baum's *The Wizard of Oz,* to contrast the potency of fantasy versus realism in providing young readers with self-exploration and discovery. Although realism would seem to offer the best chance for self-scrutiny and self-clarification, Donovan finds that fantasy allows young readers the best opportunity for imaginative projection and clear minded self-appraisal.

ALICE AND DOROTHY: REFLECTIONS FROM TWO WORLDS

Two types of juvenile fiction are currently enjoying an extended vogue. One is fantasy, a quasi- or outright science fiction with mythic overtones. The other, the diametric opposite, is the realistic novel which even on the most junior level is fraught with trauma, self-discovery, and societal clashings. Paradoxically, fantasy, descending from the old form of allegory, myth, or religious parable, can actually be the vehicle for a more vigorous affirmation of self--the humanist ideal--than the realistic novel. Although this realistic genre is the result of the self-reliant humanistic concept of life which views non-existential systems as fantastical, only fantasy allows infinite scope for the imagination to project a heroic self. However, fantasy such as Lewis' *The Lion, the Witch and the Wardrobe*, with faith and salvation implied as both absolutes and possibilities, cannot sufficiently arm a reading child to face his greatest doubt: his adequacy. The fundamental problem of self-sufficiency remains the subject which the most enduring children's books must address.

Two classic fantasies, *The Wizard of Oz* and *Through the Looking Glass/Wonderland,* illustrate the interplay of qualities that combine to meet needs which are a normal part of children's psyches and which also arise out of societal pressures they are powerless to control. The common factor which exists in both books is the struggle of the ordinary, unexceptional protagonist to pass through challenge and to emerge affirmed in a strengthened self, creating or discovering in the process an order of meaning. It is with the emergent self that the child reader identifies if the array and disposition of the story's opposing forces are acceptable and the obstacles of the proper magnitude.

The reason for fantasy's power of self-exploration for the young reader resides in the way literature operates in the lives of children. As anyone who has worked with children and books knows, the story is of primary interest to children. Ask them to tell you about the book, and you get a plot summary. With enough encouragement the child will also speak of such matters as character, realism, or even style, but he will seldom mention the underlying theme. Indeed, it is difficult to introduce this concept even to much older children in English classes. And yet, a fairly basic tenet of children's literature holds that some world-ordering system be evident and, furthermore, be benevolent and thus ensure an ending which is positive and good regardless of the traumas en route. How do we justify this convention? Why has it evolved? Who asked for it?

Simon Lesser has written that we participate in the fiction we read; it becomes our own experience. He also points out that this involvement is somewhat within our control and as we see disaster looming, we usually withdraw and assume the role of spectator, horrified perhaps, or even concurring in the appropriateness of the tragic conclusion. Thus we experience Aristotle's catharsis.[1] However, this distancing ability comes with age, maturity, and experience. Children have not the toughness to retrieve their emotional investment in the hero in time to save themselves from total participation in catastrophe. Thus, ever since gentle rearing became the accepted style of literate parents, children have been introduced only gradually and partially through literature to the grimness and random brutality of life. They learn to expect that life's fragrance will prevail over the thorns; their hope is that they can guarantee this through their own self-directed actions.

Children seek affirmation of the goodness of life through the books they read. As Norma Schlager puts it, "Children in middle childhood expend an inordinate amount of effort and energy exploring the perimeters of reality." She relates their

26

literary choices to developmental stages suggested by Piaget and Erikson.[2] Lesser describes this process in all of us as "the desire to discover what St. Augustine refers to as the dark corners of the heart."[3] What makes children's explorations significantly different is their inexperience and vulnerability, as well as their overwhelming self-interest. One could say that while children are searching for themselves as triumphant individuals, they also explore their possible future roles in the peculiar adult scheme of things. Children, concerned with themselves as somehow self-determining, ask not "who am I?", the adult's quandary, but rather "how can I be?" The child is basically torn between thinking of himself as weak and powerless to control his world ("I could ne'er do that") and capable of great things, far more than he is allowed to do ("Even *I* could do that!"). Thus, he searches for one like himself or for one with whom identification is possible and a useful strategy in the resolution of the struggle may be revealed. Children have little need to see how things don't work; they have enough experience and imagination for visions of disaster. They need to know how to master a possibly threatening environment and powerful, incomprehensible, adult demands. Norman Holland writes, "The single most common fantasy structure in literature is phallic assertiveness balanced against oral engulfment."[4] Surely, putting aside the psychological language, this describes the plight of the reading child who insists on his identity with all its rough edges in spite of society's diligent efforts to sand them into harmonious smoothness. This molding process is suspiciously perceived by the child as a restriction on growth and freedom, even though he is told it is the route to growing up.

Clearly then, literature, assumed to be an escape from reality, becomes a handbook for children as well. The obstacles of fiction represent the inexorable illogic the child observes in the world about him, the world he perceives as the domain of adults. This basic illogic of life assures the child that he must ultimately rely upon his own understanding and ability, even though as a child he has little opportunity to use either. But he knows and fears that circumstances may arise to test him; this makes the story's action critically important. Fiction, particularly fantasy, creates these circumstances for his consideration. For some children, more socially engulfed than others, literature becomes a particular oasis of nourishment and vitality. Girls, psychological studies tell us, develop verbal abilities earlier than boys. Perhaps cultural expectations tend to promote this and encourage girls to read earlier, better, and more. These same cultural expectations deny girls, even more than boys, the opportunity actually to test the parameters of their power. Thus girls, threatened with greater and earlier submergence, read for clues to escape. But what they find in literature is reinforcement of their condition. Boys may triumph; girls are saved.

Fortunately there are occasional exceptions to this situation; the two books under consideration have endured to achieve almost mythic status. The works of Lewis Carroll and Frank Baum illustrate the use of fantasy in the cultivation and celebration of the self. The commonalities of Alice in *Through the Looking Glass/Wonderland* and Dorothy in *The Wizard of Oz* are both obvious and subtle. They tend, I think, to emphasize the great importance children attach to a self-determining system of values in the teeth of any convention or pressure to the contrary. Alice and Dorothy are both ordinary little girls quite lacking in distinction or rebelliousness. Neither sets forth to find adventure. Both are, in fact, quietly at home when things come unstuck. When their worlds are transformed into a threatening new set of problems, they are apprehensive and defensive in a most acceptably feminine way and meet all obstacles, dangerous and otherwise, with the techniques they have been taught in proper homes: politeness, truthfulness, and trust. They respect authority and are obedient to powerful dominant characters. No extraordinary strength or cunning is evidenced. Dorothy does manage to melt a witch, but Alice does little worse than inflict some verbal damage. This is fair enough since Dorothy is in greater actual physical danger. Yet in chapter after chapter, incident after incident, these children extricate themselves from nightmare-like situations with complete aplomb. Here is no princely rescuer, no divine plan or direction, but a persistent emphasis on the normalcy and self-sufficiency of the heroine. Dorothy's whole inspiration is centered on her Kansas farm life, while Alice draws heavily on her Victorian lifestyle for moral support in the face of all-out weirdness.

Besides their genuine goodness and simplicity, the quality which these two children have which endears them to us is their unflinching determination and sense of self. Doubt as to what may happen keeps the reader going; but there is never any real question of the persona, even though at times both girls are challenged by authority figures who dismiss them as harmless children. How all children, but especially repressed Victorian little girls and isolated rural American ones, must have responded to these stalwart sisters. The illustrations which are most successful (Tenniel and Denslow) capture this strength of self; the more fantastical or Disney-nice fail.

Further, we might compare the success of these stories with others such as *Pippi Longstocking* or *Heidi*, which are set in a realistic environment and which also have strong central characters who never suffer serious identity doubts. Such a comparison makes it fairly clear that the fictional contrast between a fantasy-magic world and a "real" individual strengthens the image of self. One can only be so real in the real world; to achieve the archetypical, at least for children, requires the fantastical. There must be dramatic contrast between the world and the self beyond the normal. In literature for older children, the clash can occur effectively between man and society, man and God, or man (good) and man (evil), and so affirm the self. Such conflicts are too threatening for children who do not have personal enemies--or if they do, have no hope for self-affirmation through conquest because the enemy is always more powerful or combat is forbidden; nor can children confront society or God head-on.

The extraordinary attraction of *The Wizard of Oz* and *Through the Looking Glass/Wonderland*, however, can also be accounted for outside their compelling heroines or imaginative appeal. They are also something more than a subversive message to thwarted little feminists. If their placement in the literature of their time is considered, interesting implications for present-day children's reading emerge. Alice is a rough contemporary of Jo March in *Little Women* and Little Nell in *The Old Curiosity Shop*. These and other child heroines emerged from the Victorian times of conflict and conformity. They are examples of characters such as we find in present-day realistic fiction for children: drawn from life, well-rounded, facing real, overwhelming problems not of their making. And they are successful to the extent that when the stories end, after trial and sorrow, the main character has grown and become stronger, has come to rest in harmony with the society around her, largely because of her close relationships with others. Kind and loving hearts have prevailed over war, injustice, evil. It is important to remember that children of the Victorian age were generally rigidly controlled either in the environment of the respectability-conscious middle class or under the heavy yoke of child labor on the farm or in the shop. Both groups felt the controlling hand of convention equally heavily. Penalties for breaching the accepted norms were heavy for anyone in spite of the challenges to morality, religion, and asthetics from rebels such as Darwin,

Rossetti and Hardy. Indeed, under the surface of enforced order and Christian morality, horrors and abuses both great and small flourished. Quite likely children were well aware of this pattern of contradiction (more of the general illogic of things) and presumed it to be the same as naughtiness in the nursery, decorum in the drawing room. But children of all times and cultures, however oriented to the society in which they are embedded, fear the same things: their essential fragility, abandonment, catastrophe.

In a relatively stable society like that of England or America in the late 1800's, they had less cause, perhaps, than now to feel their worst fears might be realized at any moment. By and large, the established morality, even though flouted surreptitiously, or occasionally in public, gave an underlying strength to the value system. A child might be bad, but at least there was no real doubt about the matter. He could be assured that God and society would see and judge him truly sooner or later. This cultural rigidity was at once terrifying and comforting. Literature might deal with the hardships and excesses of the times, but there was little belief that the underlying order was weak or false. Pippa's song was heard in the land. From this confining but safe position, children needed and seized upon a book which successfully offered a chaotic, dangerous world with absolutely no overall religious or moral order: no rules, no boundaries, no safety. Basically amoral, they moved easily and without question into this all too recognizable dreamworld where nothing was being taught or shown apart from survival--and even triumph--of the self. Such an intoxicating experience would appeal to generations of readers.

In these two books, then, we have the essential child, culture's underdog by virtue of sex as well as age, set in opposition to forces representing all the irrational, incomprehensible power structures of adult society and overcoming them by simple persistence. It is no wonder that these books enjoyed immense popularity for years and evolved into classic works which speak not only to the questing child in us, but to the adult who knows himself now to be ranged on the other side. Both of these fantasies, emerging from stable, secure, well-ordered cultures, suggest that fantasy is, if not the best and only, certainly an effective vehicle to affirm the value of the self. The indifferent universe remains an arena of conflict between the self and annihilation. We can perhaps suggest that the fantasy-hungry readers of our own time have a similar need, for they have pirated the fantasies of the past and even grafted them at times to the rootstock of contemporary science fiction. How then, to account for the contradictory demand for realism as well as for the religious or quasi-religious tale, all of which end well?

The characteristic motif of our time is disintegration. We are hanging on and letting go at a dizzying rate. Our children are still testing their limits, but at the same time they are being tested. Our "happy ending" realism reflects our insistence that children have no illusions other than that all will somehow be well. Out of our chaotic culture is emerging not the sturdy unsupported self, but the self whose strength is affirmed by recognition from man, or even a "force": a conformist, one who finds and fits into a preordained system. But the essential paradox is unavoidable. In a society children and adults must work together for the safety and self-realization of all. No person can realize himself at the expense of others, or the fragile web of society breaks down and all fail. This is what realistic fiction promises the child with its happy ending and realization of a kind of self. It is C.S. Lewis' promise, too: trust, be strong and good, have faith. And so, we are given Harriet and Charlotte as individuals who are defined by their interrelationships with the group. But who has chosen, children or adults? Where are our Alice and Dorothy? Is Wonderwoman all we need? Where is the child, so typical she is

29

insignificant, who can stand alone and face even the Jabberwock or the wicked witch armed only with dignity and an unbounded ego? Has our culture become so threatening or so bland that we have made her impossible? I hope not. We all need her to help us find our own selves and face our own endings, for the child's persistence grows into the adult's endurance.

NOTES

[1] Simon O. Lesser. *Fiction And The Unconscious.* New York: Vintage Books, 1962, p. 249.

[2] Norma Schlager. "Predicting Children's Choices in Literature: A Developmental Approach," *Children's Literature In Education,* 9, 1978, 137.

[3] Lesser. p. 253.

[4] Norman N. Holland. *The Dynamics Of Literary Response.* New York: Oxford University Press, 1968, p. 43.

PART III   THE RELIGIOUS VIEW

5

BEYOND THE CIRCLES OF THE WORLD:
DEATH AND THE HEREAFTER IN CHILDREN'S LITERATURE

Margaret P. Esmonde

Esmonde's essay opens Part Three, The Religious View, with a very direct appraisal of the religious perspective in five powerful writers of our time: J.R.R.Tolkien, C.S.Lewis, Ursula K.LeGuin, Shirley Rousseau Murphy, and Ruth Nichols. She shows how these five fantasists have addressed death and afterlife in a serious way that separates them from secular realists. The secular mainstream has either kept death off limits for children's books or trivialized it in what she calls a "fertilizer" approach to the subject. Though often considered escapist, the best fantasy literature has projected an honest view of death with no denial of grief or presentation of easy comfort, but as a part of life.

BEYOND THE CIRCLE OF THE WORLD:
DEATH AND THE HEREAFTER IN CHILDREN'S LITERATURE*

In her novel, *The Left Hand of Darkness*, Ursula K. LeGuin has one of her characters ask: "What is sure, predictable, inevitable--the one certain thing you know concerning your future, and mine?" "That we shall die," the protagonist replies.[1] The one thing that mankind has always known is the one thing that twentieth-century man finds most difficult to accept. In a culture that venerates youth, those who in another age would have been glad of the reverence accorded grey hair, are busy disguising that grey with dyes and creams, hiding wrinkles with plastic surgery, bald heads with hair transplants, and mature figures with tight jeans and gold chains, gulping elixirs and pills that promise extended youth and frantically gyrating at discos--anything in order to blot out the quiet voice that whispers: "Dust thou art, and unto dust shalt thou return."[2]

In earlier ages, man was on better terms with death. The Judeo-Christian heritage of Western Europe stressed the fact that man, an exile and a pilgrim here on Earth, was bound for the Heavenly Jerusalem where "God shall wipe away all tears from their eyes; and there shall be no more death, neither sorrow, nor crying, neither shall there by any more pain: for the former things are passed away."[3]

The life of man was often short, violent and filled with pain. In his admonition to Beowulf, Hrothgar summed up the human condition:

> Now for a time there is glory in your might: yet soon it
> shall be that sickness or sword will diminish your strength,
> or fire's fangs, or flood's surge, or sword's swing, or
> spear's flight, or appalling age; brightness of eye will fail
> and grow dark; then it shall be that death will overcome
> you, warrior.[4]

The omnipresent icon of the grinning skeleton and the Dance of Death quickly disabused man of any illusion of "deathlessness." But, on the other hand, this same heritage held out the bright promise of the Heaven of the Just. Quoting the Old Testament prophet Isaiah, Paul told the Corinthians: "Eye hath not seen, nor ear heard, neither have entered into the heart of man, the things which God hath prepared for them that love him."[5]

But as the result of a complex concatenation of events beginning about the middle of the nineteenth century, man lost his heavenly bearings. The evidence of modern science, particularly geology which indicated that the earth was millions of years older than the five millenia implicit in a literal interpretation of the Bible, and astronomy which demonstrated that man was not the center of the universe but only an insignificant inhabitant of a small planet circling a small sun in a galaxy of millions of suns and a universe of millions of galaxies, eroded Western man's beliefs. Darwin's *The Origin of the Species,* which denies Genesis' account of man's beginning, Sir James Frazer's *Golden Bough,* which suggested that Christianity was just another version of a universal myth, and Sigmund Freud's psychological studies which indicated that man did not truly possess free will, all eroded irreparably man's religious certitude of his heavenly destination. Death became the end of all things, not a glorious new beginning.

The same science which shook the foundations of religious belief offered man the means to deceive himself about the reality of death. The steadily decreasing rate of infant mortality, the increasing longevity of man, and the relegation of the aged and the dying to nursing homes and hospitals made it quite possible for the modern child to reach adulthood never having experienced death at a personal level.

Death, which had been a staple of children's literature in earlier centuries, became taboo in children's fiction by mid-twentieth century. In his desire to protect children from all unpleasantness, twentieth-century man suppressed their experience of death. The potent symbol of the grinning skeleton which reminded earlier generations of their mortality became just another costume possibility on Halloween.

But the past decade has witnessed what one reviewer has labeled a "death renaissance" in children's fiction. And the National Education Association recently announced that "the study of death is probably the last of the old taboos to fall in the schools."[6] In classes across the country youngsters of all ages "study" death by "visiting cemeteries and funeral homes, reading novels and essays about death and even taking turns lying in coffins."[7] Only the strong possibility that the study of death might lead students into such prickly questions as "What happens after death?" dissuades some school districts from the subject.

In her critical review, "Facing the Other Fact of Life: Death in Recent Children's Fiction,"[8] Jane Abramson concluded that a large number of the "death" books recently published for children of various ages in response to this new trend are unsatisfactory because they are either "problem-solving" books which can pass only as bibliotherapy or "mediocre, soap operatic" sermons. With few exceptions these books avoid mention of an afterlife, preferring to depict death as "the great fertilizer." Dead pets (and dead relatives?) "help flowers grow." She concludes that "the best books involving death reveal an author's personal vision of life. These titles have lasting value as literature because death is part of the story not merely the raison d'etre of the book."[9]

But even in the books recommended by Ms. Abramson, the question of an afterlife is largely ignored. No realistic novelist has attempted to describe "what happens next." In this totally secular age, the hereafter, so familiar to our ancestors, has become a *terra incognita*. The mysterious land of death has been left to those writers whose stock-in-trade is unknown lands and metaphysical realities--the fantasists.

The best fantasy literature, so often reviled as escapist, has dealt with the subject of death honestly, neither disguising the pain of the survivors nor avoiding the question of an afterlife. Never has it tried to pacify children with the soul-shrinking idea of death as "the great fertilizer." Fantasists such as Ursula LeGuin and J.R.R. Tolkien have presented death and the hereafter in a sensitive and thought-provoking manner, not as a problem to be solved but, as Ms. Abramson suggests in her article, as part of their personal vision of life.

The most traditionally religious of the fantasists who have dealt with the question of an afterlife is C.S. Lewis in his *Chronicles of Narnia*. The thinly disguised Christian allegory, whose central focus is Aslan's redemptive death and resurrection, climaxes in the seventh book fittingly called *The Last Battle*. At the conclusion of the book, Aslan explains to all the assembled protagonists in Neo-Platonic terminology that they are dead "as you used to call it in the Shadow-Lands."[10] England and even the old Narnia have been mere shadows of reality. With their deaths, reality begins. "The dream is ended: this is the morning."[11] In a direct aside to the reader, Lewis concludes his chronicle with a final consoling passage:

And for us this is the end of all the stories, and we can

most truly say that they all lived happily ever after. But for them it was only the beginning of the real story. All their life in this world and all their adventures in Narnia had only been the cover and the title page: now at last they were beginning Chapter One of the Great Story, which no one on earth has read: which goes on for ever: in which every chapter is better than the one before.[12]

J.R.R. Tolkien, a colleague of Lewis' at Oxford, also examines death and the afterlife in his work. In his essay, "On Fairy-Stories," he argues that "Escape" is one of the main functions of fairy stories, particularly the "Great Escape," the escape from death. But he concludes: "Few lessons are taught more clearly in them than the burden of that kind of immortality, or rather endless serial living, to which the 'fugitive' would fly."[13] He further points out in his essay that the consolation of the fairy-story, the joy of the happy ending, does not deny the existence of sorrow and failure: the possibility of these is necessary to the joy of deliverance. "It denies . . . universal final defeat and in so far is *evangelium*, giving a fleeting glimpse of Joy, Joy beyond the wall of the world, poignant as grief."[14] Though he does not deny the sorrow of mortality, Tolkien suggests that it is not a curse but a blessing which gives meaning and joy to those who must live in a mortal world.

In his own "fairy-story," *The Hobbit*, the theme of death is introduced at the climax of the novel. Having passed succeedingly complex tests on his path to maturity, climaxing in the moral dilemma of the Arkenstone, Bilbo Baggins faces the final test of maturity--death. Since the story is essentially a fairytale, with its necessary *eucatastrophic* ending, Bilbo himself escapes death, but the child reader who has closely identified with the little hobbit, experiences the loss of a true friend in the moving scene between Bilbo and the dying Thorin Oakenshield. Thorin, "wounded with many wounds," takes leave of Bilbo and adds: "I go now to the halls of waiting to sit beside my fathers, until the world is renewed."[15] Bilbo kneels, filled with sorrow, to bid Thorin farewell. "Then Bilbo turned away, and he went by himself, and sat alone wrapped in a blanket, and . . . he wept until his eyes were red and his voice was hoarse. He was a kindly soul. Indeed it was long before he had the heart to make a joke again."[16] So movingly does Tolkien describe the death of Thorin that the child hears or reads the passage with tears running down his cheeks. Though, in keeping with his essay, Tolkien implies that Thorin looks forward to renewal in a future life, Tolkien offers no facile comfort, no denial of grief. There are tears and it is a long while until time heals the wound of loss.

Though Tolkien's *The Lord of the Rings* trilogy is not officially considered children's literature, it is widely read by adolescents. And in the trilogy, they see the further development of Tolkien's examination of human mortality. The story presents many deaths--the brave, repentant death of Boromir, the magnificent burial rites of Theoden, the fearful suicide of Denethor, the squalid end of Sarumen diminished to Sharkey--but most of all it is concerned with putting death in perspective by challenging the reader to consider the function and value of death itself.

That the question of death and immortality was a major theme in Tolkien's trilogy is confirmed by a comment he made in reply to a letter inquiring if the theme of power was the dominant motif in *The Lord of the Rings*. Tolkien answered, "But I should say, if asked, the tale is not really about Power and Dominion: that only sets the wheels going; it is about Death and the desire for deathlessness."[17]

Tolkien develops the theme of death and immortality through three characters: Elrond and Elros, the twin sons of Elwing and Earendil the Mariner, and Arwen Undomiel, the daughter of Elrond. Elwing, the mother of Elrond and Elros, was of Eldar (elven) descent while Earendil, their father, was half-elven, half-human. At the end of the First Age, the Valar gave Elrond and Elros the irrevocable choice as to which kindred they would belong. Elrond chose the immortality of the Eldar and was granted the same grace as those of the High Elves that still lingered in Middle-earth: that when weary at last of the mortal lands, they could take ship from the Grey Havens and pass into the Uttermost West. Elros chose the mortality of Man-kind, but a great lifespan was granted to him "many times that of lesser men." Though a long lifespan was granted to his descendants as well, they had to remain mortal since the Valar were not permitted to take from them their mortality, the Gift of Men (or the Doom of Men, as it was afterwards called). Elros' descendants begrudged the choice of their forefather and desired immortality within the life of the world which was the fate of the Eldar. This discontent eventually brought about their downfall and the destruction of their kingdom, Numenor.

The reader wonders at first at the choice of Elros and sympathizes with his descendants. Who would not choose to live forever if he could? Throughout the trilogy, though his purpose is obscured by the heroic action of the epic heroes, Tolkien concerns himself with justifying Elros' choice by proving that mortality is indeed a gift and not a curse. The elves, immortal beings living in a mortal world, witness the passing of many beautiful things. All else but they must grow old and die. All the things of the world that they cherish, they must inevitably lose, until at last they are almost forced to seclude themselves in retreats like Rivendell and Lothlorien where they can, after a fashion, make time stand still. But they cannot otherwise reverse the inexorable passage of time. In the end, even Elrond knows the full bitterness of his immortality when he must part from his daughter Arwen who has chosen mortality in order to marry Aragorn.

In marrying Aragorn, Arwen shares with him "the Gift of Men," but she does not fully realize the meaning of her choice until the time of Aragorn's death. As his death approaches, Aragorn declares to Arwen: "Lo! we have gathered, and we have spent, and now the time of payment draws near." Yet she "could not forbear to plead with him to stay yet for a while. She was not yet weary of her days, and thus she tasted the bitterness of the mortality that she had taken upon her." To her grief at his imminent death he says: "I speak no comfort to you, for there is no comfort for such pain within the circles of the world." Arwen replies: "But I say to you, King of the Numenoreans, not till now have I understood the tale of your people and their fall. As wicked fools I scorned them, but I pity them at last. For if this death is indeed, as the Eldar say, the gift of the One to Men, it is bitter to receive." Aragorn replies: "But let us not be overthrown at the final test, who of old renounced the Shadow and the Ring. In sorrow we must go, but not in despair. Behold! we are not bound for ever to the circles of the world, and beyond them is more than memory."[18]

As Aragorn's remarks suggest, physical death is not the end of man. Tolkien clearly implies that there is life beyond Middle-earth in "the Uttermost West" where at the end of time, man will live forever in the place prepared for him by the Creator before the beginning of the world.[19] In the end of Tolkien's trilogy, Frodo, the Christ-figure of the story, wounded with incurable spiritual wounds, is granted the grace to sail beyond this world into eternity: "And the ship went out into the High Sea and passed on into the West . . and then it seemed to him that as in his dream in the house of Bombadil, the grey raincurtain turned all to silver glass and was rolled back, and he beheld white shores and beyond them a far green country under a swift sunrise."[20]

Both Tolkien and Lewis use the conventional imagery of the sunrise, the morning, the ending of the dream, and the green country as symbols of afterlife which will be blissful, lived in union with Iluvatar, the Father of All. Both authors enjoy immense popularity with young and old readers precisely because they have successfully coupled Judeo-Christian heritage with the mythic dimension of heroic literature and dare to say unequivocally that man exists beyond death, that death is a new beginning, that we are not bound forever to the circles of the world, and that beyond them is eternal life.

Less traditional than Tolkien and Lewis is the work of Shirley Rousseau Murphy in her fantasy sequence which includes *The Ring of Fire, The Wolf Bell*, and *The Castle of Hape*. These fantasies reveal Ms. Murphy's concern with the idea of rebirth to higher levels of existence if man lives virtuously in his present life. In *The Ring of Fire*, she introduces the idea that spirits exist which all mortals long for, but which are "so far removed from Ere [her imaginary fantasy world] and from this time and place, that few can guess at the reality of their beings. To be mortal is to understand mortality. But beyond that, the next step of your spirit's life can only be grasped when you are ready."[21]

In another section of the same book she writes:

> For the spirit moves onward, born yet again in a form we do not understand, born yet again on a plane farther removed from Ere than the plane in which the Luff'Eresi (the superior but mortal beings) now dwell. So are the planes of the universe. One and another and another beyond all counting by man. And each of you must move from the one to the other in lives that shine like hours in our mortal days. Must move or, trapped in a lust for cruelty that destroys the spirit, must die bound in one body forever.[22]

This same theology is repeated in her third book, *The Castle of Hape,* in which the seer, Ramad of Zandour, is told by the Luff'Eresi that man will be

> . . . born again, Ramad, provided one equips himself to be reborn. If he does not, if he has created evil, or nurtured evil with his way of life, if he has sucked upon the misery and pain of others, then he goes not forward into new lives but dies and turns to dust. It is the choice of each.[23]

Murphy stresses throughout her fantasies that man has control of his actions and that he will achieve a higher level of existence only if he lives virtuously in this life. She acknowledges the presence of evil in her world, but also assures the reader that, though it may temporarily triumph over the good, evil brings about its own destruction--the death of the soul and the end of all existence.

While Murphy suggests we enter higher and different levels of existence, Ruth Nichols' protagonist in *The Song of the Pearl* experiences reincarnation into other earthly existences. Mary Margaret Redmond dies at the end of the first chapter of the book, but her death is only a beginning. After she has regained her spiritual bearings in the peace of a mysterious pavillion, she must go back through various previous reincarnations to discover the initial reason for the hatred which emerges in each reincarnation to prevent her from achieving a higher level of existence. She is told by a spiritual guide that "neither life nor death lasts forever"[24] and that, when she has made peace with herself, she must return to Earth to resume her pilgrimage. But first, she must "understand and finish this story, so that a new one can begin."[25]

To get back to the root of her hatred, Margaret must go all the way back to ancient Sumer to her reincarnation as Tirigan, a young monarch assasinated by a usurper. His hatred for his murderer and his own curse of that murderer has echoed down through various reincarnations. Seeing the truth, Margaret can transcend her hatred and is promised in the future that, because she has overcome hatred, henceforth she will be rich in love. She is promised by the goddess Inanna: "You have known what it is to receive help: now you shall help others, and in the future many shall be made joyous by your love . . . Your story is vaster than you can conceive, and your adventures are just beginning."[26] Ms. Nichols' book departs radically from Judeo-Christian teachings as she draws upon Eastern myth and theology as the basis of her interpretation of life after death. But her views are not essentially so different from the others, for Margaret comes to realize that hatred is sterile and that revenge can destroy the revenger as thoroughly as the aggressor. She learns that love is the key to higher existence and that man must strive to live virtuously and in doing so he can gain eternal life.

The greatest and most moving examination of death and afterlife is to be found in the award-winning Earthsea trilogy of Ursula K. LeGuin. In *A Wizard of Earthsea, The Tombs of Atuan,* and *The Farthest Shore*, she explores the meaning of death as seen through the eyes of youth. With Taoism and Jungian psychology as her ideological bases, she also draws upon the idea of reincarnation as well as the heroic epic tradition and classical mythology to explore the relationship of life, death, and the hereafter.

In the first book, *A Wizard of Earthsea*, the young protagonist, an apprentice wizard named Ged, in his pride and arrogance, misuses his great natural ability in order to summon the dead into the world of the living. Too inexperienced to control the spell, he also loosens a terrifying "shadow" which cripples him, then pursues him throughout Earthsea until he turns and faces it.

Symbolically, LeGuin indicates that the very young do not and cannot cope with the knowledge of personal mortality. When Ged first deals with death in working a spell on Gont to please the witch's daughter, he is saved from a full realization of death by the intervention of Ogion. But when he summons the long-dead princess Elfarran to prove himself better than his fellow student Jasper, he discovers too soon the truth of his own mortality. LeGuin depicts that knowledge as a shapeless black monster who severely wounds Ged before being driven off by the Archmage at the price of his own life. Though LeGuin describes Ged's wounds as physical, they symbolize the psychic wounds a child sustains who realizes his own mortality too soon. Ged's paralysis is analogous to the depression and inertia of children exposed too early to death or life-threatening experiences.

All of his subsequent adventures and perils bring Ged closer to the inevitable confrontation with the reality of his personal mortality. But each encounter strengthens him also. His friend Vetch's love, demonstrated by the revelation of his true name, awakens in Ged for the first time the ability to care about someone other than himself. His attempt to save the son of Pechvarry, the fisherman, in spite of the danger to himself, demonstrates his emotional growth. Similarly, in his encounter with the dragon of Pendor, he again puts the welfare of his people before his own safety.

His ability to resist the lure of power offered by the Terrenon Stone and the sexual temptations of Serret also indicate a growing maturity. When at last he returns to Gond and Ogion, his teacher, through his suffering he has learned humility, patience, responsibility, self-control and, most importantly, love. He can finally "hunt the hunter" and give the monster his own name. When he names "the shadow *of his death* [italics mine] with his own name"[27] he has made himself whole. Ged comes of age by accepting his own mortality.

The Tombs of Atuan, the second book of the Earthsea trilogy, offers in symbolic terms the female coming of age. The protagonist Tenar, renamed Arha the Eaten One at the time of her initiation as priestess of the Nameless Ones, must choose whether to serve the gods of darkness and death who offer her immortality as an endlessly reborn priestess, or take back her own name, and live in the service of life.

Like Ged's, Tenar's testing is intricately intertwined with the theme of death. Her consecration at age six as priestess involves her symbolic death, but it is not until she orders the sacrifices of three men to the Dark Powers that death forces its reality on her. In a conversation with Ged, she considers the choice she must make in order to free herself from the evil gods: "If I leave the service of the Dark Ones, they will kill me. If I leave this place, I will die." Ged assures her that she will not die. Only Arha will die. He adds: "To be reborn one must die, Tenar. It is not so hard as it looks from the other side."[28] Like Ged, Tenar achieves maturity by choosing to serve life.

Of the trilogy, the book concerned with death most particularly is the third, *The Farthest Shore*. Of this book LeGuin herself has written: *"The Farthest Shore* is about death. That's why it is a less well-built, less sound and complete book than the others. They were about things I had already lived through and survived. *The Farthest Shore* is about the thing you do not live through and survive. It seemed an absolutely suitable subject to me for young readers, since in a way one can say that the hour when a child realizes, not that death exists--children are intensely aware of death--but that he/she, personally, is mortal, will die, is the hour when childhood ends, and the new life begins."[29]

In this powerful book, Ged, now Archmage of Roke, and Arren, young Prince of Enlad, journey throughout Earthsea to find the reason why men are losing all joy of life. Hare, a ruined wizard, provides the first clue. "No death. No death--no!! No sweaty bed and rotting coffin, no more, never. The blood dries up like the dry river and it's gone. No fear. No death."[30] All crafts and arts falter because people are obsessed with fear of death, and to win a kind of life-in-death, they sacrifice the joy and achievement of living. Even Arren is touched by the madness engendered by the fear of death. When Ged is badly wounded, Arren does nothing to help him. Later, he confesses to Ged: "I was afraid of you. I was afraid of death. I was so afraid of it I would not look at you, because you might be dying. I could think of nothing, except that there was--there was a way of not dying, for me, if I could find it. But all the time, life was running out, as if there was a great wound and the blood running from it--such as you had. But this was in everything. And I did nothing, nothing but try to hide from the horror of dying."[31]

Ged replies: "There is no safety, and there is no end. The word must be heard in silence; there must be darkness to see the stars . . . To refuse death is to refuse life."[32] He explains that the knowledge of mortality is a great gift. "It is the gift of selfhood. For only that is ours which we are willing to lose. That selfhood, our torment and glory, our humanity, does not endure. It changes and it goes, a wave on the sea. Would you have the sea grow still and the tides cease to save one wave, to save yourself?"[33]

LeGuin does not offer any easy comfort to her readers. Again and again, Arren expresses his fear of death and the Mage agrees that death is terrible and to be feared but adds that life is also terrible and must be feared and praised.

Confronted at last in the Land of the Dead, the sorcerer who has disturbed the balance between life and death by tampering with forbidden lore, asks: "What man would not live forever, if he could?" Ged answers: "All who ever died, live; they are reborn, and have no end, nor will there ever be an end. All, save you. For you would not have death. You lost death, you lost life, in order to save yourself."[34] When the sorcerer offers to share his immortality with Arren, the prince turns from him in disgust. He has at last understood the meaning of the song called "The Creation of Ea":

> Only in silence the word,
> only in dark the light,
> only in dying, life:
> bright the hawk's flight
> on the empty sky.[35]

Nor does LeGuin soften her picture of life after death by intimating that the dead dwell in some pleasant paradise. Her description of the land of the Dead suggests analogies with the Greco-Roman Hades, a place in which the shades of the dead dwelt in neither pain nor happiness. Dryness characterizes this land whose stars are unchanging, a place where

> . . . the marketplaces were all empty. There was no buying and selling there, no gaining and spending. Nothing was used; nothing was made. . . All those whom they saw--not many, for the dead are many, but that land is large--stood still, or moved slowly and with no purpose . . . No marks of illness were on them. They were whole and healed. They were healed of pain and of life . . . Quiet were their faces, freed from anger and desire, and there was in their shadowed eyes no hope.
>
> Instead of fear, then, great pity rose up in Arren, and if fear underlay it, it was not for himself, but for all people. For he saw the mother and child, who had died together; but the child did not run nor did it cry, and the mother did not hold it or ever look at it. And those who had died for love passed each other in the streets.
>
> The potter's wheel was still, the loom empty, the stove cold. No voice ever sang.[36]

LeGuin's interpretation of life after death seems to include all of the major approaches used by various other authors. She draws on classical mythology, the heroic epic mythos, the idea of gods and dark powers, and the idea of reincarnation as well. Arren confronts death in a terrifying journey through the underworld as do many other epic heroes, and at the end of the trilogy he takes his place as the High King of Earthsea. Gods, dragons, primal powers and great heroes contribute a feeling of authenticity to her epic.

In her treatment of the spirits of the dead, she seems to suggest the idea of reincarnation. There is a land of the Dead, classical in nature, but its inhabitants such as the spirit of the great hero Erreth-Akbe seem to be merely apparitions, holographic images of spirits who once lived upon earth in that human form, for of Erreth-Akbe and the others, Ged says: "He is alive. And all who ever died, live, they are reborn and have no end, nor will there ever be an end."[37]

In the final analysis, no living man knows what lies beyond the grave, and it is this ignorance on which life is based. Again, in *The Left Hand of Darkness,* LeGuin writes: "The unknown, the unforetold, the unproven, that is what life is based on. Ignorance is the ground of thought. Unproof is the ground of action. If it were proven that there is no God, there would be no religion . . . But also if it were proven that there is no God, there would be no religion . . . "[38] Each fantasy author who attempts to expand the child's comprehension of metaphysical reality stresses three virtues: the protagonist's faith in a spiritual reality, his hope of achieving a higher level of existence in that spiritual reality when physical life is ended, and most important of all, what Paul calls the greatest of the virtues, love. Each protagonist in the novels discussed must grow in love for his fellowman even to the point of sacrificing his own good for the good of others.

Shirley Murphy's protagonists believe that man will be born again only if he has not created evil or nurtured it with his way of life, if he has not sucked upon the misery and pain of others. Having overcome hatred, Mary Margaret Redmond is reborn to give love to others and is promised a new existence vaster than she can conceive. Tolkien's Frodo wins through to a higher level of existence by sacrificing himself for the good of Middle-earth. He tells the faithful Sam: "I tried to save the Shire, and it has been saved, but not for me. It must often be so, Sam, when things are in danger: some one has to give them up, lose them, so that others may keep them."[39] Ged saves his world by sacrificing all of his mage-power to close the door between death and life.

Lewis, Tolkien, Murphy, Nichols, and LeGuin have chosen to express their beliefs about life and death in term of fantasy terms because, as LeGuin has written: "Fantasy is the natural, the appropriate, language for the recounting of the spiritual journey."[40] Realistic fiction is a most unsatisfactory medium for expressing a truth which is beyond reason, beyond mortal knowledge. Students may visit cemeteries and funeral parlors; they may lie in coffins indeed, but until educators and writers overcome their fear of the metaphysical aspect of death, children will be denied true insight into the function of death as part of life. Until then, death will be only the corruption of the grave, the great fertilizer.

It remains then for fantasies to confirm that death is "terrible and must be feared."[41] These writers dramatize for their young readers that "in sorrow we must go but not in despair. Behold! we are not bound for ever to the circles of the world, and beyond them is more than memory."[42]

*This essay is being published posthumously.

[1]Ursula K. LeGuin. *The Left Hand of Darkness* . New York: Walker and Co., 1969, p. 52.

[2]Genesis 3:19.

[3]Revelations 21:4.

[4]*Beowulf,* in *The Norton Anthology of English Literature*, 4th ed., ed. M.H. Abrams *et al.* New York: W.W. Norton & Co., 1979, I, 59.

[5]I Corinthians 2:9.

[6]Gene I. Maeroff. "Schools Take Up Study of Death," *New York Times, 6* March, 1978, p. 1A.

[7]Maeroff, p. 1A.

[8]Jane Abramson. "Facing the Other Fact of Life: Death in Recent Children's Fiction," *School Library Journal*, 21:4, December 1974, 31-33.

[9]Abramson, p. 33.

[10]C.S. Lewis. *The Last Battle.* New York: The Macmillan Co., 1956, p. 173.

[11]Lewis, p. 173.

[12]Lewis, pp. 173-174.

[13]J.R.R. Tolkien. "On Fairy-Stories," in *Tree and Leaf* . Boston: Houghton Mifflin, 1965, pp. 67-68.

[14]Tolkien. "On Fairy-Stories," p. 68.

[15]J.R.R. Tolkien. *The Hobbit* . Boston: Houghton Mifflin, 1966, pp. 300-301.

[16]*The Hobbit*, p. 301.

[17]Glen GoodKnight. "Death and the Desire for Deathlessness," *Mythlore* 3:2, Whole No. 10, 19.

[18]J.R.R. Tolkien. *The Return of the King*, 2nd ed. Boston: Houghton Mifflin, 1965, pp. 343-344.

[19]Tolkien is here following a long tradition in locating Paradise somewhere in

the West to be reached by sailing on the unknown seas.

[20]*The Return of the King*, p. 310.

[21]Shirley Rousseau Murphy. *The Ring of Fire*. New York: Atheneum, 1977, p. 194.

[22]*The Ring of Fire*, p. 177.

[23]Shirley Rousseau Murphy. *The Castle of Hape*. New York: Atheneum, 1980, p. 93.

[24]Ruth Nichols. *The Song of the Pearl* . New York: Atheneum, 1976, p. 127.

[25]*The Song of the Pearl*, p. 128.

[26]*The Song of the Pearl*, p. 151.

[27]Ursula K. LeGuin. *A Wizard of Earthsea*. Berkeley, CA: Parnassus Press, 1968, p. 203.

[28]Ursula K. LeGuin. *The Tombs of Atuan*. New York: Atheneum, 1971, p. 114.

[29]Ursula K. LeGuin. "Dreams Must Explain Themselves," *Algol,* No. 21, November 15, 1973, p. 14. Rpt. *The Language of the Night*, ed. Susan Wood. New York: G.P. Putnam's Sons, 1979, p. 55.

[30]Ursula K. LeGuin. *The Farthest Shore*. New York: Atheneum, 1972, p. 61.

[31]*The Farthest Shore*, pp. 135-136.

[32]*The Farthest Shore*, pp. 136-137.

[33]*The Farthest Shore*, pp. 137-138.

[34]*The Farthest Shore*, p. 204.

[35]*A Wizard of Earthsea*, p. 7.

[36]*The Farthest Shore*, p. 196.

[37]*The Farthest Shore*, p. 204.

[38]*The Left Hand of Darkness*, p. 52.

[39]*The Return of the King*, p. 309.

[40]Ursula K. LeGuin. "The Child and the Shadow," *The Quarterly Journal of the Library of Congress,* 32:2, April, 1975, 147.

[41]*The Farthest Shore*, p. 185.

[42]*The Return of the King*, p. 344.

6

DYNAMIC LIFE CHOICES IN THE LEWIS TAPESTRIES

Grace R.W. Hall

In Part II, The Humanist Case, Donovan explores the use of fantasy to develop a young reader's imaginative projection and self-appraisal. She uses Carroll's Alice and Baum's Dorothy to illustrate an implicit challenge to young people for deeper self-exploration and discovery of their human potential. In Part III, The Religious View, Esmonde demonstrates five writers' use of skillful fantasy to explore a common theme: death and the hereafter.

Hall joins these two to celebrate the dynamic possibilities of fantasy for the enriching of young readers. Unlike Esmonde, her focus is on one author, but a number of themes. She discusses C.S.Lewis' use of the *Chronicles of Narnia* to introduce youth to some classic Christian concepts. Lewis does not overly preach Christianity; he erects no tinsel pulpit. Instead, Hall demonstrates how he engages the reader in a fully realized fantasy of other worlds from which Christian themes organically arise.

DYNAMIC LIFE CHOICES IN THE LEWIS TAPESTRIES

Through the creation of several worlds, the characterizations of all kinds of life, and the positing of a continuing society, C.S. Lewis dramatizes his world view for the young reader in the *Chronicles of Narnia* Lewis introduces children to the landscape, architecture, and inhabitants of a Dead World, an Underworld, and a Sea World. His prime concern, however, is with Narnia, an alternate world, and with the other world, Aslan's country. Lewis' alternate world provides a basis for an evaluation of the child's own world and of the child's actions in it. Narnian history parallels human history. It affords a perspective on the latter. Its vantage point from which human history is viewed reveals the limitations and imperfections of the child's own world. The character, wholeness, and emotional quality of the Narnian experience evoke older, more complete value systems. The reader is drawn into participation with the human child characters through whose perceptions he experiences Lewis' fantastical world. Both Lewis' characters and his readers grow in awareness as they experience hardship, transformation, sacrifice, metamorphosis, and mission. No aspect of life is ignored in the *Chronicles of Narnia* and a multitude of life questions are answered as the children pursue an enemy, search for a lost friend, Prince, or father, or make the journey to the Uttermost East.

As a professor of medieval literature, Lewis immersed himself in the literature of the past. In the Narnia series he reanimated that literature, making Narnia a composite world more reminiscent of a medieval tapestry than of a modern, sterile Utopia. Lewis does not hesitate to enrich his art and delight his audiences by drawing into his world Celtic druids, a Biblical unicorn, Roman fawns and Naiads, and Greek dryads and satyrs. He introduces children to the supernatural, the mystical and the miraculous in a world where Earth's children fraternize with the very real inhabitants of another land: talking beasts, fawns, and awards. The societies which flourish within Narnia range in character from the sublime to the ridiculous and include the redemptive and the destructive. Their inhabitants, whether mice, men, or marshwiggles, exhibit peculiar traits, virtues, flaws and/or values with which a child may identify.

Despite his joy in the fantastical, Lewis maintains a fidelity to nature and life in the vivid descriptions of specific animals and their habits and activities and in his representation of the real children, with their fears and their quarrels. A beaver builds a dam and lives near it and catches fish. A lion roars. A frightened horse returns to its stable. A boy cries because his mother is dying and tries to hide his tearstained face from a girl, who, not knowing, indelicately asks him what he has been "blubbering" about. A puny little boy likes bossing and bullying other children and pinning dead beetles to a card. His realism is grounded on his appeal to the five senses: fragrance, creative music, the majesty of a castle, the brush of snow, the tang of tea and the taste of fish, "alive half an hour ago" and "out of the pan half a minute ago" (*The Lion, The Witch and the Wardrobe* , p. 60). Narnia is a land which provides a richer, fuller, more complete sense experience than our world. The animals are much larger than those in our world, more real--and talkative. Narnia is not only a land in which the senses are very real, but a land of shadows and light and intuitive knowledge. Lewis thus mixes the natural, the real, and the fantastic to create his worlds of pulsating humanity and animality. Fantasy is grounded in reality, the mystical touches the mundane, and the Divine manifests itself in animality.

All of Lewis' worlds are appropriately peopled. In non-industrial Narnia animals, trees, and rivers are alive and work in harmony with men. In Underworld the gnomes are dreadfully pale and carry three-pronged spears in their hands and pad along on large soft feet in the knobbled and twisted, walled and dark caverns with stony floors. From those dark realms "few return to the sunlit lands" (*The Silver Chair* , p. 125). Out of the marshland Lewis raises Puddleglum, a gloomy but wise Marshwiggle, who turns out to be a brick.

Besides being right for their settings, Lewis' characters retain their identity. They do not become more and more allegorical (as Ransom does in Lewis's adult fantasy). Nor do they progress until they become superhuman as in evolutionary Utopian science fiction. Reepicheep, the stalwart mouse, is as straightforward and certain of his duty and as sensitive to the feelings of the others as he has always been (though he is quivering with happiness) when he reaches the eastern end of the world and says finally, "This is where I go on alone" (*The Voyage of the Dawn Treader,* p. 206), and, as he unbuckles his sword, which has been his means of defending the King's and his own honor and flings it across the lilied sea, "I shall need it no more" (*The Voyage of the Dawn Treader,* p. 206). The children, though rising to kingship and queenship, react consistently too; given free choice, they sometimes opt poorly.

The conduit to this fantastical, but believable world is significant for the characters and the reader. In *The Lion, The Witch and the Wardrobe,* four children escape boredom on a rainy day and discover a more natural world of Narnia and the "magic" of redemption. In *Prince Caspian,* the same four children escape immediate embarkation for the routine and drill of the school year and become involved in a battle for the restoration of a king. In *The Voyage of the Dawn Treader,* three children escape from a routine spat to a journey to the Lone Islands and the experience of the transformation of one of the children. In *The Magician's Nephew,* a boy escapes the clutches of an evil man and discovers other worlds and a healing fruit for his dying mother. In *The Silver Chair,* two children escape the bullying of scholars in Experiment House and are blown from a cliff by a huge lion to an adventure which leads them into Underworld and the rescue of a prince. In *The Last Battle,* two children escape time in a railway accident and the shadowlands of the dead and enter into the morning of an Eternal Day and a Universal Kingdom where they travel with ever increasing speed "further in and further up."

Thus, Lewis avoids the sense of isolation of his fantastic world from our world by his unique transitions. Unlike scientific fantasy which depends largely upon technology for travel through space, and hence requires an immense time gap, the Lewis adventures are embarked upon when a picture comes alive, a wardrobe door swings open to conceal hide-and-seek players, or when children touch magic rings in an attic room. Furthermore, by providing a different time system for each world, he avoids boring intervals in space capsules and the necessity of the children's taking "any of our time" (*The Lion, The Witch and The Wardrobe,* p. 39) for their adventures into Narnia. The characters exist comfortably in two worlds at a time. He illustrates the independence of time systems by the differences in the progress of time in the geographical and historical development which the children discover when they return to Narnia, a hardly recognizable country after a span of only a few years in their own world. He calls attention to the dying sun (timekeeper) in another world where the children, supposedly on the way to Narnia, are mistakenly plummeted.

His transitions suggest far more than Lewis' skill as a story-teller. They show his empathy with his child characters and his young readers as well. He accepts the frustrations children have with school routines and other limits set by adult society and suggests that there are experiences to be desired, experiences that are other-worldly, which exceed in excitement, meaning, and joy those of the everyday world. A child may owe allegiance to both worlds, the world of duty and the world of joy. The alternate world provides escape, but also involves mission or redemption. Clearly, Lewis suggests that there is more to be learned than that which is found in traditional schools or in experimental educational systems.

As the fictional children of this fantasy learn resourcefulness, self-reliance, and stretch a multitude of inner reserves, so the reading child through imaginative projection can explore himself. The children of the book assimilate every aspect of reality in another world, physical, emotional, and political. They are preoccupied with the landscape, the geography, and the occupants. They learn to cope with a great variety of creatures with unique whims and traits. They learn to cope with the irregular in life, for there are moments occupied with fears of giants, frozen hands and feet, and of uncertainty of location and loyalty. The children have to whisper and tread softly for they do not know for sure, in this unfamiliar world, which side even a robin is on. The children, seeing the world with fresh eyes, are forced into weighing values and making crucial decisions. The *Chronicles of Narnia,* like good secular fantasy, allow young readers to identify with characters and consider what they themselves might do.

But Lewis' fiction goes beyond secular humanism to suggest that something more than the mundane skirmish of men and animals is happening in this world of talking beasts. The fantasy suggests ways of responding to life other than the bartering and acquiring of goods, jobs to be done other than the mundane, and values to be idealized other than the humanistic. Lewis provides a purposeful view of mankind in which creation, invaded by evil, is aided by a god "who appears in the flesh" at crucial times to aid those who oppose the evil. That god is a lion (the lion of the tribe of Judah) in a country of talking beasts. Aslan is:

·The Breath of Life for the Dwarfs and Animals whom the White
Witch had turned into Stone,
·The Lamb who provides a breakfast of roast fish at the Eastern
End of the world,
·The Guardian of the Living Water,
·The Sign-giver for the Quest,
·The Willing Sacrifice for a Traitor,
·The Dragon Peeler for a Beast of a Boy.

Aslan is All, all that anyone needs on the journey home in *The Horse and His Boy.* The Voice in the Darkness and the Unseen Companion who walked on the precipice side of the path was also the lion.

". . . the lion." "I was the lion who forced you to join with
Aravis. I was the cat who comforted you among the
houses of the dead. I was the lion who drove the jackals
from you while you slept. I was the lion who gave the
horses the new strength of fear for the last mile so that you
should reach King Lune in time. And I was the lion you
do not remember who pushed the boat in which you lay, a
child near death, so that it came to shore, where a man sat,
wakeful at midnight, to receive you" (pp. 138-9).

50

Aslan is not vicious, nor cruel: he will not cause suffering where it is not necessary, but he is interested in removing the horny dragon skin, even though it makes the victim smart, in order to get down to the real person underneath. He does offer the living water to a little girl who will die without it, but on his terms, not hers. In the face of the blasphemy of a prince and the proposal to violate a young lady's sanctity, he gives fair warnings:

> "Demon Demon Demon!" shrieked the Prince. "I know you. You are the foul friend of Narnia. You are the enemy of the gods . . . The curse of Tash is upon you." . .

> "Have a care, Rabadash," said Aslan quietly. "The doom is nearer now: it is at the door: it has lifted the latch."

> "Let the skies fall," shrieked Rabadash . . .Let blood and fire obliterate the world! But be sure I will not desist till I have dragged to my palace by her hair the barbarian queen, the daughter of dogs, the ---"

> "The hour has struck," said Aslan, and Rabadash saw, to his supreme horror, that everyone had begun to laugh.

> They couldn't help it. Rabadash had been wagging his ears all the time and as soon as Aslan said, "The hour has struck!" the ears began to change. They grew longer and more pointed and soon were covered with grey hair.

> "Oh, not a Donkey. Mercy. If it were even a horse--even a horse--e'en--a--hor--eeh--auh, eeh-auh." And so the words died away into a donkey's bray.

> "Now hear me, Rabadash," said Aslan. "Justice shall be mixed with mercy. You shall not always be an Ass."

> "You have appealed to Tash," said Aslan. "And in the temple of Tash you shall be healed. You must stand before the altar of Tash in Tashbaan at the great Autumn Feast this year and there, in sight of all Tashbaan, your ass's shape will fall from you and all men will know you for Prince Rabadash" (pp. 185-7).

This remarkable quotation characterizes Aslan's patience and control in the face of a rebellious, ridiculous prince who acts more like a spoiled child than a leader. It calls attention to Aslan's habit of mixing mercy with justice. It has, however, a more subtle implication. Aslan does not suggest that Rabadash's religious affiliation be changed, but accepts Rabadash's "god."

Standing in opposition to Aslan is the White Witch. It is she who has made it "always Winter and never Christmas" (*The Lion, The Witch and The Wardrobe,* p. 14) in Narnia. In appearance she is a majestic queen, a fairy godmother with a magic wand, a provider of Turkish delight, but she tyrannizes her subjects, renders lifeless those whom her wand touches, and induces insatiable cravings and nausea in those whom she provisions. As the originator of evil in Narnia, she is the exact counterpart of Aslan, the originator of all that is good.

Evil and human frailty take many forms in Lewis' books. Destruction of our world in *On the Beach* by an atomic bomb is tame in comparison to the crumbling walls, towers, and throne room of a majestic civilization which has been annihilated by the evil Queen who dared to say "the deplorable word" *(The Magician's Nephew*, p. 54) which even turned sun to blood. The materialistic society of the Calormenes has no respect for nature and, invading Narnia, lays waste the land in *The Last Battle*. The Dwarfs, cautious, unbelieving, and isolated even in the eternal kingdom, refuse to see its grandeur. A society of enormous physical proportions, the Giants at Harfang, serve and eat talking beasts. On Doorn and Avra, two of the Lone Islands which belong to the King in name, practices have crept in which are alien to Narnian ethics: slavery and disorder in conduct. And, although they do not deny allegiance to the King, they will not "believe" Caspian is King and his life is imperiled. In *The Voyage of the Dawn Treader* the children come upon the laughable, childish Dufflepuds who can't even get their own names straight, invisible Monopods who repeat everything the Chief says and cheer on both sides of the argument between Lucy and the Chief. They are "yes" men. Their god, like themselves, is invisible and "lives upstairs." So, also, does the Magician, his representative. The Dufflepuds are both afraid of him and think they can fool him, and are so manly and courageous that they insist that a little girl, Lucy, ascend and steal a spell for them from the Magician's book. They believe he is angry with them and are afraid he will sneak up on them for he "makes no more noise than a great big cat" (p. 116). Of course, Aslan is King here too, but the Dufflepuds do not know him very well. Against this array is clearly set the continuing society, the company of the committed, the friends of Narnia, those who share knowledge of Aslan and who have helped in his cause. As an old Professor who has been there once himself says: "Once a King in Narnia, always a King in Narnia."

Besides positing the creatures' allegiance to and reliance on a universal being outside man himself, Lewis weaves other Biblical themes throughout the seven books: themes of Creation, Sacrifice, Redemption, The Law, Resurrection, and Immortality. The creation of a world is described in *The Magician's Nephew:* Aslan breathes life into nature and man. The great theme of sacrifice and redemption is explored in *The Lion, The Witch and The Wardrobe* ; the king and creator of beasts, Aslan, who appears in the flesh to aid the children in their struggle against evil, "lays down his life" for a traitor and the world. In *The Silver Chair* a poignant passage contains a paraphrase of Isaiah 55:1. Aslan invites Jill to drink of the stream which he guards, the water of life. Nowhere else in the books are the children's choices presented with such clarity and simplicity as in this dialogue:

"If you're thirsty, you may drink."

. . .

"Are you not thirsty?" said the Lion.
"I'm *dying* of thirst," said Jill.

. . .

"I daren't come and drink," said Jill.
"Then you will die of thirst," said the Lion.

"Oh dear!" said Jill, coming another step nearer.
"I suppose I must go and look for another stream then."
"There is no other stream," said the Lion (pp. 16-17).

In *The Lion, The Witch and The Wardrobe*, the children learn of the law and justice and their claims at the Stone Table. There is a growing sense of the children's awareness of the nature of good and evil. They continually ask themselves: "How shall we behave under these circumstances?" "What is fair and just?" "Which is right?" There is a growing sense of discernment between right and wrong although, after all their experiences, they still, at times, choose their own way.

In *The Voyage of the Dawn Treader*, the light becomes more and more intense as the Dawn Treader approaches Aslan's country in a dynamic expression of the Scriptural passage: "The path of the just is as a shining light that shineth more and more unto the perfect day" (Proverbs 4:18). Aslan comes from the East over the sea; Cair Paravel is in the East by the Sea. Aslan's country is in the extreme East--where the sun never sets. "Oh, the cry of the sea gulls! Have you heard it?" (*The Lion, The Witch and The Wardrobe*, p. 148), asks Lewis, for somehow those who have heard know how that sound coming from above the waves synchronizes with the longing of the soul to be at one with its Maker.

Lewis' range is enormous. Not only does he intone a haunting sense at times, but at other times, he paints life in his world with a lively wit. A rollicking sense of humor pervades the scene where the newly-created animals converge on Uncle Andrew in *The Magician's Nephew*, christening him "Brandy" because that is what he says so often, and, after much indecision as to which way is up with him, finally opt that his bushy hair is a root system and plant him upside down. Yet even here a sense of justice prevails, for Uncle Andrew had not hesitated in sending a little girl out into space alone, not knowing what frightening beast might have awaited her there. In another amusing scene from *The Voyage of the Dawn Treader*, the children come upon a table set with a huge feast and boasting some very peculiar guests. Fearful of approaching what at first sight was discernible as "beavers," "huge birds' nests," or "haystacks," they finally arouse the three Mighty Lords, but all the conversation that can be elicited from them before they fall back into a deep sleep is:

"I'll go eastward no more. Out oars for Narnia.",

"Weren't born to live like animals. Get to the east while you've a chance--lands behind the sun", and

"Mustard, please" (p. 164).

This passage is not only amusing, but satirical, for these Lords can hardly rouse themselves to comment on the Great Journey, never mind continue it, and the last one can only remember that what he was eating didn't taste just right. The *Chronicles of Narnia* are replete with such examples.

The Magician's Nephew, The Lion, The Witch and The Wardrobe, The Horse and His Boy, Prince Caspian, The Voyage of the Dawn Treader, The Silver Chair, and *The Last Battle* are living tapestries, three-dimensional, yea, four-dimensional, making available, with clarity to children (and to those who once were) a dynamic tradition. Lewis offers in them real humanity and the hope of human kindness, yet his most important contribution is that he offers a continuing account of an adventure in another, more real world and a glimpse into Aslan's country.

The struggles of man in the world of nature and other men require the best efforts of man. But man is insufficient for the test and must rely on something beyond his power. Whatever else Lewis says to children, he makes it clear that they are not alone in an alien universe, for in addition to the strength and devotion of the company of the committed, there is Aslan. In Narnia, children are not subjects, but Kings and Queens in their own right, active participants and sharers of responsibilities in an on-going Kingdom, which begins with the "magic from before the dawn of time" *(The Voyage of the Dawn Treader*, p. 116), which works backwards when a willing, innocent victim forfeits his life for another, and which continues after "Time" *(The Last Battle*, p. 150) shall be no more.

BIBLIOGRAPHY

------, *Proverbs* 4:18, *The Holy Bible*. Authorized (King James) Version.

Lewis, C.S. *The Horse and His Boy*. New York, The MacMillan Company, 1954.

Lewis, C.S. *The Last Battle*. London: The Bodley Head, 1958.

Lewis, C.S. *The Lion, The Witch and The Wardrobe*. New York: The MacMillan Company, 1950.

Lewis, C.S. *The Magician's Nephew*. New York: The MacMillan Company, 1955.

Lewis, C.S. *Prince Caspian*. New York: The MacMillan Company, 1951.

Lewis, C.S. *The Silver Chair*. New York: The MacMillan Company, 1953.

Lewis, C.S. *The Voyage of the Dawn Treader*. New York: The MacMillan Company, 1952.

7

THE DIVIDED WORLD OF LOUISA MAY ALCOTT

Abigail Ann Hamblen

Hamblen's essay shows the division between two polar perspectives within the religious world view of one writer. She finds Louisa May Alcott's works salted with the spiritual transcendentalism of her father and peppered with the Calvanistic common sense and reasoned practicality of her mother. Alcott seemed to have equal concern for both of these poles of understanding. Her triology, *Little Women, Little Men,* and *Jo's Boys* , is peopled by those who soar to religious peaks and by others who seek refuge in reason and practicality. The two groups love and respect one another, but can never be wholly united.

THE DIVIDED WORLD OF LOUISA MAY ALCOTT

One of the most popular writers of children's fiction grew up in a curiously double-faceted environment. From her infancy Louisa May Alcott was subjected to both the amiable Transcendentalism of her dreamy father and the stern religious orthodoxy of her highbrow mother.

As every student knows, Bronson Alcott was constitutionally unable to earn a living in a harsh world. (In modern slang, he simply could not "hack it.") He could spend hours happily reading ancient philosophies and then writing down his own confused (and often confusing) ideas about what being alive was all about. "Thou art," he wrote, "my heart, a soul-flower, facing ever and following the motions of thy sun, opening thy self to her vivifying ray, and pleading thy affinity with the celestial orbs . . . . "

He believed, with Wordsworth, that each human being is born with a divine *core*, and that it is the function of education to exploit this divinity. But his innovative pedagogical efforts had to be cut short: early nineteenth-century New England was not ready for his idealistic Plumfield where children were encouraged to speculate on death and -- more amazingly -- on how they happened to be born.

Bronson Alcott was a man who cherished the intellect but it is clear that he gave man's spiritual yearnings his primary allegiance. "Believe, youth, that your heart is an oracle; trust her instinctive auguries, obey her divine leadings; nor listen too fondly to the uncertain echoes of your head." And, because he attended so strongly to the former, we may be sure poor Alcott never did the latter! He seemed wholly controlled by an inclination toward the ideal. And though his daughters loved him tenderly all their lives, and looked up to him with a kind of reverence, they could not live on saintly smiles and poetic thoughts; they needed food and clothes and housing. Such an unearthly religion, with its firm belief in man's divinity and God's goodness, is not able to provide what demands intelligent effort.

Abigail Alcott, adoring her husband but having a more traditional Calvinist streak in her, knew terrible hours of anxiety and depression, both of which Alcott himself seemed incapable of experiencing. Her religious posture was not nearly so ethereal; she was deeply conscious of man's need to do God's will in a corrupt world. Her girls had to learn to make their way - and in the mid-nineteenth-century if you were descended from the Boston Mays you did not clerk in shops, and you were very desperate indeed when you had to take in sewing, or go out as a governess. (We know that Louisa, as a very young woman, did actually "go out to service" as a housekeeper for a short time; her doing so was an episode that neither she nor her family ever cared to dwell upon.)

The Alcott story has been told over and over again. We know the various idealistic experiments the dreamer initiated or took part in: the Temple School, the fiasco of Fruitlands. We know that time and again some kindly relative or friend came forward with a little cash or a box of discarded clothing. We know of Abigail Alcott's tears, and her taking a position as a kind of "social worker" in Boston. We know that Louisa, fierce and hungry soul that she was, tutored, sewed, and wrote feverishly, determined, somehow, to survive. We know about her sisters, each of whom cultivated her own talents and, with the exception of one who died young, eventually achieved marriage and motherhood, both of which were denied Louisa.

"The worldling," wrote Bronson Alcott, "living to sense, is identified with the flesh; he dwells amidst the dust and vapors of his own lusts, which dim his vision, and obscure the heavens wherein the saint beholds the face of God." We shall never truly understand how much of such a statement his most famous daughter took to heart. But we do find, curiously, the blend of his "other-worldliness" and her mother's common sense orthodoxy advocated in her many books for children.

Like her father, Louisa seemed to have a deep belief in the power of some form of communion with a divine presence and trusted in the ultimate goodness of her God. She saw God as the eternal comforter; it was, she believed, his function to look after his children. Like her mother, however, she was a stern advocate of the Puritan work ethic, and had a deep orthodox conviction that man was responsible for his actions and must use his common sense to make his way in the world.

To trace the dichotomy of Transcendental spirituality and Calvinist practicality in all of her fiction would require volumes. We can see it very satisfactorily, however, in her famous trilogy, the last volume of which, *Jo's Boys,* was written at the end of her career.

One finds it difficult to explain just why *Little Women* achieved such success in its day, and later became a classic. Undeniably it has a fresh charm that never grows stale; one can read it at sixty with as much pleasure as when one read it at ten. Perhaps the reason for its success is that it celebrates life as only the great works of the world do, by showing in a spirited fashion the contrast of light and darkness, of despair and courage. In short, it is a mix of airy transcendentalism and a more down-to-earth orthodoxy.

Alcott herself was concerned, not with being great, but with making enough money to live on for her family existed perennially on the edge of poverty. So when her publisher suggested she write "a girls' story," she reluctantly consented to try her hand at one. And since "a girls' story" must offer moral uplift to its young readers, she incorporated in her tale what her dreaming father had taught her, mixing in a stiff dose of her mother's more clear-headed thought. The result is a tension between these starkly contrasting views which is woven into a delightful account of the growing-up years of four attractive girls.

Her mixed religious world view is made explicit in the first chapter. It begins with the four sisters complaining of their poverty, of the fact that there are to be no presents at Christmas, and the sadness of having their father off in the war. Then the mother reads them a letter from him, a letter in which he says that he knows it is difficult for them to wait a year before the family is reunited, but:

> while we wait we may all work, so that these hard days need not be wasted. I know they will remember all I said to them, that they will be loving children to you, will do their duty faithfully, fight their bosom enemies bravely, and conquer themselves so beautifully that when I come back to them I may be fonder and prouder then ever of my little women.

Here we have a clear statement of a fundamental religious "truth": each individual is beset by "sin," the father's gentle "bosom enemies." And it is the duty of each human being to conquer that sin. Just what is the "sin" of each of these girls? Selfishness; rebellion against one's lot; vanity; dislike of household drudgery; envy. Each of these, we note, is a "worldly" trait; each must be eradicated. But how this is to be accomplished is left unsaid.

The more practical mother provides "guide books" on Christmas morning: a copy of the New Testament for each daughter -- "the beautiful old story of the best life ever lived." The "spirituality" of Christ is to help these girls live in the material world.

They nevertheless discover that the problems they confront are unyielding. Jo finds controlling her fierce temper an almost insurmountable task; on one occasion her resentment almost results in great sorrow. After the episode, she has a quiet talk with her mother, who confesses that she, too, has had to fight this "bosom enemy." When Jo asks how she manages, Marmee explains that she has a "friend to comfort and sustain" her. She goes on gently:

> My child, the troubles and temptations of your life are beginning, and may be many; but you can overcome and outlive them all, if you learn to feel the strength and tenderness of your Heavenly Father as you do that of your earthly one. The more you love and trust Him, the nearer you will feel to Him, and the less you will depend on human power and wisdom.

So, although we have a vague suggestion followed by a more practical bit of guidance, the solution to living in a hard world is, in both instances, religious.

Later one of the sisters has a taste of so-called "fashionable" life, and finds herself out of her depth in a world of elegant clothes, vapid manners, exhilarating balls, and flirtatious schemes. She is glad to return home and describe it all to her mother who listens sympathetically and finally explains her "ambition" for her daughters, beginning, "I want my daughters to be beautiful, accomplished, and good; to be admired, loved, and respected, to have a happy youth, to be well and wisely married, and to lead useful, pleasant lives, with as little care and sorrow to try them as God sees fit to send."

If this hope for her daughters in any way exhibits a preoccupation with human affairs and material goods, it is balanced by a subsequent homily:

> Money is a needful and precious thing -- and, when well used, a noble thing, -- but I never want you to think it is the first or only prize to strive for. I'd rather see you poor men's wives, if you were happy, beloved, contented, than queens on thrones, without self-respect and peace.

Here we see a practical and socially conscious woman who nevertheless places all of these values inside the context of a devout religious "peace."

Reliance on God rather than self is made even more explicit in the chapter that tells of Beth's serious bout with scarlet fever. The young girl nearly dies in spite of careful nursing. At the moment of crisis, Jo is overcome with despair. Laurie takes her hand, holding it tight, and "the warm grasp of the friendly human hand comforted her sore heart, and seemed to lead her nearer to the Divine arm which alone could uphold her in her trouble."

Alcott's presentation of Jo's newspaper work again presents the tension of practical striving within the bounds of religious piety. Jo, striking out on her own, desperate to make money for her family, takes to writing sensational stories for a paper that caters to the less educated. She is brought up short eventually by the good Professor Bhaer, who makes her realize that she is doing emotional harm both to her readers and herself.

Conscience-smitten, she ponders the question as to whether or not she should keep the money paid her for these lurid tales. She has been saving it to take her ailing sister to the seashore in the summer. After some agonizing, she decides it is "right." "I think I haven't done much harm *yet,* and may keep this to pay for my time . . . I almost wish I hadn't any conscience, it's so inconvenient. If I didn't care about doing right, and didn't feel uncomfortable when doing wrong, I should get on capitally."

Alcott snares poor Jo in a very practical dilemma here: she can earn money, much-needed-money, at the expense of her religious ideals. The clash between the "spiritual" well-being of religious duty and the material advantages of worldly gain produces both pain and inconvenience. But the religious resolution of this and other conflicts is obvious.

Little Men, the second novel in the trilogy, is really a series of lively stories about the goings-on at Plumfield, the quite unorthodox school set up by Jo and Professor Bhaer after they were married. Today we would call their methods "progressive education," for they constantly stress spiritual growth as even more important than intellectual development.

Jo tells Nat, a newcomer, "I want my boys to love Sunday, to find it a peaceful, pleasant day, when they can rest from common study and play, yet enjoy quiet pleasures, and learn, in simple ways, lessons more important than any taught in school." A great deal of emphasis is placed on such ethical training and "spiritual" enrichment at Plumfield. So here again we see the primacy of the religious world view over that of the rational or practical one.

Nat first hears the story of Jesus from Demi, the small nephew of the Bhaers: "He liked poor people, and was very good to them. He made them well, and helped them, and told rich people they must not be cross to them, and they loved Him dearly, dearly." Nat asks if this great man were "rich," and Demi assures him he was not: "O no! He was born in a barn, and was so poor He hadn't any house to live in when He grew up, and nothing to eat sometimes, but what people gave Him, and he went round preaching to everybody, and trying to make them good, till the bad men killed Him."

We smile at this over-simplified version of the beginning of Christianity, but its very uncomplicated innocence fits in with the general tone of the Alcott system of ethics promulgated so energetically at Plumfield. As Alcott describes these two young boys we gain a fuller sense of the religious tension in her books. In Demi we see one

> very fond of books and full of lively fancies, born of a strong imagination and a spiritual nature. These traits made his parents anxious to balance them with useful knowledge and healthful society, lest they should make him one of those pale, precocious children who amaze and delight a family sometimes, and fade away like hot-house flowers, because the young soul blooms too soon, and has not a hearty body to root it firmly in the wholesome soil of this world.

As for the waif Nat, taken into the school, his teachers discover that "though his body had suffered, his soul seemed to have taken little harm." The hard realities of the material world had not injured the spiritual side of his nature. Thus we see in these two young boys a coalescence of Transcendental ideals and orthodoxy's concern for man's less ethereal nature.

The book ends on an explicit affirmation of the two-fold religious perspective. The elderly father compliments Jo on the work she and her husband are doing "to help on the good time." And Alcott remarks that "the good man never lost his faith in humanity, and still hoped to see peace, good-will, and happiness reign upon the earth."

Apparently Jo does not quite share her father's optimistic view of man. She

61

tells him she is not ambitious about changing the world. She simply wants to see that the children learn "honesty, courage, industry, faith in God, their fellow-creatures, and themselves." The merry, fun-filled *Little Men* is a dramatization of the trials and efforts to instill such qualities, qualities we see at a glance comprehend both religious perspectives.

Jo's Boys does not enjoy the popularity of *Little Women*. Louisa Alcott was understandably tired when she wrote it, and it lacks something of the verve and energy that make her great classic immortal. In her preface she apologizes: "Having been written at long intervals during the past seven years, this story is more faulty than any of its very imperfect predecessors; but the desire to atone for an unavoidable disappointment, and to please my patient little friends, has urged me to let it go without further delay."

Whatever its faults, it certainly encapsulates her religious philosophy, a philosophy which she felt her young readers should adopt as their own. We read the book with pleasure and with a sense of wonder that a hundred years can change the face of the world so much and leave untouched certain fundamentals.

In all her novels, Alcott stresses the importance of the "spiritual" life, that is, the necessity for Divine guidance. There is more than a touch of religiosity in them all, though never any orthodox sectarianism. But the reader does not feel overcome by this spirituality, for embedded within ther novel is the recognition of material necessity and the work ethic: stand on your own feet; do your job as best you can; use common sense. Her view is two-fold in that it seems to be spiritual, yet clearly recognizes that we are organisms grounded in a material world.

Jo's Boys tells of the struggles, the dreams, the hopes, and the successes of several young people. Some of these are Jo's sons and nephews and nieces. Others are those she and her Professor have had as students in their unconventional boarding school. Still others are attending the college established by a wealthy friend's will. All of these adolescents, at some time or another, come to her with their problems, and to all of them she gives compassionate advice. In her advice we see both the Transcendentalist father and the orthodox, practical mother.

Alcott's first chapter gives an account of the earlier fortunes and misfortunes of her principal characters, characters with whom the reader is presumably familiar. And here, as clearly as anywhere in her writing, we see her acceptance of Providence and man's achievements within that framework: "All manner of happiness, peace, and plenty came in those years to bless the patient waiters, hopeful workers, and devout believers in the wisdom and justice of Him who sends disappointment, poverty, and sorrow to try the love of human hearts and make success the sweeter when it comes."

The same practicality within the context of God's will is seen in a description of her own mother: "She had lived to reap the harvest she sowed; had seen prayers answered, hopes blossom, good gifts bear fruit, peace and prosperity bless the home she had made; and then, like some brave, patient angel, whose work was done, turned her face heavenward, glad to rest." Poor Abigail Alcott achieved her peace the hard way, even though her daughter does not emphasize the fact. Child of Boston Puritans, she had full need of such pious comfort after a life of marginal security with the idealist Bronson Alcott.

Louisa's lack of concern with material or "worldly" affairs is tempered in this book too. Jo's success as a writer is obviously due to her persistent work and patience. Jo apparently not only ran a large establishment (we know she does much of the actual housework herself), but she managed to write so much and so effectively that she became a well-known author. The Professor had had his long hours of labor, too. He took his teaching duties seriously, and the discipline requiring common sense was not always easy to handle. In other words, both Jo and the Professor had had to use their *minds* and *hands* to achieve successful careers. They relied on their Heavenly Father's loving attention but added their own measure of hard work to insure success.

One of the most interesting characters in light of Alcott's religious perspective is Dan, the "black sheep." In *Little Men,* Dan had come to the Bhaers' school at fourteen or so, already street-hardened. A passionate, black-browed boy (he reminds one faintly of Emily Bronte's Heathcliff), he is the most difficult child his teachers have ever encountered. His escapades, his language, his whole being, seem to run counter to romantic notions of childhood innocence. He rebels at discipline, and even runs off, to come back, finally, bruised and beaten, but still fiery.

In *Jo's Boys* he is still a wanderer, going out to make his fortune here and there. At one time in the story he comes back for a visit, preparatory to going West. He has earned a little money, and considers ranching, but explains that he doesn't care to amass any wealth; the pursuit of money, rather than the money itself, is the fun, and he looks "as if his little fortune rather oppressed him." At that point Dan seems motivated solely by benign materialistic impulses. His whole character, and it is a strong one, is clearly formed outside any religious concern. He believes that to get money, indeed to survive, one must work, and one must rely on oneself. He has no expectation that God will grant him any favors.

Jo knows his predisposition and advises him to be a good steward of his talents: "If you marry and settle somewhere, as I hope you will, you must have something to begin with, my son. So be prudent and invest your money; don't give it away, for rainy days come to all of us, and dependence would be very hard for you to bear." At the same time, however, "she liked *to see that the money-making fever had not seized her lucky boy yet."* (Italics added.) So, man must be prudent but not consumed by the fever for material goods. Jo is plainly under the influence of both the parable of the talents and the Biblical injunction: "Lay not up for yourselves treasures upon earth." Thus she represents Alcott's basic affirmation of religious orthodoxy which celebrates work and prudence only within the confines of a life in tune with the will of God.

In a later, long, heart-to-heart talk, she cautions Dan about his fiery temper, urging him to curb it: he must, she implores, turn to his heavenly Father, for "There is no other help or hope for human weakness but God's love or patience." She seems to recognize that a violent temper would be a great impediment to success and might even lead to physical trouble (as indeed it does later), and that the way to control it is to reach out to the spiritual source of help. Worldly wisdom within a context of religious concern seems to characterize her view of life. Interestingly, as they go on talking, Jo seems to see some spark of "dumb desire" in Dan's eyes, a longing that shows her "a glimpse of the divine spark which smoulders or burns clearly in every human soul." Here again the Transcendental ideas of her philosophic father seem to be creeping into her orthodoxy. But the advice she gives the young man moves away from that notion of the universal divinity of man a bit because of the evangelical tone with which she concludes her guidance:

> "Never sneer at good things or pretend to be worse than you are. Don't let false shame make you neglect the religion without which no man can live. You needn't talk about it if you don't like, but don't shut your heart to it in whatever shape it comes. Nature is your God now; she

has done much for you; let her do more, and lead you to know and love a wiser and more tender teacher, friend, and comforter than she can ever be. That is your only hope; don't throw it away and waste time; for sooner or later you will feel the need of Him, and He will come to you and hold you up and when all other help fails."

Alcott makes it clear that self-reliance and innate goodness are not sufficient, for in spite of the fact that Dan goes off to invest his money wisely and settle down, his strong passion (his basic depravity) masters him and in a moment of fury he kills a man. Alcott does not judge him harshly, for we are hastily assured that Dan kills in self-defense and that the world is better off without the victim (he was a ruthless card shark, intent on cheating an inexperienced young boy). The murder, moreover, was the result of Dan's passionate sense of injustice: he was incensed that a schemer would take advantage of an innocent young person. As the act was purely manslaughter, with extenuating circumstances, Dan's prison sentence is just a year.

We know, however, that in Louisa Alcott's eyes and those of her religious contemporaries he is still a sinner, a murderer. But because he comes to know despair and man's insufficiency, he is gently guided to repentance and reliance on God. And because of this turn to an external source of strength he is moved to acts of goodness: he keeps a prisoner from trying to escape, and later when he is released and working in a mine, saves the lives of twenty men, at great peril to his own.

Eventually Dan does get back to Plumfield, acutely conscious of his "stain." He is finally persuaded to tell his story to Jo, and is assured of her continuing affection, though her words seem strange today: "I *am* shocked and disappointed by the sin, but I am also very glad and proud and grateful that my sinner has repented, atoned, and is ready to profit by the bitter lesson . . .. "

A more modern, humanistic reader is drawn to Dan, feels a kind of exultant admiration for his courage, his strength, his passion. But because Alcott is wedded to the religious views of a century ago she views him as merely a "sinner" who has "repented and atoned." To Alcott he is never purified of his stain. For when it looks as if the beautiful, petted niece Bess is the object of Dan's love (though he tries to conceal the fact), Alcott has her taken away on a long trip. The girl is charming and gifted and almost supernaturally good and pure. She has known nothing but love and luxury and beauty and, though by modern standards Dan may be the more appealing of the two and in Alcott's eyes redeemed in many ways, he remains in her view dark with "sin." "Light and darkness," Alcott tells us, "were not farther apart than snow-white Bess and sin-stained Dan."

In many ways this curious mismatch sums up the strange blend of Alcott's parents' world views. We see here as throughout her work the Transcendental ideals of her father, his eternal hopefulness for mankind. But overshadowing this optimistic yearning is her mother's certainty that no individual can escape his basically finite and depraved nature, and the clear-headed practicality which is a part of that notion. At times a clear-headed practicality seems to assert itself over and above this pious perspective, but it is always seen in the final analysis to be a worldliness which lies clearly within the bounds of that orthodox faith.

PART IV POLAR PERSPECTIVES

8

SACRED AND SECULAR VISIONS OF IMAGINATION AND REALITY
IN NINETEENTH-CENTURY BRITISH FANTASY FOR CHILDREN

Anita Moss

Moss's essay shows how the fantasies of two nineteenth-century friends, Lewis Carroll and George MacDonald, pay homage to two contrasting worlds. MacDonald believed that the human imagination imitates the "prime operation of the power" of God and thus serves as the basic tool of revelation. In the imaginary fictive world MacDonald creates, he expresses his strong religious convictions in the hope that children can apprehend their divine dimension and enact their moral implications in the ordinary world. Carroll's work, in contrast, stresses the need for children to rely on their own intelligence and initiative in order to make sense of the complicated and baffling world of adults. He even mocks the conventional moral tales and instructional verse, the usual fare of nineteenth-century children. Thus, Alice grows to emotional maturity through her spirited, tenacious self-reliance, while MacDonald's lesser known characters seek to attain spiritual purity by looking beyond themselves for their ultimate spiritual resources. The fantasies of two of their contemporaries, Dinah Maria Mulock and Mrs. Molesworth (Mary Louisa Stuwart), reveal the influence of their original creations and the differing world views of the sacred and the humanistic.

SACRED AND SECULAR VISIONS OF IMAGINATION AND REALITY
IN NINETEENTH-CENTURY BRITISH FANTASY FOR CHILDREN

Writing classic British children's fantasies in the 1860's and 1870's, George MacDonald and Lewis Carroll essentially established the traditions of modern fantasy. Though they were personal friends and admired one another's work, these two writers held profoundly different views of reality. MacDonald, strongly influenced by Romantic conceptions of childhood and imagination, saw the universe as an orderly and miraculous creation, the work of a loving God whose will would finally prevail. Carroll, despite his conscious expressions of faith, seemed in the *Alice* fantasies acutely aware of disorder and chaos, of an uncertain and ever-shifting reality. These contrasting visions of reality provide the bases for two distinct traditions of fantasy which have found rich expression in the work of many other nineteenth- and twentieth-century fantasy writers. MacDonald established what has often been called "sacred" fantasy, a term which suggests that the imaginative quests and heroic efforts of human characters are performed in the service of a higher and divine order of reality. Lewis Carroll's fantasies, on the other hand, issue entirely from the imaginative faculties, the emotional fears and wishes of the child character. Carroll's *Alice* fantasies begin and end in the same place; they refer only to themselves and do not lead the reader into an awareness of divine reality. MacDonald's view of the imagination suggests that it is a mode of receiving divine revelation, while Carroll views it as a vehicle for the child's emotional survival and growth.

In many ways the fantastic works of George MacDonald assimilate ideas and techniques of emerging forms of fairytale and fantasy in nineteenth-century England. In the aftermath of the first expressions of Romanticism early in the century, some of the finest creative and critical minds increasingly turned to the imagination as a source of inspiration and sustenance in an age of anguished religious doubt and shifting values.[1] John Ruskin's literary fairy tale, *The King of the Golden River* (1851), combined an emphasis upon spiritual purity and social responsibility with a magical sense of nature and an idealized vision of childhood. In his famous fantasy, *The Water-Babies* (1863), Charles Kingsley attempted to reconcile the miracles of science with religious and social concerns. But George MacDonald explored these issues in the largest and most significant body of fantasy written in nineteenth-century England.

Several factors probably account for MacDonald's achievement. Born in Huntly in Aberdeenshire, Scotland, on December 10, 1824, MacDonald experienced in his childhood both the moral rigors of Calvinism and the picturesque landscape and the mysterious stories, legends, and ballads of the Celtic imagination.[2] A student of Romantic conceptions of nature, the imagination and the child, a Congregationalist minister who had to leave his pastorate for preaching what his congregation believed to be heretical German Romantic theology, an avid reader of German Romantic fairy tales, and an explorer of dreams, the unconscious, and psychic states such as mesmerism, MacDonald was uniquely prepared to weave these varied threads of conventions and ideas into a rich new tapestry. In so doing, he essentially established the conventions of modern British fantasy. In addition to his own Scottish background, MacDonald also had a clear understanding of the intellectual currents of his time. Like Kingsley, MacDonald was compelled in some way to compensate for anxieties resulting from religious doubt.

M.H. Abrams has explained that one of the major characteristics of Romantic writers is their penchant for attempting to make up for the loss of God, for a universe drained of supernatural meaning.

> In its central tradition Christian thought had posited three primary elements: God, nature, and the soul; with God, of course, utterly prepotent, as the creator and controller of the two others and as the end, the *telos,* of all natural process and human endeavor. The tendency in innovative Romantic thought (manifested in proportion as the thinker is or is not a Christian theist) is greatly to diminish, and at the extreme to eliminate the role of God, leaving as the prime agencies man and the world, mind and nature, the ego and the non-ego, the self and the not-self, spirit and the other, subject and object.[3]

Thus Wordsworth sought to unify the mind, the imagination, and nature. Poets such as Coleridge and Shelley manifest a marked interest in unconscious states of mind as a means of perception through which a higher reality is apprehended entirely and truly. And John Ruskin sees divine symbols not only in nature, but also in art. Nancy Mann has shown in her excellent dissertation that Victorian fantasy writers were occupied with similar concerns. While some of these writers, such as Lewis Carroll and William Morris were, either consciously or unconsciously, secularizers, Mann maintains that others such as Kingsley and MacDonald attempted to restore the "lost divine third term."[4] The revolution in ideas created by the Romantic movement, however, made it necessary for both Kingsley and MacDonald to embody the divine in significantly new ways. In *The Water-Babies,* then, Kingsley places his central character, Tom, in a totally secular and evil world and redeems him in the divine elements of nature. MacDonald's characters also begin their adventures in the context of the ordinary world. But they enter a fantasy world in which they encounter a divinely "other" presence, and then return to the ordinary world, where they may enact visionary truth in a social and ethical context. This characteristic pattern perhaps allows MacDonald to combine his visionary propensities with his Victorian (and Calvinist) need to keep his eye steadily upon duty in the social world.

Robert Lee Wolff, Richard Reis, C.N. Manlove, and Nancy Mann have all commented upon the "ordinariness" of MacDonald's intellect. Indeed he was not an original thinker, and he did not significantly modify ideas which came to him from theological writers of the past or those which came from the great seminal minds of the nineteenth century. For ideas on childhood, MacDonald drew heavily upon Wordsworth; he is indebted to Coleridge for conceptions of the imagination. The transcendentalism of Carlyle permeates MacDonald's works of fantasy, though in MacDonald this quality becomes a radical kind of immanence, rather than transcendence.

In matters of religious doctrine, MacDonald increasingly turned away from Calvinism (especially after the resignation of his only pulpit as a result of controversies over divine love and such questions as the damnation of the heathen and the place of animals in eternity). Having finally joined the Broad wing of the Established Church, MacDonald associated with religious liberals. He was influenced by the religious writers Jacob Boehme and William Law, who emphasized mystical experience, and by those who stressed tolerance and the importance of ethics, such as the Cambridge Platonists and F.D. Maurice.[5] MacDonald's theological notions began in childhood:

I well remember feeling as a child that I did not care for
God to love me if he did not love everybody: the kind of
love I needed was the love that all men needed, the love
that belonged to their nature as the children of the Father, a
love he could not give me except he gave it to all men.[6]

Despite some private struggles with religious doubt resulting from the deaths of
four of his eleven children, MacDonald's faith was never really in question. He
believed unswervingly in a divine reality in which all dimensions of nature,
including man, participate. Ultimately, through his fantasies, essays, and
"unspoken sermons," MacDonald constructed a divine order of his own, using
ideas from Pietism, Platonism, and Christian Socialism. In many respects the
writing of fantasy became a way for MacDonald to embody his most deeply and
profoundly felt convictions about the place of the divine spirit in the material world,
and the relationship between adult and child, creature and creator, the imagination
and spiritual growth. His ideas on the imagination are especially potent and have
exerted a significant influence upon subsequent writers of fantasy. The imagination
enables man to penetrate the divine essence and the productions of the pure
imagination necessarily express the truths of that divine reality.[7]

In discussing the role of the imagination in his essay "The Imagination: Its
Function and Its Culture," MacDonald explains that the imagination is "that faculty
in man which is likest to the prime operation of the power of God."[8] Yet in
MacDonald's view, man's imagination is only capable of revelation, not creation.
Thoughts in man, he says, arise unconsciously. If the man is good, his perception
of revelation will be the surest way to truth:

We dare to claim for the true, childlike, humble imagination,
such an inward oneness with the laws of the universe that it
possesses in itself an insight into the very nature of things.[9]

Hence the miner boy, Curdie, and his father, Peter, in *The Princess and Curdie*
(1883) see the Grandmother as a beautiful woman, "the whole creation . . .
gathered in one centre of harmony and loveliness in the person of the ancient lady
who stood before him in the summer of beauty and strength."[10] But the Mother of
Light explains: "For instance, if a thief were to come in here just now, he would
think he saw the demon of the mine, all in green flames" (p. 55). Thus the
imagination, if the person is not good, can be a dangerous faculty which may lead
one away from the truth. MacDonald explains:

The imagination will work, if not for good, then for evil; if
not for truth, then for falsehood; if not for life, then for
death. The power that might have gone forth in conceiving
the noblest forms of action, in realizing the lives of the
true-hearted, the self-forgetting, will go forth in building
airy castles of vain ambition. Seek not that your sons and
daughters should not see visions, should not dream
dreams; but that they should see true visions, that they
should dream noble dreams.[11]

MacDonald demonstrates the dangerous possibilities of an impure imagination in several of his fantasies. Princess Rosamond in *The Wise Woman* (1875) imagines ravening wolves and other horrors which inhibit her progress and spiritual growth; Mr. Vane in *Lilith* (1895) imagines creatures of horror as he journeys through fairy land unless he is in the pure light of the moon. Invariably in the fantasies of MacDonald, a narcissistic imagination turned in on the self is at best self-centered and shallow, and at worst, diseased, perverse, and evil, a pattern prominent among Romantic writers. For MacDonald, the true end of the imagination and its activity is not excess but harmony: "A right imagination, being the reflex of the creation, will fall in with the divine order of things."[12]

In his essay "The Fantastic Imagination," originally published as a preface to a volume of his fairy tales, MacDonald reaffirms and amplifies his convictions on the nature of the imagination. A writer of fantasy may "invent a little world of his own, with its own laws; for there is that in him which delights in calling up new forms--which is the nearest perhaps he can come to creation."[13] In creating such an imaginary world, though, the writer of fantasy must create harmonious and consistent laws: "And in the process of his creation, the inventor must hold by those laws. The moment he forgets one of them, he makes the story, by its own postulates, incredible."[14]

The writer has no such freedom to invent in the moral world, however: "In physical things a man may invent; in moral things he must obey--and take their laws with him into his invented world."[15] MacDonald also believes that the lessons acquired through imaginary or visionary experience must be enacted or embodied concretely in the ordinary world. This conviction is expressed in many of his fantasies. In *Phantastes,* Anodos begins his experience in the ordinary world, and comes out renewed and ready to act upon his knowledge in the context of his moral and social life. The same pattern occurs in *At the Back of the North Wind* and *Lilith.*

MacDonald's solution to problems of faith is most persuasively expressed in those fantasies in which he can express intimations and suggestions of the divine without having to spell out its meaning. Again in "The Fantastic Imagination," MacDonald explains the symbolic nature of fairytales. He compares them to a sonata because they evoke "a suitable vagueness of emotion: a fairytale, a sonata, a gathering storm, a limitless might seizes you and sweeps you away . . . The greatest forces lie in the region of the uncomprehended."[16] The fairytale and fantasy provided forms, then, which enabled MacDonald to recreate manifestations of divine truth. Whatever doubts man may experience, MacDonald insists, the divine reality exists. And we can receive that truth by responding to it imaginatively rather than intellectually.

MacDonald's artistic success is greatest when he follows his own counsel and lets his unconscious imagination work without the interference of his conscious need to make morals explicit. When MacDonald the preacher works too hard and gets in the way of MacDonald the Romantic writer, the resulting fantasies often exhibit divided structures. For instance, the protagonists of *At the Back of the North Wind* and *Lilith* bounce back and forth between the ordinary world and the imaginary world. Likewise *The Wise Woman* (1875) manifests this split structure, a feature which C.N. Manlove has argued results from a divided vision of reality.

MacDonald, however resolutely he turned away from Calvinism, was not always entirely successful in unifying the Romantic and mystic dimensions of his thought with his unmistakably Victorian emphasis upon work, duty, and obedience. In some sermons, for example, MacDonald expresses the Romantic notion that knowledge results from the imaginative identification of subject with object: "To know a primrose is a higher thing than to know the botany of it."[17] And "I trust we shall be able to enter into its [nature's] secrets from within them--by natural contact between our heart and theirs."[18] If doubt interferes with such mystical identification, MacDonald advocates obedience and action: "He who does that which he sees, shall understand; he who is set upon understanding rather than doing, shall go on stumbling and mistaking and speaking foolishness."[19] MacDonald suggests, then, that in matters of faith, human beings had best suspend their rationalist analytical faculties in favor of the imagination and the spirit. Yet his Calvinist upbringing undoubtedly causes him to insist that faith must also be accompanied by good works in the context of the social and ethical world.

Yet in his best works of fairy tale and fantasy, such works as *The Golden Key, The Princess and the Goblin,* and *The Princess and Curdie* in which MacDonald allows his own imagination to work freely, he achieves artistic unity through his skillful use of the quest romance form and through consistently used symbols. In these fantasies the child protagonists move through the fantasy world, where they are tested and where they acquire spiritual and moral truths which can then be enacted in the ordinary world.

The Romantic strain of fairy tale and fantasy which had slowly germinated in the early years of the nineteenth century evolved, then, to a rich culmination in the fantasies of George MacDonald. His use of such forms significantly modified images and ideas of childhood and imagination. MacDonald not only wrote fairy tales and fantasies, but actually created fully realized imaginary worlds of his own where characters apprehend divine truth and so attain higher and purer spiritual states of being.

Lewis Carroll also created an imaginary world of his own, controlled by its independent rules, and in doing so, his first two books for children, *The Adventures of Alice in Wonderland* (1865) and *Through the Looking Glass* (1871), broke free of the didactic tradition in unprecedented ways and changed the subsequent course of children's literature. They were, Harvey Darton has noted, "the spiritual volcano" of children's literature.

The facts about Charles Lutwidge Dodgson's (Lewis Carroll's) life are well-known. He enjoyed a relatively happy childhood in the rectory at Daresbury, where, despite the strongly religious atmosphere, he nevertheless learned at an early age to entertain the children with games, puzzles, drawings, puppets, plays, and stories. Later, Dodgson studied at Oxford, completing his Bachelor of Arts in 1855 and his Master of Arts in 1857. Although he took a deacon's orders in the Anglican Church, he spent most of his career in the secular role of lecturer in mathematics and logic at Christ's Church, Oxford. While Dodgson outwardly affirmed an orthodox faith, some writers have interpreted his fantasies as an indication of his deeply ambiguious views towards religious truth. The terrors and the chaos of the *Alice* fantasies suggest indeed that Lewis Carroll lacked the unswerving convictions in a divine order of reality which are manifested in MacDonald's best fantasy.[20] Carroll repeatedly relies on the humanistic and ordering processes of the mind and the imagination to maintain a precarious balance in the face of a terrifying and uncertain reality.

While the significance of Carroll's two *Alice* fantasies has been analyzed from almost every conceivable perspective, no account of nineteenth-century fantasy could be complete without investigating the role of Carroll's classic works in the evolution of the genre. And in a discussion of the secular and the sacred in children's literature, his work interestingly contrasts with MacDonald's. Intensely aware of the controversy between the didactic forces in children's literature and defenders of fairy tale, Carroll often mocks or parodies moral tales, instructional verse, and school lesson books. He thereby reveals fantasy and the imagination as means through which children may celebrate an unabashed and joyously free anarchy of their own. Unlike MacDonald's heroes and heroines who move through fantastic worlds to acquire moral virtue and spiritual vision, Carroll's character Alice confronts in her fantasy world some of her profoundest wishes and fears, conquers or rejects them, and so grows toward emotional maturity, rather than spiritual wisdom or purity. Carroll thus realizes an entirely new vision of childhood as a time when children use their imaginations and their intelligence, not in the service of redeeming a fallen creation, but as a way of protecting themselves from stifling adult authority and of acquiring more secure identities for themselves in the face of emotional terrors which threaten to annihilate identity and to impede initiative. At the same time that Carroll created his revolutionary "secular" image of childhood and the imagination in the *Alice* fantasies, he also helped to encourage the conventional and idealized myth of the Victorian child in articles, public addresses, and in his last fantasies *Sylvie and Bruno* (1890) and *Sylvie and Bruno Concluded* (1894). Thus, while Carroll consciously idealized a pastoral vision of childhood and its "golden summer afternoon," his *Alice* fantasies embodied the subterranean forces at work in the child's unconscious and thus revealed the minds and imaginations of children more vividly and complexly than any of his predecessors. He stresses the child's capacity to grow and to rely on his or her own capacities in order to make sense of the world.

Celebrating the uninhibited play of the child's intelligence and imagination, Carroll, unlike earlier writers of fairy tale and fantasy, sustained a commitment to both the pleasures and terrors of fantasy throughout the *Alice* books. Through parody and burlesque of the didactic tradition and through games, puzzles and language, Carroll deflates the adult world of authority and puts the child in control. He does not, as earlier writers of fantasy had done, whisk children off to fairy land only to place them under the dominion of powerful figures who provide all the answers, solve all the problems, and neutralize the child's spirit, initiative, and curiosity. Rather Carroll creates for them a fantasy world which renders the arbitrary authority and institutions of adults incoherent and ineffectual and which permits Alice to exercise her own judgments and to make her own decisions. Thoroughly familiar with the characteristic features of traditional fairy tales and other kinds of entertaining stories and amusements for children, Carroll mines this rich source in writing his *Alice* books, modifying such traditions to liberate children from the confining strictures of conventional moral tales, matter-of-fact educations, and arbitrary adult rules. In the two *Alice* books he does not impose upon his spirited child heroine the necessity to acquire conventional moral lessons and useful information. Rather, he imbues his early fantasies with all the more significance for children. Thus, he allows Alice to confront a threatening and sometimes terrifying psychological reality and dramatizes her aggressive assertion of identity in the face of it.

Alice's Adventure in Wonderland begins as Alice tumbles down the rabbit hole after the elusive White Rabbit. While intentionally pursuing the nervous creature, she clearly does not mean to plunge into a seemingly bottomless black hole. The fantasy begins, then, out of control, with a familiar but terrifying nightmare sensation--endlessly falling into darkness. As she falls, Alice consoles herself with language. She wonders about latitude and longitude, assuring herself that "Dinah'll miss me to-night, I should think."[21] Carroll thus shows that language, even the language of nonsense (because Alice does not know the meanings of the words that she utters) can help the child to conquer uncontrollable fears. (Indeed Carroll writes in the preface to *Sylvie and Bruno* that the most effective way to deal with "unholy thoughts" is through useful mental work.)[22] In the *Alice* books such mental work consists of riddles, puzzles, games, and nonsense. Carroll thus creates a new order of fantasy in which the minds and imaginations of children are engaged not only to provide them with amusement, but also with a means of warding off their terrors. This tendency is exemplified aptly in "The Mouse's Tale." The small, helpless creature confronts his fears of violent and arbitrary extinction in the form of a shaped verse with letters growing even smaller and trailing out almost altogether at the end of the "tale." By imposing his own comic shape and order, that of his "tail," upon his worst fears, the Mouse thus faces up to cunning old Fury, embodies him in a ludicrously humorous form, and through a language puzzle, conjures him into nothingness.[23]

Carroll's creation of Alice also marks a new and liberated vision of childhood, one which is all the more authentic because it depicts the emotions, hostilities, and necessary pretensions which real children experience in attempting to make sense of the adult world and in trying to accommodate themselves to the baffling demands of that world. The chaotic quality of the garden, for example, is a telling vision of a child's coming to terms with the fallibility of adults. From the perspective of children, adults, though apparently free to do as they please, may seem to inhabit an attractive and carefully controlled world. Once children reach the "garden" of adulthood, however, they find it full of the same chaotic and baffling anxieties, fears, frustrating constrictions and imperfections which trouble childhood. Carroll reverses the usual adult-child roles in his fantasies, but when Alice finds herself joining the adult game, she is just as muddled and confused as everyone else; as the Cheshire Cat observes, "We're all mad here."

In many ways Carroll suggests that we all remain confused children looking for the right rules in an ever-shifting and unmanageable reality. For Carroll, the imagination is "the necessary angel" which enables human beings to impose their own artificial constructs of order and meaning upon a reality which is essentially meaningless and disorderly. Alice thus achieves a kind of mastery in the fantasy world which she cannot achieve in the real world. She can acquire control over her own unwieldy fears and hostilities, shake the Red Queen into a helpless kitten, and thus face with more equanimity and self-assurance the domineering adults who scold her away from the warmth of the fire (a fitting emblem, perhaps, for adult pleasures and privileges). MacDonald takes children into a fantasy world and gives them spiritual nourishment in order that they may enact moral truth in ordinary reality. Carroll takes them into a fantasy world and gives them emotional sustenance and psychological confidence which they will need to survive in the wilderness of adult passions and desires. In the first, MacDonald implies that children must look beyond themselves for their ultimate resources. For Carroll, no omniscience resides in Wonderland for Alice to discover and depend upon. Alice's trust must be in her own human potential.

In MacDonald and Carroll, then, we find two distinctive modes of fantasy, each representing a different view of childhood, the imagination, and reality itself. In MacDonald's fantasies child characters appear as conventional emblems of innocence, like Little Diamond in *At the Back of the North Wind*, while Carroll explores the psychological and imaginative complexities of his little Alice. MacDonald sees the imagination as a rather passive faculty which enables the child to receive divine revelation, while Carroll's fantasies suggest that the imagination is a much stronger and more active force which works hard on chaotic experience to create what American poet Robert Frost has aptly called "a momentary stay against confusion."

Inevitably, subsequent fantasists have written in the shadow of these two original giants of fantastic invention. Their impact was immediate. One could discuss literally dozens of nineteenth-century fantasy writers who adapted these two traditions of fantasy for their own purposes. In the 1870's, Dinah Maria Mulock's *The Little Lame Prince* (1874) and Mrs. Molesworth's (Mary Louisa Stewart's) *The Tapestry Room* (1879) both reveal the influence of MacDonald and Carroll. In its vision of childhood, imagination, and character, *The Little Lame Prince* exhibits the sacred or visionary mode of fantasy and draws rather specifically upon MacDonald's classic work *At the Back of the North Wind* (1871), while Mrs. Molesworth's *The Tapestry Room* presents a humanistic vision of the child's fantastic world. A brief discussion of each of these successors may enrich the distinctions already explored between MacDonald and Carroll.

The Little Lame Prince is the story of Prince Dolor who, upon the occasion of his christening, is dropped by a careless nurse and made lame for life. A white-haired, but beautiful, fairy godmother (reminiscent of MacDonald's goddess-like grandmother figures who appear prominently in *The Princess and the Goblin* and *The Princess and Curdie*) comes to honor the child and to bring the sad news of the queen's death. Thereafter, she is the child's only friend and protector. When Prince Dolor's father, the King, dies of grief for his wife, the child's wicked uncle banishes the little lame prince to a remote tower and proclaims Prince Dolor, rightful king of the kingdom, dead.

Prince Dolor lives a tediously boring and unhappy life in the sealed tower with his ill-tempered nurse until his fairy godmother visits him and presents him with a magic traveling cloak. Thereafter the Little Lame Prince flies about on the cloud, seeing strange, disturbing sights, much as MacDonald's Little Diamond flies about with the North Wind. After viewing a bloody revolution following the death of his uncle, Prince Dolor returns to the tower to find that his nurse has deserted him. Five days later she returns with a legion of Prince Dolor's subjects who take him back to the palace and restore him to his throne. After ruling wisely and justly for many years, Prince Dolor turns his throne over to his nephew, bids his people farewell and departs on his magic traveling cloak, never to be seen again. Presumably he has entered a higher spiritual reality.

In her vision of childhood, Mulock follows MacDonald closely. Like MacDonald's Princess Irene of *The Princess and the Goblin* and Diamond of *At the Back of the North Wind,* Prince Dolor is a blessed child who effects a spiritual conversion in the iciest hearts. Prince Dolor is, moreover, an essentially passive and static character. His adventures are initiated for him by his fairy godmother. His imagination does not create; it merely allows him to receive revelation from the fairy godmother who is clearly the representative of a spiritual world of ideal value. She sounds in fact much like MacDonald's "Mother of Light":

> . . . the little lame Prince forgot his troubles in looking at her as her figure dilated, her eyes grew lustrous as stars, her very raiment brightened, and the whole room seemed filled with her beautiful and beneficent presence like light.[24]

Even in his adult years, Prince Dolor remains childlike, refusing to marry because "no wife in the world would have been found so perfect, so lovable, so tender to him in his weakness, as his beautiful old godmother" (p. 110). The prince is, in fact, passive to the point of being regressive, making up his mind to die because the world is so ugly. But the ultimate victory of the prince is assured from the beginning because he is so clearly aligned with both beneficent spiritual powers and the righteous human order.

Although Dinah Mulock's fantasy is derivative of MacDonald's fantasy in most respects, her writing lacks the literary power of MacDonald's best work. Mrs. Molesworth is a more original and more powerful writer than Mulock. Mrs. Molesworth's fantasy, *The Tapestry Room* (1879), contains features resembling the fantasies of both MacDonald and Carroll. However, like the *Alice* books, her fantasy reveals the imagination as a human, rather than divine, faculty, which enables children to create visions and to alleviate loneliness and boredom.

The Tapestry Room is set on a large estate in the French countryside where a lonely and bored little girl, Jeanne, plagues her old nurse, Marcelline, constantly for stories. She is much more like a real child than the idealized vision of children in the fantasies of MacDonald and Mulock. (One recalls, too, that Carroll's Alice embarks upon her fantasy to relieve boredom.) Unlike Alice who must venture into the fantastic world alone, Jeanne is accompanied by her cousin Hugh, who comes to live with Jeanne when his parents die. Hugh is given the tapestry room where he is quickly ushered into a strange fantasy land by Dudu the Raven and Houpet the Chicken. He visits the Forest of Rainbows and Frogland with Jeanne, and they experience a transcendent moment of vision. In ordinary reality Jeanne does not seem to remember this fantastic journey and, to the consternation of Hugh, appears to be content with mundane, childhood games, dolls' teaparties, and the like. One day, as the two children play a make-believe fairy game, they re-enter the world of fantasy. They are given luminous wings by Dudu the Raven and they enter a lovely chamber of white cats where a beautiful white lady spins stories for children. At the end of a fairy tale, the children are astonished (but the reader is not) to learn that the lovely white lady has been transformed into their old nurse Marcelline. Finally, in the last segment of *The Tapestry Room*, Dudu tells the children the adventurous history of their family and then unaccountably disappears.

In *The Tapestry Room,* the fantasy world is essentially the creation of the inventive imaginations of the children themselves. Magic and fantasy issue from an interweaving of ordinary reality and imaginative revery. Jeanne and Hugh endow the raven, the chicken, the guinea-pig, and the tortoise with magical power. The fantastic adventures of the two children are initiated, not by an external supernatural agent, but by Hugh's imaginative engagement with the mysterious tapestry, the portal into the fantastic world. The pictures on the tapestry in the moonlight lead the children to imagine both unspeakable terrors and visions of unutterable beauty. In the very center of the fantasy, at the height of their fantastic adventures in Frogland, Hugh and Jeanne listen to song of a dying swan and experience a transcendental, Wordsworthian "spot of time":

> The children listened breathlessly and in perfect silence at
> the wonderful notes which fell on their ears--notes which
> no words of mine could describe, for in themselves they
> were words, telling of suffering and sorrow, of beautiful
> things and sad things, of strange fantastic dreams, of
> sunshine and flowers and days of dreariness and solitude.
> Each and all came in their turn; but, at the last, all melted,
> all grew into one magnificent song of bliss and triumph . .
> . too pure and perfect to be imagined but in a dream. And
> as the last clear mellow notes fell on the children's ears, a
> sound of wings seemed to come with them, and gazing

ever more intently towards the island, they saw rising upwards the pure white snow-like bird--upwards ever higher, till at last, with the sound of its own joyous song, it faded and melted into the opal radiance of the calm sky above.[25]

This central passage seems to hold the key to the essential meaning of *The Tapestry Room*. Beauty, spirit, enchanted vistas of heavenly firmament come from "the joyous song" of the swan, a traditional emblem of poetic creation and the workings of the imagination. When the song fades, so the enchantment fades. Transcendence comes through the child's imagination, permitting an "incredible glimpse," to borrow Eleanor Cameron's term, but only for a fleeting moment. Though the children try hard to sustain their vision, there was at last "no longer a trace of the swan's radiant flight . . . the children withdrew their eyes from the sky and looked at each other" (p. 98). Like Shelley's fading coal, the children's imaginative visions disappear and leave them with a sense of loss because the dream cannot be sustained. This pattern reminds us of the ending of *Through the Looking Glass* when Alice questions her own visions and asks, "Whose dream was it, kitty?" In the end, the children have moved away from their own visions, away from fairy tales into the harsh social, political histories of their families, and old Dudu the Raven, the emblem of the children's creative imaginations, has disappeared. The children sadly acknowledge, "I fear he will not come back . . . We shall have no more stories nor fairy adventures." The disappearance of Dudu suggests that the world of childhood imagination inevitably yields to the business of growing up.

In *The Tapestry Room*, then, Molesworth suggests that the world of fantasy exists only in the imaginations of children; Hugh, Jeanne, and Alice find themselves standing squarely in the gray pavement of ordinary reality, wondering whose dream it was. MacDonald and Mulock, in contrast, take their characters into a divine reality which is itself palpable and real. MacDonald's vision of this reality appears as an eternal possibility for the pure and the childlike. Hence in *The Golden Key* the most ancient and the wisest spiritual being is the Old Man of Fire, who appears as a tiny child, and Tangle and Mossy enter the column of rainbows, the bright vision which had initiated their quest. Little Diamond in *At the Back of the North Wind* is taken up into the wondrous country at the back of the north wind, while Mulock's Prince Dolor departs for the spiritual realm on his traveling cloak. In the fantasies of Carroll and Mrs. Molesworth, however, growth is towards emotional maturity, not towards spiritual purity. The characters and the reader are left wondering with the poet Keats, "Whither has fled the vision? Do I sleep or wake?"

[1]See C.N. Manlove, *Modern Fantasy* . Cambridge: Cambridge University Press, 1975, Nancy Mann, "George MacDonald and the Tradition of Victorian Fantasy". Diss. Stanford University, 1973, and Stephen Prickett, *Victorian Fantasy*. Bloomington: Indiana University Press, 1979 for comprehensive discussions of the relationships between shifting religious views and the emergence of fantasy in nineteenth-century Britain.

[2]Greville MacDonald. *George MacDonald and His Wife*. 1924; rpt. New York: Johnson, 1971, p. 20. The biographical facts concerning Charles Lutwidge Dodgson's life, his famous pseudonym "Lewis Carroll," his famous picnic with Alice Liddell and her sisters and the subsequent publication of *The Adventures of Alice in Wonderland* and *Through the Looking Glass* are so well known and have been so often recounted that I have not mentioned them in this text. However, the best biography on Lewis Carroll is still Derek Hudson. *Lewis Carroll* . London: Constable, 1954.

[3]M.H. Abrams. *Natural Supernaturalism: Tradition and Revolt in Romantic Literature*. New York: W.W. Norton, 1971, p. 91.

[4]Mann, p. 26.

[5]Mann, p. 56.

[6]George MacDonald. *Weighed and Wanting*. 1882, as quoted in Greville MacDonald, p. 85.

[7]In his chapter on MacDonald in *Modern Fantasy,* C.N. Manlove explores in some detail what he conceives to be a rather pervasive division in MacDonald's thought and literary art. According to Manlove, MacDonald avoided intellectual controversy because he was not skilled enough to handle debate. Behind MacDonald's affirmations Manlove sees fears and doubt: "MacDonald's personal involvement [in Victorian religious doubt] is given away not the least by his obsession with these themes in his writing--there are few of his sermons where they do not appear in some form, especially the word 'obedience,' to which he is almost pathologically addicted: he is in part attacking the impertinence of his own intellect. Obedience now becomes not only a means of his unconscious self-surrender, but of conscious suppression of self" (p. 63). Manlove documents rather carefully his argument that MacDonald experienced a conflict between his conscious role of zealous preacher and his identification with Christian Romanticism and mysticism. While there is some justice in Manlove's discussion, he seems to me somewhat unfair to MacDonald in failing to note that MacDonald's Romanticism can accommodate vagueness and even what seem to be contradictions and inconsistencies. His reluctance to enter into open debate surely is a manifestation also of his deep Romantic conviction that infinite truth cannot be pinned down concretely, rather than an issue of his limited intellectual capacities, as Manlove suggests. MacDonald's best fantasies embody spiritual truth which MacDonald believes cannot be apprehended by the intellect. Each fantasy is, in at least one sense, an apologetic for faith which MacDonald did see as threatened. He is least successful when he tries to make these lessons explicit. See Manlove, p. 55

ff.

[8]George MacDonald, "The Imagination: Its Function and Its Culture," *A Dish of Orts* . London: Edwin Dalton, 1908, p. 2.

[9]MacDonald, "The Imagination," p. 13.

[10]George MacDonald. *The Princess and Curdie* . Middlesex: Penguin Books, 1966, p. 49. Subsequent quotations from this text will be taken from this edition and page numbers indicated in the body of the text.

[11]"The Imagination: Its Function and Its Culture," p. 29.

[12]"The Imagination," p. 35.

[13]"The Fantastic Imagination," *A Dish of Orts*, p. 314.

[14]"The Fantastic Imagination," p. 314.

[15]"The Fantastic Imagination," p. 316.

[16]"The Fantastic Imagination," p. 319.

[17]George MacDonald. *Unspoken Sermons*. London: Longmans, Green, 1885, II, 236.

[18]*Unspoken Sermons*, II, 237.

[19]*Unspoken Sermons*, II, 119.

[20]For complete details concerning Lewis Carroll's life, his famous friendships with children, etc., see Derek Hudson. *Lewis Carroll* . London: Constable, 1954. All biographical information on Carroll in this article is taken from this source.

[21]Lewis Carroll, *Alice's Adventures in Wonderland*, in *The Complete Works of Lewis Carroll,* ed. Alexander Woollcott. London: Nonesuch Press, n.d., p. 20. Subsequent quotations will be taken from this edition; page numbers will be indicated in parentheses immediately following quoted passage.

[22]Lewis Carroll. *Sylvie and Bruno* . London: MacMillan, 1890, p. xv.

[23]For a detailed analysis of Carroll's use of nonsense language, see Elizabeth Sewell, *The Field of Nonsense* . London: Chatto and Windus, 1952.

[24]Dinah Mulock. *The Little Lame Prince* . 1874; rpt. Garden City: Doubleday, 1956, p. 36. Subsequent quotations will be taken from this edition; page numbers will be indicated in parentheses immediately following quoted passage.

[25]Mary Louisa Molesworth. *The Tapestry Room*. London: MacMillan and Company, 1879, pp. 97-98. Subsequent quotations will be taken from this edition;

page numbers will be indicated in parentheses immediately following quoted passage.

9

A CRITICAL EXPLORATION OF THE IMAGE OF THE ABORIGINE IN AUSTRALIAN BOOKS FOR CHILDREN

Marilyn Jurich

Jurich's essay critically surveys a group of contemporary Australian children's and young adult literature to introduce tthe Aborigine, both their ancient myths and their present realities. She finds some of the work stereotypical and unfaithful to the lives of the Aborigine. She concludes that they are best understood as a people in tension between their desire to retain their roots and their hope for a European future. Two qualities of the Aborigine are equally alive in the best Australian fiction: an earthy, primordial ecstasy and a stolid perseverance to grasp the modern.

A CRITICAL EXPLORATION OF THE IMAGE OF THE ABORIGINE IN AUSTRALIAN BOOKS FOR CHILDREN

> Given this legacy of the Dreamtime it is we who must waken the images, absorb their ambivalent power and explore them in ourselves--cannibal, totem and taboo, the wild man and the sage. We have to become our own ancestors--no great feat in terms of myth--and receive from ourselves the Dreamtime teachings.

--P.L. Travers[1]

Alienation is a term used to describe what contemporary people feel about their situations and about themselves. Not only are we denied understanding of the vast technological conglomerates on which we depend, an understanding possible--and only in a piecemeal way--to experts, but we are also "on the fringe" of our own existences. We are cut off from institutions which should provide more total and intimate connections: the church, the school, the family. We do not even know where to seek "roots." Who we are, who we can or should be, may depend on what we were when tradition rather than technology regulated life, when community survival and individual success had scarcely any differentiation, when nature and human nature were so inextricably bound, that to control nature, meant to control oneself. The fascination of primitive peoples--how they live, what they believe, as realized through their tales, rituals, and myths, and what experiences they encounter in becoming "civilized"--lies in what they can tell us about our "original" identity.

In recent years Americans have sought to understand the native American -- the Indian. They have found in this people another oppressed ethnic group, slandered through stereotypic representation in academic and popular media. More profoundly, American Indians are perceived as people who can help us recover a religious awe, a respect for nature, a self removed from television commercials or shopping malls. The interest in the native American is apparent from the large number of recent collections of Indian folklore and myths and from a new insurgent historical novel which represents Indians as heroes to their people, as victims of exploitation, or as non-violent figures often forced into violence. Literature with more contemporary settings often depicts Indians forced into the degradation of assimilation, Indians succumbing to white man's vices, or Indians defying the ignominy of that majority culture to acclaim a heritage of greater spiritual truth.

Even more than the American Indian, the Australian Aborigine is still in touch with these spiritual truths, in touch with his own past, a past reaching back to that special primordial existence called "Dreamtime."[2] Like the American Indian, the Aborigine has been "civilized" (the Tasmanian Aborigine was "civilized into extinction"). However, it has been more difficult to separate the Aborigine from his culture since it has been more difficult to wrest him from his lands in a country so thinly populated, with many of these tribal lands virtually uninhabitable for white men.[3] Few live in towns;[4] as long as they can remain close to tree, rock, or billabong,[5] there is still the sense of the mythological ancestors, still the communion possible through going on "walkabout."[6] Because the Aborigine is a vital proof that man can "connect" to the earth and the dream of sacred ancestral events, he has deep meaning for all of us. His myths can inform us of basic human relationships, can incite us to a sense of supernatural wonder. His life pattern can suggest our most elemental fears, needs, and hopes, and what of that elemental past *we should have kept.*

A group of contemporary Australian children's books have the effect of introducing us to those myths and that life pattern. The significance of the Aborigine in Australian literature for children and young adults will become evident through an examination of the Aborigine's own myths and folktales which have been collected for children; through stories and novels depicting current conditions where Aboriginal beliefs may influence the plot or Aborigines may appear as leading or secondary characters; through novels which reveal the Aborigine as he lived in the past recounting how he was treated by Whites. Before beginning an examination of those three categories of books, some general statements seem useful, first about the appeal of such books and then some fundamental ideas they share. Contemporary Australian literature has notably "returned to the bush."[7] Contemporary Australian children's literature reflects this turn as well. The magic and meaning of "the eternal present," Dreamtime, may have a greater hold on the child's imagination than the limited future suggested in science fiction. Aboriginal myths and folkways express the unique powers of animals and the special obligations regulating family and community behavior. The appeal to wonder and the urge towards stability are remarkably combined. The excitement in these tales derives, as well, from the knowledge of how animals and human beings can survive dangerous natural elements, sometimes only by using unusual physical powers. The unpredictable and harsh Australian climate and its challenge to human energy and ingenuity has a special appeal to children (and has played a vital part in the novels of such juvenile writers as Ivan Southall and Dal Stevens). To be able to conquer nature, as well as to trust in her, is the very means to psychological salvation in H.F. Brinsmead's *Pastures of the The Blue Crane* and to physical survival in Joan Phipson's *The Way Home.* The Aborigines, who with the simplest of tools not only endure in the most brutal of climates and topography, but, who also experience a mystical union with their land and ancestors, are *real* fictional characters for children, contemporary analogues of Robinson Crusoe or Tarzan. For it is far more difficult to be heroic and, at the same time, exist within a binding social tradition, far more difficult to be glorious when your opponent is not a mortal, but the irresistible forces of nature.

Strongly implied in all of the collections and novels in which the Aborigine appears, either as a dominant figure or as some lesser influence, is the necessity of the white, or Western Culture, to become more fully human by absorbing mystical elements in a way comparable to that of the Aborigine. The Aborigine's sense of the supernatural world has given him not only a particular awareness of nature, society, and his own identity within a tribe, but this sense has given him, in fact, the practical ability to function in conditions most people would regard as inimical, if not impossible. Psychological and physical survival is possible for the Aborigine who exists and acts in a *total world*; the gods, nature, and man are inseparable and move together through an indivisible continuum of space-time.

How that single dimension of the spirit world and the real world can be cognitively realized and sensuously evoked is determined by the fiction writer's craft. That craft must be especially skillful if the reader is to believe that such a mythos is valuable; that in some instances, it needs to be restored; and that in all instances, it needs to be respected. Subtle interplays in structure and technique, free from editorializing or preachment, are essential if the reader is to perceive the insufficiency of his own culture. Indeed, most of the writers under discussion are united in their perceptions of that insufficiency. Most suggest that whites have lost and need to recover a supernatural dimension, that the supernatural, once recovered, be more than a superfluous appendage or convenience. Divinity is all of being and must infuse our total sense of who we are. Transcendence is necessary not only for a sublime understanding of self and others, but it is crucial to our very survival. Only if we acknowledge the sacred forces in the universe can we overcome the denatured and degenerate powers of technology. Some of the books are more successful than others in communicating that basic perception persuasively.

Three excellent collections of myths provide an entrance to the Aboriginal world view both for young people and adults. Two of the collections, *The First Sunrise* and *The Dawn of Time*, written and edited by Charles P. Mountford, are wonderfully illustrated with paintings by Ainslie Roberts. These delicately wild visions forcefully realize the myths, creating a suspending timeless, time-fullness which reverberates beyond the page. The other collection is by Daisy Bates, entitled *Tales Told to Kabbarli*, as retold by Barbara Ker Wilson. Characters act out the events and the situations are closely detailed. Aboriginal words are occasionally interspersed to give a pleasing flavor to the narrative. For instance, a myth relating a man's indebtedness to his "elder brother" or totem, the Janga Woggal (Carpet Snake) who cures him of a spear wound, begins:

> Kura, kura, long long ago there was a man called Bladwa
> who lived at Nyeerrgoo Gabbi. He had two wives, and
> the three of them lived very well together. Each day
> Bladwa would go to hunt possum, kangaroo and other
> game, while his two wives gathered roots, berries, fruits,
> ants and lizards with their diggingsticks.[8]

While the narrative moves easily and dramatically, it still retains the distance and dignity of a certain and established culture.[9] We are persuaded of a rare intimacy, the human self related to other selves deep within and inseparable from natural elements. Thus, in other myths the tree-frog was, at creation-time, the mother of Pakadringa, the man of the thunderstorms; Tomituka, the woman of the monsoon rains; and Bumerali, the lightning woman. Should the frog be badly treated, her children will punish the people by bringing them a flood.[10] The curlew's wailing cry is the continuous lament of Uldanami, "the little mother" who lost her two sons when they were driven to the sky by a bush-fire. Now Uldanami's sons are the two bright stars in the southern sky; but the curlew, who is Uldanami, never ceases her calling, so convinced is she that one day her sons will answer this cry.[11]

Beyond the philosophical assumptions expressed in these three collections, the reader also realizes the Aboriginal use of myth to regulate behavior. These fable-like qualities are best realized in stories about the distribution of food. Lengo, an old man, constantly takes the fish his son, Mandabulabula, brings, retaining the best portion for himself, distributing the rest, and leaving his son only scraps and shreds. One day Mandabulabula flings down his miserable "no-good fish" and turns himself into lightning, vanishing across the sea. Thus, to his sorrow does Lengo learn that old men must grant manhood to their sons and give them proper portions.[12] Sons too may be at fault for not obeying the food-gathering laws, such as those sons of Wata-Urdli, the Morning Star, who for their miserable greediness were cast by their father into the southern sky. Now Wata-Urdli can be far removed from his disobedient and selfish sons.[13]

One of the primary lessons of the myths of the Aborigines, like others, is the appropriate sexual roles of their culture. Not surprisingly, many myths suggest that women are less worthy than men and stress the need for women to be subservient. "The Great Kalligooroo" (Totem Board)[14] describes how women are forbidden even to look on sacred objects. In Dhoogoorr (Dreamtime), a totem board connected earth and sky; womba (men) and jandu (women) could at will travel between these two places--in both places were abundant wallee (meat) and mai (vegetables); no one was ever hungry. But once a group of women, feeling cold on their way to sky country, made such a big fire that it burned right through the totem board, creating an irreparable gap. Sky and earth would never by joined again. No women can ever again burn a fire when the totem board is in the sky. The sky men, knowing what the women once did, would severely punish them for daring to look up at what was lost.

Yet, other myths suggest that women are admirable and have been unfairly treated. Kunta, devoted to her husband, the blinded hunter, Wamili, arranges that he will find the Waratah blossoms he enjoys by persuading the bush spirits to make the blossoms rigid to the touch.[15] Other wives, like the two kestrel wives of Wildu, the eagle, may even save their husbands' lives, insisting, moreover, with vigorous moral rigor, that their husbands not kill members of another tribe in revenge. One should kill only when hungry.[16] Despite such virtues, women have met with unjust treatment. They had been the sole possessors of boomerangs until the men diverted their attention and stole their weapons.[17] At one time women had refused to live with men, had preferred hunting to gathering vegetable food *as prescribed by law,* and these defiant females had refused to be warned until Tchooroo, the Great Snake, turned them into termites' nests which are now in the Great Australian Blight. Another law which prescribes that brothers-in-law remain peaceable, results in a husband's unjust and fatal punishment of his wife. Instead of punishing his brother-in-law for the drowning of his sons, Woominya spears his own wife who had been only indirectly responsible for the sons' tragedy. (She had sent her sons away from camp to search for their own food, so that they would not consume their father's portion. The brother-in-law sent to find them might have prevented the accident, but he was too lazy to search.)[18]

Women, often victims of their husbands, are understandably not eager to marry. Mardyet is stolen by a powerful sorcerer who sucks out all her blood and drives "all the bad smell from her." Immobilized each night by her "husband's" thunder magic, she cannot escape. Mardyet's mother, who finally visits her, finds her daughter "clean and well"; the mother accepts male brutality as normal, and she sanctifies the "marriage." In time Mardyet no longer runs away. She is, presumably, happy.[19] Another girl, Brolga, defies marriage by changing into a tall graceful bird, the Broga bird, a beautiful grey dancer on the flood plains of Northern Australia. The myth approves of such defiance, not because Brolga's preference of freedom is condoned, but because of a taboo tribal relationship.[20] Woman's saving grace in Aboriginal myths is that after all, *she* is the sun (sometimes Wuriupranili) and *she* is the creator of earth (sometimes Mudungkala).

In the potential for evil, the Aborigines are equalitarian. Both men and women, in human and spirit form, can be evil. The sun-woman Bila is cannibalistic. The Nabudi women kill with barbed darts from their own bodies. The male Namarakains try to steal spirits of sick people. Gurumukas will attack solitary travellers with their long projecting teeth. Then there is the spirit dingo, Mamu, who captures and eats the spirit of any child who wanders away from the light of a campfire. If you escape from him, there is always the Bunyip who will grab you from a waterhold. Good chilling (or scalding) fun! The heroes are those who

83

protect men--the two spirit brothers who show Willilambi men how to make strong spears and effective spear-throwers, and Joonga-bilbul (Chicken Hawk) who teaches the people to make fire.

The myths of the Aborigines, of which these three collections are samples, have clearly influenced Australian writers of children's and young adult novels. "The Stone Axe" by Patricia Wrightson, (an excerpt from her novel *The Rocks of Honey),* illustrates that influence: the characters, the quality of the narrative, the philosophical assumptions.[21] When Warremai, the father to Yulgelbon, is inadvertently responsible for his son's breaking a taboo that may result in a fatal judgment from the Council, the father becomes desperate. He keeps the sacrilegious act secret. Then in a dream, he finds a means of expiating his sins; the spirit of an old headman advises him to slay the tortoise, his son's totem spirit. As the axe strikes, a currawong (an Australian bird), the father's totem, seizes it and it ascends to the sky. The dream signals Warrimai to deliver this same axe to sacred ground as a means of atonement and Yulgelbon is saved. The story is a convincing account of how for the Aborigines, the spirit world, and the real world exist in a single dimension.

An Older Kind of Magic, also by Wrightson, is less convincing. Set in modern times, the novel incorporates Aboriginal myths and mythical spirits as a warning to those who thrive on "commerce" and technology. The villain is the technocrat, Sir Mortimer Wyvern, to whom the Botanical Gardens in Sidney are mere "sentimental waste." What the city needs, he asserts, is another parking lot, not the green lawns, trees, pools and statues. The Potter children, Rupert and Selina, and their friend, Benny, heartily disagree and mean to prevent the men at Parliament House from destroying the one bit of natural world where they can enjoy themselves in the mechanized city. Assisting them in their protest is Mr. Ernest Hawke who represents the better part of commerce. He likes children and cats and, unlike Sir Mortimer, is good-humored, generous, and helpful. The "Save Our Gardens" demonstration works: the gardens remain and everyone, except Sir Mortimer, is jubilant. The successful demonstration depends on magic and on the resurrection of Aboriginal spirits. Both of these devices are artistically unsuccessful. Wrightson's strategy of appropriating the primordial for practical purposes simply does not work because of her failure in creating either believable characters or situations. As if the Hawke demonstration composed of store-mannikins were not silly enough, there is a whole comet rigamarole, the basic device for the happening. The comet, "the thousand-year magic," calls to earth the Aboriginal spirits. Among these are the Net-Nets who abduct Sir Mortimer, making his appearance at the Council impossible, so that the vote is finally decided against the parking lot and in favor of the gardens. Other spirits roused from streams and bush by the power of the comet are Turongs who used to play secretly with native children in the bush. In the confused lamentation of these ancient spirits who grieve for their past, Sir Mortimer manages an escape. Stepping out into a thicket, he stumbles over a dog. Out of habit he exclaims "Excuse me," and the dog snidely responds. Immediately Mortimer turns to stone! The belief in Australia, we are told, is that hearing a dog will effect such a transformation. Swiftly the moral follows:

> For stone is stone; and men whose drills break into the
> living stone should take care. They may find what they do
> not expect.[22]

The Aboriginal spirits, deeply rooted in the earth, are those who will protect us from the machinations of all Sir Mortimers who, without family attachments, abiding friendships, without feeling for children or cats, would destroy the element necessary for human survival.

But the reader can feel little for the flat human beings in this story. Selina as the restorer of earth, valuing kittens, lizards, and even a cockroach named Morris, may possibly be accounted as quasi-mythical. Like the "real" mannikins, the others are neither human nor mythical. The Aboriginal spirits, aside from a generalized moral function, briefly appear in catalogue form and disappear with the comet. They are never sensed or even understood as strong cultural forces. Their presence or meaning does not unify a story so filled with distracting points of view and with irrelevant episodes--for example, Benny's attempt at conjuring a toad and producing a Pot-koorok, another Aboriginal spirit.

Better, but still flawed, realistic stories about contemporary times in which Aborigine characters appear, are those by Axel Poignant and Reginald Ottley. Alex Poignant's *Piccaninny Walkabout* is a picture story illustrated with photographs of Millingimbi Island. It describes the adventures of Nullagundi, ten, and his sister, Rikili, nine, who lose their path as they seek their parents and thereby spend a fearful night in the bush. The tension is released the next day when they are reunited with their parents and celebrate by having a corroboree (celebration). The book stresses the skills necessary for survival in the bush by indicating how the children, in their games, prepare for adulthood and, later, actually use these abilities killing a goanna, finding water, making a shelter during their night in the bush. What is also noticeable is the sister's dependence on her brother, her inability as a female to perform certain functions, and her acceptance of inferiority. The book, though fictive, is more informative than literary.

Reginald Ottley's books, particularly *Boy Alone*, have been highly regarded; however, the two read for this chapter, *Boy Alone* and the last in the three-part sequel, *Rain Comes to Yamboorah*, were found dreadfully tedious. They were unchanging in pace (all the perils or near calamities sound like one grinding pencil sharpener), unchanging in tone, loaded with tedious detail, strained with people constantly thinking to themselves, stymied with rambling interchanges. Some critics rationalize the main character's having no identity other than "the boy" as a device to demonstrate his lone position, his apartness from the people at the cattle station; however,the reader needs to know something of the boy's background, if not his proper name. The other characters are equally abstract and lifeless. The Aborigines in these books we know only as caricatures who sound very much like the "Ug"-muttering American Indian of the Old Westerns. ("You savvy?" is the Aborigine's favorite expression.)

The implications of both Ottley's books are consonant with other books of this genre. In both *Boy Alone* and *Rain Comes to Yamboorah*, the Aborigines are sympathetic to the boy. *Boy Alone* shows Wahreema promising to teach the boy to ride horses; Wirranoona leads him to a group of kangaroos and provides companionship for him during the big day-off expedition to the bush. In *Rain Comes to Yamboorah*, Alice and Maheena, the serving girls, are generally helpful on the station, responsible for preventing a spreading fire and for saving the life of a cattle man by preparing a special paste to remove the toxicity from a snake bite. Each girl is deeply drawn towards the boy. Maheena, when she accidentally kills the boy's favorite rooster, is heart-broken. When the boy not only forgives her, but keeps her "mistake" a secret from the ranchers, her devotion to him is assured. Alice, unconvincingly, feels such an affinity for this boy who validates for her a shared discontent with daily routines that she is persuaded not to go on "walkabout." She suppresses what were urgent stirrings and resumes her duties in the kitchen. Thus, the message is that Whites and Aborigines are more similar than they know; both have fervent "walkabout feelings." Both must recognize that such feelings must be channeled into the performance of duties to the community, the community being commercial enterprise.

The White-Aborigine encounter seems far more genuine in *The Min-Min* by Mavis Thorpe Clark, a beautiful story about a fourteen-year-old girl coming to self-awareness. The "min-min" is an Aboriginal term for a beckoning light, suspended just above the earth, gleaming and swaying "as though on an invisible thread," moving towards those who see it, but ever eluding those who try to catch it. Sylvia Edwards, the main character, vows she will catch it, and so she does for the light above is also the light within, the recognition of her own maturity, which is demonstrated in her determination to provide for the welfare of her brothers and sisters and so to help her parents--on her own terms.

The Aborigines in this story and the references to Aboriginal history are included in minor ways to suggest the displacement of the white children, Sylvie and her brother Reg, both of whom, for different reasons, leave home. In seeking another family, the Tuckers, who Sylvie hopes will help them, they journey through the Woomera area and come upon Maungawalla Rock, where they refill their water bags. In this sacred place where the Aborigines held corroborees they feel the Rock "seems sad," holding the memories of those who, removed by the government, died, their spirits unable to live apart from their ancestral earth. Later, at another water tank, they find Old Knobby, an Aborigine tracker and his two wives, one old and one young, both clad in ragged cotton dresses. Knobby, a skillful carver of miniature tools and animals, receives a token sum for his efforts, only enough for the three to buy tobacco. For all their poverty and squalor, the Aborigines invite the children to share their meal and their shelter. When the brother and sister set out the next morning, Knobby gives them food to eat on their journey and presents Sylvie with a carved kangaroo. Knobby is generous and trust-worthy. Later he reluctantly tells Mr. Tucker Reggy's confidence, that Reggy had planned to leave his sister and run away "for good." While the Aborigines parallel the children's own economic deprivation and social exclusion, they also suggest the affection and generosity that are possible when human beings are accepted for what they are and not for what they have, or from where they derive. And it is just such affection and generosity that enable Sylvie to find her "min-min."

The need for civilized people to recognize positive qualities which the Aborigines still retain and they have lost, the need for both Whites and Aborigines to become "assimilated" to each other's society, the Aboriginal values outweighing white ones, is a theme that is unevenly, but forcefully, struck in two novels by James Vance Marshall, *A Walk to the Hills of the Dreamtime* (1970) and the earlier, more widely known *Walkabout* (1961) (the basis for a popular film and probably the basis for the more recent book). The stories have remarkable affinities; in both, the main characters are an attractive teen-age sister and a younger brother whom she protects and about whom she is possessive. While her brother accepts the Aboriginal customs and mores, even excels at understanding the Aborigine disposition or demonstrating abilities the Aborigine values (in *Dreamtime,*[23] eleven-year-old Joey makes a spear as strong as an adult man can make), the sister experiences uncertainties about Aborigine folkways and beliefs, even expresses a personal repugnance, and certainly (for a better reason in *Dreamtime)* has active fears of what these natives may do to her. The natives, in both novels, belong to the Bindibu tribe which lives in the Central and North Australian desert. It is somewhere in this region that both groups of children are stranded as a result of accidents--in *Walkabout*, a plane explosion, in *Dreamtime*, a dust devil which

86

causes the stockman driving their car to be killed.

In neither book do we learn anything about the children's backgrounds, certainly not their religious backgrounds, only stray facts. Mary, thirteen, and Joey, eight, the characters in *Walkabout*, come from a comfortable home in Barbados; Sarah, fourteen, and Joey, eleven in *Dreamtime*, were raised in a mission, their mother having been an Aborigine, their father a Japanese pearl-diver. To an extent, this tendency to abstract characters, a practice Ottley negatively employs, is necessary here; for if the children are to connect to the Aborigine experience, they must immediately become absorbed in a new dimension of timelessnes. Nonetheless, such a complete elimination of past influences prevents the children from having memories that would not only humanize them, but would also provide them with a standard for comparison and would permit the reader to make more critical judgments of modern and Aboriginal societies. (Of course, for Mary and Joey, we can assume the usual modern comforts, but what in their peer group relationships would have compared with the assistance--the very means to survival--the Aborigine boy freely provides?)

One assumption we can make about background derives from the girls' strong fears of sexual assault. Obviously, each has felt the predatory lust of white males in her own society. Sarah's encounter we learn about early in *Dreamtime*; while the stockman loads provisions the storekeeper makes sexually offensive remarks to her. Not only these remarks, but his whole manner becomes so threatening to her that later in a dream, she is snared by his fixating eyes which strip her and his slurping mouth which devours her. In *Walkabout*, Mary's fear of sexual violence from the "darkie" certainly seems more related to her equating nakedness with sexual abandon than to any "situation" in her past. The insinuation is unmistakable--in white society, the uncovered human body is sinful, prone in this state, to succumb to vile animal lusts; in white society, a male who clearly admires the physical being of a female, means to possess her and often by force. Mary, who has learned such shame and fear, cannot know of natural and necessary nakedness and the passive and innocent delight at sexual beauty. Mary's unconcealed horror of the native boy and Sarah's unwillingness to be sexually exploited by a white male society, that is, the sexual attitudes of each girl, move the plot in a distinct way.

The plots of both books contain similar incidents: the sharing of a barley sugar to avert hunger, salt pans being mistaken for the sea, pardalote who lead the parched wanderers to water. Two factors cause key differences in the stories: in *Walkabout*, the rescuer is a single Aborigine and the children--especially Mary--have little access to his language; in *Dreamtime*, the rescuers are a group of Aborigines and the children--even Sarah--come to a closer understanding of their language and ways; in *Walkabout*, Mary's sexual inhibitions lead to the native boy's death; in *Dreamtime*, the sexual mores of the tribe--forbidding a brother and sister to sleep together--and particularly the sacred beliefs of the medicine man, lead to Sarah's death. Thus, Marshall's books have a similar theme, the somber theme that only through death--here self-inflicted death--is cultural misunderstanding resolved and the gap bridged that may effect mutual recognition and appreciation of the other's values and beliefs.

In *Dreamtime*, Sarah had partly succeeded in closing the gap with Thoomee, a pregnant lubra (young girl) with whom she shared pleasures, tasks, and even conversation. Sarah tries to explain to Thoomee the idea of cultural norms, that different societies may have varying notions of right and wrong, that Sarah's sleeping in the same tent with Joey is an expression of natural affection, as well as the concern of an older sister for the safety of her brother. Her explanation is

87

futile. Thoomee responds, "There is one lore . . . for us all. And those who break it are lost."[24] Sarah's action accomplishes more; her carrying Thoomee's dillybag through the oppressive heat and drought expresses a kindness that needs no analysis. For the tribe, for herself, and particularly for Thoomee, Sarah demonstrates the sacrificial love of her Christian upbringing. Sarah sacrifices her own life to bring rain. Her act will assure Thoomee's survival and the well-being of the fetus Thoomee carries. The tribe will persist through the birth of its newest member.

Her sacrifice provides the bridge and is the bridge between the two cultures. Marshall assures us that her act is not a proclamation (is it instinct? desperation? what?), only the feat of a frightened child. For in becoming the tree, the rainpole which is axed down, she also becomes a believer in Aboriginal ritual, an adherent of Wulgaru, the Bindibu god. Her death climaxes in wild thunder and radiant rainfall. The medicine man, who would have destroyed both himself and Sarah in an Aboriginal ceremony to bring rain, is aghast at his own continued existence and must convince himself of ancestral powers by assuming a trance. But while he may not believe in Sarah's God, he is affected by Sarah's person and power; in grief, he gashes the body, severely lacerates himself, then disappears. Thoomee finds the bridge. Remembering that Sarah had promised that Jesus would save her unborn child, now feeling that child stir once again, among the stones where Sarah is buried, Thoomee finds Sarah's crucifix and prays. Symbolically, Thoomee plants a root from an everlasting in Sarah's grave. "Everlastings don't really last forever; but their seed will often take root in unpromising soil, so that great drifts of flowers, unbelievably beautiful, will sometimes spring from the most unlikely plant."[25]

In *Walkabout* as the native boy is dying, it is the White girl that "bridges the gap"; but Mary's sudden revelation of "one world" is the last crescendo to a sentimental sweep of maudlin nonsense. Marshall forces the plot by emphatically insisting that the Bindibu sees only the Spirit of Death in Mary's shocked face when she expresses alarm at his overt admiration of her. Supplying a whole chapter (11) that documents the natives' propensity towards auto-suggestion (they can "believe" themselves to death), Marshall, nonetheless, fails to convince us that adequate motive exists for the Aborigine's determination to die. Realistic encounter is replaced by melodrama--the bushboy's frenzied war dance, a natural expression of sexual energy is countered with Mary's violent withdrawal; the confirmation of Mary's sexual fears is played in a scene equivalent to one in a 1940's sexually coy cinema. Swimming naked, innocent of observers, Mary is approached by the native; immediately she sees a potential rapist and faces him snarling, threatening him with a stone. Once again he is cruelly misunderstood, for he had appeared only to give her instructions about his burial table. Defeated, he retreats to a muggawood tree. The reader is informed that this tree, to the Aborigines, symbolizes a broken heart, its appearance "sad and drooping" and its flowers "perpetually wet with a crimson fluid, seeping out like blood."[26]

Right before he dies, the boy's eyes smile at Mary and now we are told, that smile breaks Mary's heart. "And in that moment of truth all her inbred fears and inhibitions were sponged away, and she saw that the world which she had thought was split in two was one."[27] From where does this sudden recognition arise? Trust is certainly easy enough now: a dead Aborigine is also a safe one.

Marshall often, too obviously, steers character and plot in order to affirm an attitude, to document a fact, or to dramatize a scene. In both *Walkabout* and *Dreamtime*, he seems overly fond of melodramatic scenes with sexual overtones.

Sarah's presupposition that should she go to the lagoon, the medicine man would make love to her or strangle her, has no basis in antecedent action. It is another one of Marshall's gory enticements.

Though these intrusive elements sometimes disturb credibility of character, distract from the plot, distort the tone, Marshall's stories are still engaging. The writer's deep respect for the Aborigines, his knowledge of their beliefs and folkways, his ability to translate their feelings and to convey the scenes and sensations of the Australia they inhabit, provide the great truths for the novels. The threat of the medicine man's pointing stick; the wonderful significance of a boy's initiation rites; the men's ability to snare their quarry through a perfect mimicking of that quarry's movement; the perfect relationship between adults and children; all this we come to understand. We hear the drum and the didgeridoo,[28] see the magnificence of the forest, "graceful blue-gums soaring to two hundred feet, coral trees festooned in rose-pink bloom, kurrajongs like weeping cascades of ivy . . .",[29] are at the water's edge with egrets, jacanas, and bitterns, become exhausted and thirsty walking on and on, looking for a well. Marshall is accurate in information, compassionate in attitude, and creates images that can powerfully affect. Such images persuade us that we in "civilized" society are poor in what we do *not* possess -- the sense of nature as both ordinary and extraordinary, as removed from us, yet intimately affecting us.

The interaction of supernatural and secular is perfectly realized in Nan Chauncy's *Hunted in Their Own Land.* Can a novel about traditional Aborigines, tribes living generally without conflict before the coming of the White Man, be engrossing? These tribes were without a time sense, their pace unvaried except for the variations within a cycle, themselves forming repetitious patterns. Since tradition regulated behavior, a novel about Aborigines would also contain little psychological development of characters. That rare dissension would be regarded as so trivial by modern standards of non-conformity as to be shrugged aside. Thus, how does Nan Chauncy for one-half of the novel *Hunted in Their Own Land,* the portion concerned with traditional Aboriginal culture, succeed in holding the reader's attention? The interest--and this occurs frequently in fantasy and in science fiction--comes from language, the strange names of people from another culture, their ways of communicating; through the rhythm and innuendo of language comes the psyche of the people. The people are the *Parlevar* whose place is among the *Parllerde*, the spirit cliffs, sacred to *marmanuke*, the fathers whose memory gave their lives meaning and linked them to the earth. While the tribes observed separate customs and occasionally had territorial disputes, they generally lived in harmony. Their experiences at the *korobarra*, gatherings, let them enjoy song, dance, and story-telling. Then the *num*, the white men--or white devils--came, and the tribes were hunted and forced to remove to a harsh alien land. There, apart from their spirit earth, denied their hunting ways, their ways of eating and dressing, their own language, their very names, they lost all sense of selves. Within a short period, they perished.[30]

The tragedy of that genocide, the extinction of the Tasmanian Aborigines (they are racially distinct from the mainland natives), may well be realized by the reader's perceiving through Aborigine eyes. The structure of *Hunted in Their Own Land* allows for the penetrating recognition that a whole way of feeling and existing has been lost, for the novel begins several generations before the White violence--exactly how long ago is not determined--and the action shifts between the Toogee and Loonty peoples. The expansive sense of earth and time; the tranquility in following traditional expectations, is rarely disturbed, except by the "flying whale" or "floating island," the first sightings of White men's ships. Thus the reader becomes *Parlevar*, one with their spirits and their past. When Towterer, the chief of the Pyonduc, is desperate to return to his own country, we know his yearning. His spirits are ours--we have felt his *marmanuke's* death by the *num's* fire sticks; we have been with Wyrum, another Poynduc chief of long ago who mourned his own *marmanuke*, disturbed as he had been in a dream that some horror would spring from the sea. That horror later has many echoes. One is *Tyree! Tyree!* A man blinded by the *num*-devils who have taken his people, his *lore* (wife) and his children repeatedly makes this call. He thinks his wife, Tyree, will hear and come to him now that he cannot see. When she does not, he throws himself off a cliff.

We have lived not only with the human ancestors, but with the supernatural beings intimately related to the tribe, *Moinee*, the Good-Spirit-Over-All who made Moon, Sun and Sun's children, the Rainbow and the Stars. The Universe was ours; thus its loss not only obliterates the people to whom it belonged, but also part of ourselves, the readers. The "Black Man's Home," the island that is their prison, is outside of the Universe.

> Each 'cottage' was stuck to the next, pressed closely together like mussels on a rock; they made long lines like men about to dance. Inside were strange, unneeded things like 'stool' to sit on. There was place for Fire, but Fire was not free; Fire must climb a long hole to get out, so that only smoke went up to see the stars. Sitting wearily outside, they watched the flies settle in swarms on walls where Sun had breathed.[31]

In the Afterward, we learn that Towterer's only remaining descendant, his daughter Mary, is befriended by a Lady Franklin who had visited Flinders Island. To Lady Franklin the native girl becomes Mathinna (the name means "necklace"--Aborigine girls often wore shell necklaces) and is reared at Government House on Van Diemen's Land, where she enjoys the luxury of elegant living. But when Lady Franklin returns to England, Mathinna is left unprotected, abandoned to the depravities of natives who had been settled on Oyster Cover in the remains of a former penal station. Soon afterwards she is discovered dead (and drunk) in the river near that settlement.

The historical Mathinna is probably the inspiration for Merrina, another Aborigine girl in an earlier book by Chauncy entitled *Tangara*, also about the persecution of the Tasmanian natives. Here, however, the incident is more reminiscent of the Lieutenant Bowen convict raids (which came after a famine caused them to be deranged and violent). Merrina is not the main character; rather she becomes the "historical vision" of the white girl, Lexie. To the child Lexie, Merrina is the delightful "playmate," even "soulmate." To the fourteen-year-old Lexie, Merrina becomes more symbolic, the spirit of The People who will wait until white men find the need to resurrect it.

Once again the story spans generations. Lexie reenacts the experience of her great-great-aunt Rita Pavemont who had played with an Aborigine girl, Merrina, and who had been given a shell necklace by Merrina which Lexie inherits. It is by this necklace that Lexie is recognized by this new Merrina who calls Lexie "Weetah sent by the sun, her yellow hair just like Rita Pavemont's." Time is all one and nothing need change. Only catastrophe produces change at a time when the very survival of the natives is threatened.

Blacks' Gully, the meeting ground for the white girl and the native girl, is first realized as a hiding place for remaining Blacks, later as the spiritual power of the natives that will ever remain as part of the earth itself. Until the housekeeper and her aunt, who will be Lexie's governess, return, Lexie lives in the bush with the Malleys, some old friends. Each day Lexie manages the walk to the Gully where she is sure to be surprised by the sudden appearance of Merrina. Always Lexie experiences "Tangara," a setting off for another place in the Aboriginal culture, a landscape of mind as well as of place. For Lexie learns how to find a wombat's lair, how to dig for taoorela, "blackfellow bread," how to throw a stone at a quarry. She joyously swims with Merrina's baby brother, Trewella, and meets Merrina's people who wonder at her appearance, are delighted by her clothing, and are eager to share with her all their delicacies.

When Lexie tearfully informs Merrina that she must soon return home, Merrina promises, "I'll always know when you want me Weetah--always."[32] On her last day with Merrina, Lexie is invited to a kangaroo feast; the "fathers" hope for Weetah's assistance in driving away "the bad spirits." During the festivity, "Namma" himself appears, the reincarnation of evil, and two white men blast the sky with shots. The people are trapped. While Merrina pushes Lexie to safety, she herself does not follow.

For years afterwards Lexie has only the faintest awareness of her experience at Blacks' Gully, only sub-consciously experiencing sadness or panic at moments when the Blacks are being discussed, sometimes expressing her distress in dreams. The mention of Blacks' Gully rouses tremendous fear; and she never goes there until she is fourteen, when her brother, lost during a geological expedition, is believed to be in that region. Following the yearning cry of Weetah, she discovers in the gully her brother and learns that it was Merrina who had rescued him. Determined to thank Merrina, Lexie moves towards the cliffs where she is, to find the black girl surrounded by shadows--mothers and children and fathers and hunters. There Merrina is, calling for her dead; " . . . one by one they came towards her in their proud dignity."[33] Lexie can bear no more and she promises never to forget Merrina. Her older brother knows differently; he knows that for both of them the sense of Merrina will fade until memory is fantasy--not till the very end will they see her when she calls them to her little fire. As if to confirm that statement, a gum tree mysteriously crashes across the Cleft Rock and the hole is blocked forever. The indication is that Blacks' Gully is no longer necessary. The past cannot rejoin the present--until some time when the Whites are ready.

Chauncy's books, *Hunted in Their Own Land,* far more than *Tangara,* are the only ones to vivify the Aboriginal culture from the Aborigines' own perspective. (Marshall *reports* on how the natives feel; the natives do not sense for themselves.) No books for children show through Aboriginal perspective the current dilemmas of the people: the conflict between kinship group and European culture; their suffering from the white-instilled perversities of drinking, gambling, and sex; their difficulty in acquiring an education that demands they be competitive and in securing good jobs, when few means are provided for their getting any jobs and when a traditional nonacquisitiveness has made them unsusceptible to materialistic goals.

Yet the books which capture the world view and experience of their past and present their can have a powerful impact. Such books written for children might suggest to the toy-grabbing, fad-minded, junk-buying population of youngsters that Aboriginal values are unusually sane. Elspeth Huxley makes an interesting distinction between primitive and civilized man: the primitive transmits and preserves what has already been created in the past, while the civilized are themselves the creators.[34] Knowledge of the past does more than inform; it has the sacred function of uniting each individual with his mythical ancestor of the Dreamtime; it assures the continuity of the earth, periodically renewed through performing events that duplicate those originally acted out by those Dreamtime ancestors.[35] Myth, in essence, creates for the Aborigine (more specifically for the male Aborigine during puberty) an entirely new dimension--perhaps, we can call it "inter-time"--so that recollection of an ancestor's life becomes a special kind of revelation. At his initiation, the Aranda boy, for example, "not only learns what happened . . . but ultimately discovers *that he was already there*."[36]

The exposure of children to this Australian literature with its strange underpinnings of the Aborigine world view might connect them to some of the deeper truths of our shared human heritage. It is not Aborigines who need to be assimilated, but we who need to be enlightened by their practice of sharing, their distrust of competition and dislike of accumulation.

> Fair shares among tribesmen is not an ideal; it is the norm.
> And what an irony that our own society whose religion
> teaches this ideal should, in the name of progress, so
> totally extinguish the only human societies on our planet
> that have achieved it! The tribesmen reproach us, perhaps
> with their success.[37]

The success of the Aborigines derives, in large part, from their ability to merge the sacred and the secular, to make self-interest correspond to divine purpose. Clearly, we need to explore for ourselves how the urge towards religious belief may become the positive expression of humanistic aspirations.

[1]From "The Legacy of the Ancestors" in *Parabola: Myth and the Quest for Meaning*, Vol. II, No. 2, Spring 1977, p. 17.

[2]In *The World of The First Australians* by Ronald M. and Catherine H. Berndt (Chicago: University of Chicago Press, 1964), the concept is extremely well defined. It is the formative or creative period when mythological creatures determined the shape of the earth, when they produced the progenitors of the present Aborigines. These beings do not belong to a past; they are eternal in the persons and places that will continue to exist as long as men obey their instructions. See pages 186-188 for an extensive analysis.

[3]O.H.K. Spate. *Australia*. New York: Frederick A. Praeger, 1968. As of the date at which the book was printed, there were 4,000 semi-nomads.

[4]In her 1967 travels which she records in *Their Shining Eldorado: A Journey Through Australia* (New York: William Morrow, 1967), Elspeth Huxley notes that of 45,000 full-blooded and 80,000 part-blooded Aborigines, only 800 live in towns. Reservations, missions, and pastoral lands account for the majority, the largest percentage living on pastoral land.

[5]A billabong is a section of a river or creek, a term usually applied to a cut-off point which meanders or to an anabranch.

[6]"Walkabout" refers to, most commonly, the visit a man or woman makes to a scene of his (her) origin or to a place where an ancestral spirit lives. Only the male can view shrines or *churinga* (wood or stone slabs recording totemic legends).

[7]T. Inglis Moore in *Social Patterns in Australian Literature* (Berkeley: University of California Press, 1971) remarks on this as a striking literary trend. As society grows more and more heavily urbanized, he states, "the spell of the bush" seems to flourish even more potently. See p. 68.

[8]Daisy Bates, Collector, *Tales Told to Kabbarli*, retold by Barbara Ker Wilson. New York: Crown Publishers, 1972, p. 65.

[9]Compare the collection of K. Langloh Parker entitled *Australian Legendary Tales*, selected and edited by H. Drake-Brockman (New York: Viking, 1966), which seems, to me, to be over-written. Perhaps, though, since the concentration here is on *tale*, not on myth, the simple and stark quality is not as important.

[10]Charles P. Mountford. *The First Sunrise: Australian Aboriginal Myths*, paintings by Ainslie Roberts. New York: Taplinger Publishing Company, 1969, p. 26.

[11]Charles P. Mountford. *The Dawn of Time: Australian Aboriginal Myths*, paintings by Ainslie Roberts. New York: Taplinger Publishing Company, 1969, p. 36.

[12]Bates, pp. 78-80.

[13]Mountford, *The Dawn of Time*, p. 48.

[14]Bates, pp. 21-22.

[15] Mountford, *The Dawn of Time*, p. 60.

[16]*Ibid.*, p. 26.

[17]*Ibid.*, p. 46.

[18]Bates, pp. 28-31.

[19]*Ibid.*, pp. 12-14.

[20]Mountford, *The Dawn of Time*, p. 72.

[21]Patricia Wrightson, "The Stone Axe" in *Australian Kaleidoscope*, Barbara Ker Wilson, ed. Sydney: Collens, 1968, pp. 180-192. *The Rocks of Honey* could not be located by this writer. As with this title, many other Australian children's books are not available in the United States.

[22]Patricia Wrightson. *An Older Kind of Magic* . New York: Harcourt, Brace, Jovanovich, 1972, p. 182.

[23]*Dreamtime* will be used to refer to *A Walk to The Hills of Dreamtime*.

[24]James Vance Marshall. *A Walk to The Hills of Dreamtime*. New York: William Morrow, 1970, p. 116.

[25]*Ibid.*, p. 140.

[26]*Ibid.*, p. 90.

[27]*Ibid.*, p. 96.

[28]A didgerido is a musical instrument made out of a hollowed log, five feet long with no stops. According to Elspeth Huxley (p. 311), the sound is a single one, and is played over and over, "Gibba-yerra, gibba-yerra."

[29]Marshall, p. 65.

[30]Nan Chauncy. *Hunted in Their Own Land* . New York: Seabury, 1967, p. 152.

[31]*Ibid.*, p. 112.

[32]Nan Chauncy. *Tangara*. London: Oxford University Press, 1972, p. 59.

[33]*Ibid.*, p. 112.

[34]Huxley, p. 337.

[35]Beane, Wendell C. and William G. Doty, eds. *Myth, Rites, Symbols--A Mircea Eliade Reader,* I. New York: Harper Colophon, 1976, p. 51.

[36]*Ibid.*, p. 31.

[37]Huxley, p. 304.

BIBLIOGRAPHY

This bibiography contains books referenced in this chapter, as well as books consulted on Aborigines, Australian literature, functions of mythology and ritual. A single asterisk (*) indicates fiction (novels, folktales, myths) intended for children or adolescents. Double asterisks (**) indicate non-fiction written for adolescents.

* Brinsmead, H.F. *Pastures of The Blue Crane.* New York: Coward-McCann, 1966.

Baglin, Douglass and David R. Moore. *People of The Dreamtime: The Australian Aborigines.* New York: Walker/Weatherhill, 1970.

* Bates, Daisy, Collector. *Tales Told to Kabbarli* as retold by Barbara Ker Wilson. New York: Crown, 1972.

Beane, Wendell C. and William G. Doty, Editors. *Myth, Rites, Symbols--A Mircea Eliade Reader,* Volumes I and II. New York: Harper Colophon Books, 1976.

Bjerre, Jens. *The Last Cannibals.* Estrid Bannister, trans. New York: William Morrow, N.D.

** Blunder, Godfrey. *The Land and People of Australia.* New York: Lippincott, 1972.

* Chauncy, Nan. *Half A World Away.* New York: Franklin Watts, 1962.

* Chauncy, Nan. *Hunted in Their Own Land.* New York: Seabury, 1967.

* Chauncy, Nan. *Tangara.* London: Oxford Unversity Press, 1972.

* Clark, Mavis Thorpe. *The Min-Min.* New York: MacMillan, 1969.

Greenway, John. *Down Among the Wild Men.* New York: Little Brown, 1972.

Gunther, John. *Inside Australia.* Completed and Edited by William H. Forbis. New York: Harper & Row, 1972.

Haviland, Virginia. *Children and Literature: Views and Reviews.* Chicago: Scott, Foresman, 1973.

Huxley, Elspeth. *Their Shining Eldorado: A Journey Through Australia.* New York: William Morrow, 1967.

* Marshall, James Vance. *A Walk to the Hills of the Dreamtime.* New York: William Morrow, 1970.

* Marshall, James Vance. *Walkabout*. New York: Doubleday and Company, 1961.

** Massola, Aldo. *The Aborigines of South-eastern Australia As They Were*. Melbourne: William Heinemann, 1971.

Moore, T. Inglis. *Social Patterns in Australian Literature*. Berkeley: University of California Press, 1971.

* Mountford, Charles P. *The Dawn of Time: Australian Aboriginal Myths*. Paintings by Ainslie Roberts. New York: Taplinger Publishing Company, 1969.

* Mountford, Charles P. *The First Sunrise: Australian Aboriginal Myths*. Paintings by Ainslie Roberts. New York: Taplinger Publishing Company, 1972.

* Ottley, Reginald. *Boy Alone*. New York: Harcourt, Brace and World, 1965.

* Ottley, Reginald. *Rain Comes to Yamboorah*. New York: Harcourt, Brace and World, 1967.

* Phipson, Joan. *The Way Home*. New York: Atheneum, 1973.

* Poignant, Axel. *Piccaninny Walkabout: A Story of Two Aboriginal Children*. Sussex, England: Angus and Robertson, 1957.

Spate, O.H.K. *Australia*. New York: Frederick A. Praeger, 1968.

Travers, P.L. "The Legacy of the Ancestors," *Parabola* Volume II, Number 2, Spring 1977.

* Wilson, Barbara Ker, Editor. *Australian Kaleidoscope*. Sidney: Collins, 1968.

* Wrightson, Patricia. *An Older Kind of Magic*. New York: Harcourt, Brace, Jovanovich, 1972.

10

THE FEMALE PASTORAL JOURNEY IN
JULIE OF THE WOLVES AND *A WILD THING*

Lois R. Kuznets

Kuznets calls attention to the parallels between Jean George's *Julie of the Wolves* and Jean Renvoize's *A Wild Thing* which make them a part of the pastoral genre. She sees the female protagonists, Miyax and Morag, retreating from civilization and then attempting unsuccessfully to return to it. Kuznets' essential point is that at the root of their estrangement from civilization lie two crucial contemporary issues: environmentalism and feminism. Interestingly, the authors' approaches to these issues clearly align them with humanism's affirmation of the individual, but distance them from other humanistic assumptions about human rationality, civil organization, and social progress.

THE FEMALE PASTORAL JOURNEY IN
JULIE OF THE WOLVES AND *A WILD THING**

In realistic terms, the protagonists of Jean George's *Julie of the Wolves* (1972) and Jean Renvoize's *A Wild Thing* (1970) are both runaway girls.[1] In literary structuralist terms, one can view and study them as "female heroes" in pastoral variants of the "monomyth" described by Joseph Campbell in his *The Hero With a Thousand Faces*.[2] Similarities of character and structure in the two books make them interesting subjects of comparative study. In the process of comparing them in terms of Campbell's ideas of monomyth, two of the crucial issues of our time, questions of women and of the environment, emerge as interrelated and central in these books. George's and Renvoize's treatment of these two issues suggests clearly a humanistic world view: these two young women struggle to determine their own destinies with only their own inner resources.

Julie of the Wolves is well-known, having won the 1973 Newberry Medal for the best contribution to children's literature. *A Wild Thing,* classified as young adult literature, is less famous. Both books depict the attempts of adolescent girls, Julie-Miyax and Morag, to run away from intolerable, "civilized" situations into a wilderness that forces them to come to terms with nature and themselves and from which they attempt to make ambivalent (in the case of Julie) or abortive (in the case of Morag) re-entries into society.

Much of the immediate appeal of both these books for children and adults lies in detailed and realistic survival lore embodied in the girls' adventures and their meeting the immediate demands of the environment. But Jon Scott, in considering *Julie of the Wolves*, finds beneath the realistic surface of this work a deeper structure that he links with the pastoral tradition.[3] He sees Julie as taking a journey into an Arctic "Arcadia" and out again. *A Wild Thing* might be seen in a similar light as a "Highland pastoral."

A summary of some important aspects of Campbell's analysis seems a useful preface to an exploration of a deeper structure in both novels. The hero of Campbell's monomyth follows a common pattern of adventure consisting of three stages: "a separation from the world, a penetration to a source of power, and a life-enhancing return."[4] Stories may dwell on any one of the three stages: the difficulties or necessities of "separation and departure" in the first stage; the dangers or delights of "trials and victories of initiation" in the second stage; the triumphs or disasters of "return and reintegration into society" in the third stage.[5]

An important and more controversial aspect of Campbell's analysis is his application of Freudian concepts to this structure. The hero in the otherworld journey is seen as working through what Freud calls the Oedipal conflict, meeting and dealing with symbolic representations of both parents, separating from and uniting with them in appropriate ways to bring about self-integration. So the journey is not merely one of physical adventure but of psychological discovery as well; successful self-integration then permits reintegration into society at a more effective level.

Stories categorized as "pastoral" may be seen as a special development of the monomyth arising from the gradual urbanization of human life, as distinctions began to evolve between city and country and conventions to develop about the symbolic nature of each. In the pastoral form of the monomyth, leaving the city is the hero's means of leaving the world in order to find the source of power and rebirth in the country; the hero returns to the city to bring back to the world the life-enhancing power of the country. Some pastorals de-emphasize the dangers and emphasize the delights of the stage of trial and initiation; all play upon the difficulties but postulate the inevitability of the return to the world. Pastoral can, but need not, be sentimentalized, turning the country into an unrealistic "Arcadia" inhabited by dainty shepherds and shepherdesses.[6]

This overview of the monomyth, its Freudian overtones, and pastoral form prepares us to discern in plot summaries of both books a pastoral variation upon the structure of Campbell's monomyth. The three sections of *Julie of the Wolves* do not in their order correspond to the stages of the monomyth. Rather, George employs one of its common variants and begins, as classical epics do, *in media res:* the audience first hears about the stage of trial and initiation, then goes back to the stage of separation and departure, and finally returns to the re-entry into society.

The first section introduces us to Miyax, a fourteen-year-old Inuit (Eskimo) girl whose *gussak* (foreign) name, Julie, we do not learn initially. She has already been on her journey from Barrow to Point Hope for several days; she is lost and starving and must use the wolf lore taught her by her father in order to be adopted by the wolf pack that will feed her while she gradually learns to be self-sufficient on Alaska's North Slope. Her feelings of abandonment introduce the second part of the story after the pack has helped her and then resumed its normal winter nomadry.

This second part takes us back in time to the death of Miyax's mother when Miyax was four and swiftly through the subsequent ten years. During these years Miyax first lives with her father, Kapugen, in a seal camp. At the age of nine, Miyax is separated from him by her Aunt Martha and moves to town where she can attend school and where she learns of her father's death and becomes Americanized. At thirteen, having found her aunt uncongenial, Miyax accepts the alternative of a traditional arranged-marriage to Daniel, the retarded son of her father's best friend. A year later, when Daniel attempts to consummate the marriage, she runs away from Barrow. At the moment of running away, she plans to journey by boat (the North Star) to San Fransisco to live with Amy, her pen pal, but she underestimates the practical difficulties of the journey.

By part three, both Miyax and the reader are forced to reassess the present and the future in terms of both her immediate past with the wolf pack and the far past of Miyax's childhood. Miyax discovers that the wolf pack has not completely abandoned her and that she, in turn, can be protector to a golden plover, a beautiful bird that has somehow failed to migrate. She begins to see the traditional Inuit lifestyle as an attractive alternative to her dreams of San Fransisco. By the time the heavenly North Star rises over the horizon, she is not particularly worried about catching the boat by that name. However, she uses the star to move closer to civilization and in so doing discovers the ravages of civilization on a landscape now beautifully alive for her.

These ravages are tragically epitomized by the death of her wolf father, Amaroq, and the wounding of her wolf brother, Kapugen, both shot from an airplane. She succeeds in nursing Kapugen back to life and leadership of the pack and discovers from a passing Eskimo hunting couple that her father is really alive in a nearby settlement. All is not well, however, for when she finds him, her father is much changed, moving in a direction opposite to her own recent development. He is married to a *gussak* school teacher and, worse, hunts from airplanes. Miyax runs away once again, but she is forced by the death of the golden plover to accept the idea that the day of the Eskimo and the wolf is over. At the story's close, she returns to her father and presumably to his compromises with the *gussak* civilization.

Rather than inserting the past, as a whole, into the middle of the narrative structure, as *Julie of the Wolves* does, *A Wild Thing* integrates the past bit by bit into the present of Morag's psyche. Carrying a newspaper picture of the Scottish Highlands and little else in pack or mind, Morag is dumped by bus at the Scottish foothills, far less equipped than Miyax to deal with the wilderness. She has, nevertheless, consciously chosen to journey into it, driven not by a single traumatic incident but by the cumulative effect of years of failure to make emotional and intellectual contact with anything in her urban environment. Her wish to come to the Highlands seems to be the last surge of life in this fifteen-year-old, whose inability to function has led her to be placed in a school for retarded children. Like Miyax, Morag was separated at four from her mother, though not by death. The state declared her mother unfit to care for her and a baby brother after the death of a younger sister. Morag has never known her sailor father.

Gradually Morag learns to survive, partly, like Miyax, by becoming a member of an animal family (she finds a lame nanny goat and her kid) and by discovering a sheltering cave. Unfortunately, she also raids most of the crofts in the countryside, stealing supplies before she learns to live off the summer land. Her learning to survive physically opens her to experience at all levels. Early in the story, the most prominent figures in her psychic life are a series of foster mothers from the first, a warm country woman, to the last, a practical, sternly puritanical woman from whose home Morag has fled. Then she begins to recall buried memories, both good and bad, of her profligate and infantile, but fascinating mother, her disapproving grandmother, and her sick sister who died in her arms when four-year-old Morag attempted to nurse her. The agony of this return to the past is considerably greater for Morag than are her initial physical agonies of near starvation and unaccustomed labor. This suffering, however, leaves her, like Miyax at the beginning of part three, prepared both physically and psychologically to consider a future hitherto unenvisioned.

The initial result of Morag's journey into the psychic past is her naive plan for finding a casual mate, one who will impregnate her with a daughter to replace her lost sister. Leading her nanny goat, she appears, ragged and tanglehaired, to a hiker, who, frightened out of his wits by this apparition, naturally flees from her. At this point, Renvoize makes clear, the road begins to divide for Morag into two paths, one of which seems to signal, at a realistic level, insanity and death, the other sanity and life. She finds a skeleton which, in her isolation, she begins to worship in elaborate and obsessive ways, weaving a legend around him, linking him with a castle on the seashore that she has seen in her wanderings. Then life and sanity seem to win over when she finds an injured climber, crumbled upon his dead partner. Morag nurses the climber back to life and shares a brief rural idyll with him. Arthur Figgs, as his name sardonically suggests, is a rather ordinary young man, an engineering student with a romantic streak, which is initially stimulated by Morag. Figgs, however, can barely sustain this repressed aspect of himself long enough for him to impregnate Morag; it is not strong enough to permit him to accept her wildness. He leaves by the end of his projected three-week holiday.

Through the fall, Morag, who has failed to make adequate provisions for winter, is forced to make a number of raids on the countryside. When the snows come, she realizes that she and her unborn child will not survive alone. She walks down to a village where her slow approach brings out the mass of villagers with guns to hunt down this wild thing that has ravaged outlying homes. They do not succeed in catching her; she plunges back through the wilderness, finally arriving at the castle on the seashore where she miscarries and dies. By the following spring, her bones have mingled with the sands.

Julie, of the wolves, survives; Morag, the wild thing, dies; both of these endings, apparently opposite, are nevertheless similarly ambiguous. Julie's survival has its negative aspects for those things she has learned to deal with and come to value seem doomed. Morag's death, with its merging into the landscape that has given her a brief but intense and satisfying sense of her own existence, has its positive elements. Particularly in the case of Julie, the ambiguity is limited largely to the difficulties at the third stage of the monomythic structure: re-entry and re-integration into society. The ambiguity in Morag's case is more diffused over the whole adventure because of the nature of Morag's character itself and the particular direction that her attempts at self-integration take. Still, one might say that the possibilities of re-integration into society--as the natural result of their trials and initiations--are rather bleak in both cases, so that worldly survival does not necessarily make an affirmative ending in the one, nor death an entirely negative ending in the other.

Campbell recognizes that the third stage, although less spectacular in most cases than the second, is often the most difficult for the hero; certainly many versions of the monomyth, both ancient and modern, exist in which this re-entry is ambiguous, if not abortive. Even if failure is not unusual, the problems of re-entry in any age can be of great moment to contemporary readers who identify with the central figure; therefore, it is important to consider and attempt to pinpoint the particular nature of these problems. In the case of our two books, re-entry problems might be seen as connected with contemporary feminist and environmentalist concerns. Julie-Miyax's and Morag's problems of reintegration into society seem to arise from two similar general aspects of these books: the substitution of a female for a male hero in the monomythic adventure and the use of the pastoral journey as a means of trial and initiation in the late twentieth century.

The problem of the "female hero" is a familiar one in feminist criticism. A section of the MLA meetings in 1978 was devoted specifically to the question of "Woman as Mythic Hero: The Quest in Twentieth Century Literature."[7] Papers on authors such as Doris Lessing and Margaret Atwood pointed out where and why the fates of men and women deviate and divide in the process of the mythic quest: the male hero finds a proper mate, a heroine whom he can master as he can't his mother, and returns to society to take his father's place in it. Neither the love resolution nor the power resolution is permitted the female hero, who at that point, must become the conventional heroine.

In recent years, the difficulties of transferring the Freudian model of the Oedipal situation to women also have been a matter of hot debate among psychoanalysts and psychologists. In using Freud, Campbell, writing in the Forties, does not, of course, acknowledge any such difficulties, although he does not deal exclusively with male heroes. A single paragraph can be said to dismiss the possible conflicts in the "female hero":

> When the child outgrows the popular idyl of the mother breast and turns to face the world of specialized adult action, it passes, spiritually, into the sphere of the father--who becomes, for his son, the sign of the future task, and for his daughter, of the future husband. Whether he knows it or not, and no matter what his position in society, the father is the initiating priest through whom the young being passes on into the larger world. And just as formerly, the mother represented the "good" and "evil," so

now does he, but with this complication--there is a new
element of rivalry in the picture: the son against the father
for the mastery of the universe, and the daughter against
the mother to *be* the mastered world.[8]

The end of the quest for the male hero is "to master" and for the female "to *be*
mastered." Only at the highest level of metaphysical speculation and in a state of
Nirvana beyond the limits of human life can these two states of being be conceived
as one and the same.[9]

Some feminist critics note that the solution to the problem of the female hero in
both ancient and modern literature has often been for the central female never to
accept a mate but rather to become a kind of "virgin goddess," not necessarily
chaste but never married. How do our two books deal with the problem of the sex
of the hero? Interestingly enough, in two quite different ways: George depicts the
stage of trial and initiation as a postponement and practical sublimation of the
problem of sexual role; Renvoize adds a male hero on his own pastoral journey and
contrasts the male and female versions of trial and initiation.

Julie-Miyax's journey into the Arctic can be seen as a postponement of solving
the Oedipal problem in the way that females are supposed to deal with it, that is, by
learning to be mastered. Her journey begins after a frustrated attempt at rape on the
part of Julie's retarded husband and towards the end of the journey we learn that
she has not yet menstruated. In fact, the young Eskimo woman whom Julie meets
towards the end assumes at first that Julie has been sent out into the wilderness to
become a woman--that she is in traditional initial menstrual exile. In reality, this is,
of course, exactly opposite of the case, for Julie-Miyax, although married at
thirteen, attempts to postpone being a woman by becoming a man in imitation of
her lost father, not her dead mother. We are continually reminded of the role
reversal involved in her journey by the fact that sex roles are highly differentiated in
the Inuit culture itself; there are even male and female knives for the various tasks
that must be undertaken; Miyax uses both of them. And, drawing our attention
specifically to the Inuit ceremonial differentiation in sex roles, George notes, when
Miyax kills her first bird:

> Had she been a boy this day would be one to celebrate.
> When a boy caught his first bird in Nunivak he was
> supposed to fast for a day, then celebrate the feast of the
> bird (p. 46).

Miyax decides to sing the song of the Bird Feast for herself, with its significant
words:

> Tornait, Tornait
> Spirit of the bird
> Fly into my body
> And bring me
> The power of the sun (p. 47).

Just as she has rejected Aunt Martha, Julie-Miyax throughout her journey continues to
relate to males rather than females, choosing instead of the wolf mother Silver, the wolf
father and his son, not only as protectors but as role models; she fights not with a

104

female wolf but a male, Jello, for his place in the pack. Only after her initial disappointing contact with her changed father does she contemplate becoming part of an Eskimo couple in order to continue to live in the wilderness.

At the end of the novel, the death of Tornait, the bird that she harbors in her hood, is not simply a signal of the death of Julie's capacity to revive a way of life doomed by the encroachment of a technological civilization, but also the death of the male power in her that the song of the Bird Feast celebrates. She cannot return as a son might, in one of these monomyths, to fight the father and redeem a culture that has degenerated under his rule, but as a daughter to accede to his compromises. In addition, she must also now face the Oedipal conflict embodied by her stepmother, who is a representative of the encroaching culture. Miyax's competence at meeting the trials and initiations of the second stage can be an inspiration to young girls, yet her sex adds only another level of irony to the fact that she has acquired the male skills and power of a doomed culture.[10]

Julie-Miyax's period of initiation and trial can be seen as a postponement of sexuality and a prolongation of what psychologists call the period of latency. According to a well-known student of Freud, Erik Erikson, during the latency period the seven- to twelve-year-old school child develops the competency and skills that will eventually enable him to enter adult society in its work aspects.[11] Morag, although older than Julie-Miyax by about a year, can be seen as having much more catching up to do than Julie with respect to this competency; her development and change in the Highland period is not a postponement of sexuality, but a compression of two stages of development into a short period of time.

Arriving in early spring, Morag has acquired the competency and skills of the latency period by early summer, at least enough of them to sustain herself through a Highland summer; she moves quickly on to the next stage as she blossoms into a sexual being and specifically a woman. In a scene in the bedroom of a croft that Morag has raided while the inhabitants are away for several days, Morag sees her developing body in a full length mirror for the first time and also tries on some of the accoutrements of "civilized" femininity--stockings, frilly slips, etcetera. However, just as those skills that she learns in the Highlands are not necessarily the ones that she would have to practice in urban survival, the type of feminine development and attraction for the opposite sex that she will develop during the summer will not be associated with the world of feminine clothing, cosmetics, and deodorants. Her sexual and sensual development is of a much more earthy sort.

Renvoize chooses to deal with the problem of the female hero by developing Morag gradually into a kind of earth mother, close to the "virgin goddess" model. Renvoize accomplishes this transformation by having Morag (in contrast to Julie) deal psychologically mainly with women--her mother, grandmother, sister, and foster mothers--and to resolve her inner conflicts with them as the important part of her development. She is associated also with the female nursing goat rather than, as Julie is, the hunting male wolf. Renvoize also has Morag discover that neither the "Mossman," the male skeleton that she worships (perhaps a kind of father?), nor Arthur are necessary to her psychologically once she has that baby (whom she envisions as a daughter) inside her. This emphasis upon female identification and relationships, in which males are seen as brief intruders, is an element of Earth Mother myths, like Demeter (Ceres) and Persephone, prevalent very early in human history and surviving in later mythology mainly in tales of Artemis (Diana).[12]

Renvoize also uses time as a *leitmotif* that contrasts the time of the city, measured by watches and calendars into seconds, hours, and days, with the seasonal time of the country, which becomes Morag's time. This sense of time holds a sense of eternity both in its daily lack of time consciousness and its inexorable cyclical pattern where the death of the individual is not as important as nature's continuity. This view of time not only gives a special earth goddess aura to Morag while she is living, but adds much affirmation to her death at the end of the book. Morag seems to have many moments of timeless ecstasy during the Highland summer and her body's disintegration through the Highland winter is seen as a reintegration with nature, part of the cyclic pattern in some ways more important here than re-entry into an unwelcoming society.

Thus, although she realistically recognizes and depicts Morag's final inability to function effectively in either the Highland winter or society, Renvoize creates another level of reality by emphasizing certain earth goddess aspects of Morag, and in so doing, manages to avoid irony in the depiction of Morag's death and to suggest affirmation in her return to nature, redeeming her failure to find a viable life style. What irony there is in the book, Renvoize saves for Figgs and his pastoral journey. As a climber in the Highlands who almost dies and is reborn in the arms of a goat girl, Arthur is also a pastoral hero. This particular goat girls stinks, however, to put it bluntly, for *A Wild Thing* is certainly an unsentimentalized version of the pastoral. It is partly the earthy nature of his journey that Arthur eventually rejects. This rejection and return to society could still function within the monomythic tradition where the hero returns to the world having rejected threatening female temptresses along the way; however, Renvoize connects Arthur's lack of earthiness with his being an engineer and his profession links him, like Kapugen, with the destructive forces of civilization that make the late twentieth century pastoral journey seem so ironic.

These links of Kapugen and Figgs with modern civilization bring us to the second aspect of the problem, involving the use of the pastoral in modern times. The pastoral has been, through the beginning of the twentieth century, a fairly affirmative form of the monomyth. To be sure, there was always a certain elegiac nostalgia about it, a mourning for the death of innocence that the return to the city signaled, but although the city may be corrupt and renewal by country virtues necessary in every generation, the possibilities for such renewal seemed, like nature itself, to have a cyclic inevitability--if winter comes, can spring be far behind? As the Industrial Revolution progressed, however, the city took on a technological dimension and threatened more and more to engulf the countryside; as Leo Marks put it in discussing nineteenth-century American literature, the Machine threatened to invade the Garden.[13] One can see the threat of the machine in the garden in children's as well as adult literature of the turn-of-the-century; *The Wind in the Willows* is an excellent example. Still, at that time, material progress, especially through the wonders of scientific discovery, seemed mainly to promise the extension of the garden rather than the end of it. For instance, we are not surprised to find in *The Secret Garden,* another exemplar of the pastoral for children, that Colin is rightly inspired to scientific study of the mysteries he experienced in that garden.

Much has happened to the world in the last seventy years to make scientific technology seem more like a threat than a boon to human existence: the annihilation of the human race quickly through atomic explosion, or slowly through pollution, seems to fulfill certain apocalyptic mythic patterns other than those we've discussed. Apocalyptic anxiety, when expressed in pastoral form, no longer produces elegies for a lost innocence, but more ironic prophecies of an end to the natural world and human life itself. The irony that I have already noted in Julie-Miyax's story and the Arthur Figgs portion of *A Wild Thing* is of this apocalyptic prophetic type.

In both these books there are signs of distrust of the twentieth-century Western culture based on scientific technology; that culture is seen in clear conflict with the life-enhancing experiences of the protagonists. Jean George's conservationist stance is no secret; she is particularly severe here in alluding to the American presence in Alaska. The Americans are laughed at for "discovering" secrets about the cold in laboratories that Eskimos have known for centuries; the alcoholism among the Eskimos seems attributable to the foreign presence; technological trash in the form of oil cans and the like is shown as eternal in that climate; those who shoot wolves from airplanes are virtual murderers, not just of a species but of ecological balance. The day of the wolf and Eskimo is over, not through evolution, but through genocide, George appears to say.

In *A Wild Thing*, we are not dealing with a conflict of two cultures, the losing one of which is made to represent nature and the other scientific technology, so the apocalyptic anxiety is not quite as pronounced as in *Julie of the Wolves*. Yet, at some level, Morag and Arthur are also made to represent these two opposing forces, nature and scientific technology. The couple have their first quarrel when Arthur tells her that he is planning to help build a dam in the Highlands near her cave:

> She was appalled. She refused to believe him. The more
> she defended the wildness of the land, the more he argued
> how improved it would be, how magnificent modern dams
> were and how time must march on (pp. 210-211).

Then they see a rabbit in the last paroxysms of myxomatosis (which has become science's answer to rabbit overpopulation) and Arthur is too squeamish to kill it quickly, saying, "They don't suffer much . . .They're only animals" (p. 217). Morag, who has hunted for food, takes the rabbit out of its misery. Arthur has, in his accident, significantly broken both his watch and his glasses. Renvoize indicates that in his final rejection of Morag and return to the land of watches and spectacles, he is rejecting the best, the most eternal and paradoxically clear-sighted, part of himself: Arthur's being an engineer bodes no good for the Highlands.

The two problems that I have attempted to delineate above, that of the female hero and the late twentieth century pastoral journey, can and do exist separately in other works of art. They could also be seen as interconnected in the manner that Dorothy Dinnerstein, a feminist psychologist, finds them to be.[14] In *The Mermaid and the Minotaur,* Dinnerstein postulates that two great issues of our time, "the woman question" and "the environmental question" are inter-related: the traditional view of man as mastering and woman as being mastered is played out not only in family relationships but in civilization's relation to nature. "Mother Nature" becomes a woman to be mastered and, in the case of such traditionally masculine weapons as scientific technology, ultimately destroyed. In Dinnerstein's view, too complex to be delineated fully here, our rape of nature will stop only when we alter our subconscious views of women, fostered first by our child upbringing patterns and perpetuated, as well as expressed, by those very monomyths with their rejection of the mother that we have been discussing here.

Renvoize's book in particular, seems a model illustration of Dinnerstein's theory, for Arthur initially rapes Morag, the earth goddess, and may well, as an engineer, go on to rape the countryside. Renvoize, I think, makes such a connection consciously. I doubt that George does. George represents Eskimo men as either demoralized or co-opted by civilization and that civilization is also represented by a woman, the *gussak* stepmother. So in *Julie of the Wolves,* sexual symbolism in relation to the environmental issue is not clear.[15]

The appeal and strength of the survivalist aspects of both these books--even with their ambivalent or abortive endings--should not be underestimated. The degree to which either George or Renvoize would admit feminist concerns and their interconnection with environmentalist concerns is arguable. The argument, however, is worthwhile. It points to the presence in these two books of levels deeper than physical adventure. Both books confront (or barely skirt, depending on the degree of consciousness we are willing to attribute to their authors) two of the major issues of our day, feminism and environmentalism. The realistic nature of that confrontation would seem to locate George and Renvoize squarely in the humanist camp, although in a curious way their treatment undermines some implicit assumptions of humanism: beliefs in man's rationality, civil organization, and human progress. Control of nature through the use of man's superior intellect has been central to the idea of the humanistic ascent of man. Still, George and Renvoize are humanists in that they affirm the basic belief in the self as the final arbiter of one's destiny, for neither finds hope or solace for their main characters in reaching to a God beyond themselves. The race of men may create many of the problems both heroines confront, but only individual human beings can resolve them.

NOTES

*The chapter was delivered as a paper at the Midwest Modern Language Association Meeting, November, 1979.

[1]I have used the following editions: Jean Craighead George. *Julie of the Wolves.* New York: Harper and Row, 1972 and Jean Renvoize. *A Wild Thing.* Boston: Little, Brown and Co., 1971. Page numbers in parentheses in the text will refer to these editions. The English edition of the latter was published in 1970.

[2]Joseph Campbell. *The Hero With a Thousand Faces,* 2nd ed. Princeton, N.J.: Princeton Univ. Press, 1968.

[3]Jon Stott, "Jean George's Arctic Pastoral: A Reading of *Julie of the Wolves." Children's Literature* 3, 1974, 131-9.

[4]Campbell, p. 35.

[5] Campbell, p. 36.

[6]I have deliberately ignored theorists such as Northrop Frye and William Empson and also have not tried to discuss the question of the "romance genre" and its relationship to both myth and pastoral.

[7]For a listing of participants see *PMLA* 93, November, 1978, 1193.

[8]Campbell, p. 136.

[9]Parts of Campbell's analysis suggest that for some of the more godlike heroes there is a fourth stage, going beyond this world and becoming androgynous, incorporating both passive (female) and active (male) elements.

[10]Pre-adolescent girls make particularly good protagonists in children's books and many share Julie's being still in the latency or "tom boy" stage. One should never underestimate the inspiration that these protagonists give to young girls to acquire skills and competency and the self-esteem that goes with that acquisition. The child reader will not necessarily experience the irony of the ending of *Julie of the Wolves,* which is perhaps for the best--but that doesn't mean the irony is not there.

[11]Erik H. Erikson. *Childhood and Society.* 2nd ed. 1950; New York: W.W. Norton and Co., Inc., 1963, Chap. 7.

[12]Those who talk of these earth mother myths as an earlier form do not necessarily all postulate, as Robert Graves does, that a matriarchial culture produced them.

[13]Leo Marks. *The Machine in the Garden, Technology and the Pastoral Ideal in America.* 1964, rpt. New York: Oxford Univ. Press, 1967.

[14]Dorothy Dinnerstein. *The Mermaid and the Minotaur, Sexual Arrangements and Human Malaise.* New York: Harper and Row, 1967.

[15]One should point out that there are females in *A Wild Thing* who are by no means earth goddesses. Examples include Mrs. Skinner, the puritanical stepmother, and, more importantly, one of the owners of the castle on the seashore who rides by Morag's unnoticed grave, quarreling with her husband and saying, "I'm so bored." They seem a part of Renvoize's implied political and social criticism of society, issues other than those considered in this chapter.

PART V BEYIND AND BEFORE POLARITIES

11

SCIENCE, MAGIC, AND THE TEST OF LUCK

Bruce Vogel

Vogel begins Section Five, Beyond and Before Polarities, with a method for determining whether a book resides in the world of science where rational and consistent laws of physics govern, or in the realm of magic where superordinary forces can intervene and overcome the orderly principles of science. The analytical tool for detecting the presence of magic, or the supernatural, is the test of luck. Vogel affirms that no successful book can assume both these world views at once, yet he finds that there is room for sub-species or variants from this dichotomy. Ellen Raskin's absurdist works are an example. He further argues that though two works may have opposing world views, their positions on salient questions such as nature, determinism, and will might be quite similar.

SCIENCE, MAGIC, AND THE TEST OF LUCK

Given the marvels science has achieved and the marvels projected for the future, one wonders how it is that magic and superscience have not become thoroughly confused in children's literature. What need is there for old-fashioned magic when science, human or alien, can produce any effect achievable by sorcery? If one adds the claims of parapsychology to those of future science, then where is there any scope for magic to provoke wonder?

And yet it is only in the poorest specimens of contemporary children's literature (those undisciplined wish fulfillments found chiefly in the media) in which real confusion of science and magic exists. Even there the two concepts are usually distinguishable. Why do both remain popular? What can wizards do that a superscientist cannot? What griffin or chimera could science create with recombinant DNA, or find ready-made in the vast realms of space? What exists in Narnia that could not be electronically duplicated in a galaxy far away?

The fact is that science and magic, now, as in the past, serve very different functions. They relate to fundamentally different views of the universe. The two principles clash when mixed together in the same story. An author with real insight into either magic or science does not try to combine the two principles. Only the hack who lacks an understanding of either tries to mix them.

Good science fiction is, first of all, good science. No matter how speculative it becomes, it presents a rational and consistent view of the universe. A scientist believes that the laws of physics operate everywhere all of the time. The universe is governed by principles and people, being within that universe, are strictly subject to those principles. The world, viewed scientifically, is not a dull or graceless world. In it the possible is delimited by the order of things, and yet for humanity, there are breath-taking opportunities which open up whenever a new insight is achieved.

In Phyllis MacLennan's charming book *Turned Loose on Irdra,* for example, a boy confronts a variety of alien life-forms including "whizzers" and "creepers" and "vot vines." These creatures are unintelligible sources of trouble to most of the colonists, but the boy has an implicit faith that they can be understood--that their nature is determined by the same laws of survival that govern more familiar life-forms. By the power of his faith he is enabled to study the whizzers and the creepers and comprehend them in terms of the planet's total ecology. Once their roles are understood, a whole new life style opens to the human colony. Whizzers are so neat (once we meet them socially) and vot vines so useful (once their properties are discovered) that the reader cannot help wishing they flourished on earth. The alien creatures of Irdra are imaginative creations, but they are firmly grounded in a rational universe.

Ready examples of bad science fiction come to mind, not from children's books, but from literature for somewhat older readers. The books of the *Boys Life* "Time Machine" series or Brian Earnshaw's *Dragon Fall Five* novels are certainly weak science fiction, but they fail on so many levels that they serve poorly as examples. The well known Danny Dunn series offers a faulty picture of how scientific knowledge is achieved, but the integrity of the rational universe is suprisingly well respected.

The clearest examples of bad science fiction are found in the cinema and television. When the "Six Million Dollar Man" hefts a huge boulder with his mighty bionic arm, he does that which is impossible or else pointless in any rational universe. For every action there is an equal and opposite counteraction. That is the law. The weight of the boulder must be transferred from the marvelous arm to the merely human scapula and backbone. Now it is lawful in science fiction to speculate about a universe in which Newton's third law of motion did not obtain, but in any rational universe the law must be the same everywhere all of the time. In a universe without Newton's third law, anybody could throw boulders around. A bionic arm would not be necessary. The child who watches "The Six Million Dollar Man" beholds a fuzzy universe in which science (and six million dollars) can do whatever is convenient.

A magical universe is one in which there are cracks in the rational order through which powers beyond the rational may be observed to operate. These chinks may be few, but may exist. Magic (like miracle) discloses them. Proper magic does not serve the mere convenience of the magician anymore than science serves the scientist. But, as a technology may, with careful work and preparation, exploit a scientific principle, the magician may succeed in using the supernatural. A good feat of magic is a comment both upon the personality of the supernatural agency and on the human being with which it interacts.

The author who introduces magic into a tale does not do so merely to evoke gasps of surprise from the reader. She does so in order to posit a world in which there are more powerful forces than humanity, a world in which events are controlled by providence, destiny, or fate, or by forces of good and evil.

It does not follow that all uses of magic in children's literature ought to be weighty and important. Mrs. Pigglewiggle and Mary Poppins, for instance, employ quite astonishing magic just to teach children small lessons in manners and morality. One of the facts about the supernatural which is repeated over and over in folklore is that children are more entitled to a helping hand from the world of magic than are adults. God does not show his power to adults lest they abandon their own efforts, but God retains his credentials as a parlor magician and will from time to time pull off a small miracle for a child if no one else is watching. Poppins, Pigglewiggle and their many kin relate quite distinctly to the supernatural. Through them the child perceives a world in which the social order is slyly maintained by persons in touch with something beyond mere adulthood.

Then, of course, we have children's books which present fully defined magical systems with explicit roots in the supernatural. Ursula LeGuin's work *A Wizard of Earthsea* and its companion volumes form a treatise, almost, on systematic magic.

For an example of a bungled use of magic we turn again to the media -- this time to the Disney version of T.H. White's *Sword in the Stone*. The book, in this case, is nearly as bad as the absurdity which results from mixing magic and science. In the film the wizard Merlin appears as a time traveler in love with 20th century science. As young Arthur's tutor he drills and drills the boy in the precepts of modern science. The effect is insulting to the dullest viewer. Here we see Merlin using a marvelous magic spell which causes the dishes to wash themselves so that the boy can be freed to study science. Any intelligent child is going to think, "To blazes with science. I want to learn how to cast spells on dishes."

Despite the fact that children's literature has, on the whole, maintained a clear-eyed distinction between science and magic, the advent of the culture-molding film series "Star Wars" suggests that we may see an increasingly blurred use of the two concepts. Is "The Force" of "Star Wars" nature or divinity? Is psycho-kinesis science or magic?

Fortunately there is an acid test for detecting the presence of the supernatural in any story. I call it the test of luck. No intervention of magic or miracle can masquerade as a natural event if the test of luck is applied. The purpose of this chapter is to illustrate the uses of this analytical tool.

Provided that we define our terms correctly, it can readily be demonstrated that most *good* books will exhibit a distinct bias toward humanism or else toward a religious/mythic view of life. A good author has little choice but to make clear his attitude toward the supra-natural. He cannot straddle the fence because he must dispose in one way or another of the problem of luck.

A good author does not allow fortuitous circumstances or long-odds interventions of luck to go unexplained. If the author is writing from a humanist perspective, he will either avoid challenging the odds or he will educe some rational determinant to justify the unexpected outcome. An author writing from a mythic point of view will deliberately introduce odds-defying outcomes in order to explain them as interventions of the supra-natural.

There are but two ways in which an author can preserve his neutrality respecting the supra-natural. One way is to push the luck of his characters to an artfully ambiguous degree. A character is lucky enough to tax the reader's credulity but not quite so lucky that the reader demands an explanation. The reader is left with a feeling that *perhaps* more than luck stands behind the character. If the luck of the character is artfully developed, the reader would rather savor the uncanniness of it than to understand the how or why of it. A few good books and tales have been constructed upon this principle.

A good example of delicate neutrality can be found in Richard Chase's *Jack Tales*. There are very few real strokes of luck in these stories. Most events proceed logically from Jack's cleverness. No stroke of fortune is really implausible once the reader has caught on to the quality of Jack's wits. And yet there are fortuitous turns. Jack happens to have saved some leftovers from dinner in his leather apron, and these slops provide him with just the ammunition he needs to trick an awful two-headed giant into destroying himself. That lucky coincidence is as much help from chance as Jack needs. From there he proceeds to rid the land of giants. In no one tale does Jack experience enough pure luck to cause wonder. But in adventure after adventure luck continues to provide whatever small help his invention does not supply. At last the reader begins to admire Jack's luck and to wonder what elusive charm or magic power clings to his destiny.

Another way in which it is possible for an author to remain neutral on the question of the supra-natural is to introduce into his story an entity which is ambiguously poised between the supernatural and the merely alien. For reasons which I hope to make clear, this kind of ambiguity is extraordinarily hard to achieve. I cannot think of a children's work in which it has even been attempted. It is, however, a possible ambiguity and I think that Stanislas Lem's adult work *Solaria* is a rare example.

As a rule the supernatural and the alien are easily distinguishable. Where there is doubt, the test of luck will reliably differentiate.

In Tolkien's book *The Hobbit* the reader encounters dwarves, a wizard, giant spiders, trolls, goblins, and a dragon. Some of these creatures possess unfamiliar powers and traits (such as turning into stone if exposed to sunlight), but are they in fact supernatural beings or are they merely alien? The author's use of magic in this tale is so restrained that one is deep into its unfolding before one first detects the unmistakable presence of the supra-natural.

It is not in the alien nature of Smaug the dragon that the reader perceives the supra-natural, but in the remarkable luck by which the dragon is slain. Bilbo Baggins, the hobbit, notices a small chink in Smaug's armor of scales. He chances to tell his friends about this chink within the hearing of a bird which happens to be in the service of Bard of Esgoroth. The bird reports the information to Bard, and subsequently the dragon attacks Bard's town. Taking advantage of the intelligence supplied to him by the bird, Bard slays the dragon, making a spectacular shot with the last arrow in his quiver.

This remarkable chain of events is palatable only because the reader understands that Smaug's death was ordained. Bilbo and the bird and Bard of Esgoroth were all in the service of a secret destiny greater than each of them and greater than Smaug.

Again it is not the magic of Bilbo's ring which reveals the supra-natural but the luck of its finding. The power of the ring could have a rational explanation as the work of a superior and alien science. But only the supra-natural can be responsible for the stroke of chance which delivered the ring into Bilbo's keeping. Of course the hand of destiny is not immediately perceived by the reader. At first the reader accepts the ring's finding simply as a stroke of fortune. He does not yet realize how momentous an event was Bilbo's discovery nor how long were the odds against it. For all the reader knows, rings of power may be fairly common in Middle Earth. As the sequel to *The Hobbit* unfolds, the reader begins to appreciate the remarkable chance which delivered the ring to the fittest person in all the world to receive it. At the same time the reader is led to perceive the operation of some supra-natural design in the event.

Let us now apply the test of luck to a more challenging case. Let us consider the curious guest appearance of the supernatural in Kenneth Grahame's mainly rational classic *Wind in the Willows*. Apart from allowing animals a nearly human condition, the book contains not a hint of magic and nothing at all fabulous except in a single chapter titled "The Piper at the Gates of Dawn." In this chapter a lost otter child, for whom the community has been searching, is discovered sleeping in the lap of the demigod, Pan, who spellbinds the searchers with pipe music and then vanishes. What does it mean?

It is possible to maintain that Pan does not represent an intrusion of the supernatural into the story at all. Perhaps he is merely a bit of symbolic shorthand for the kindlier aspects of nature. It is after all possible for children to fall asleep in the lap of nature and come to no harm. It cannot be said with certainty that Pan rescued the child nor that he intruded upon the story at all.

And yet Pan does intervene in a sense. He shows himself. He communicates his mystery and elusiveness. Perhaps he is more than a personification of nature. Perhaps he represents the role which the supernatural plays in Kenneth Grahame's world. The supernatural exists, but we rarely perceive it. It avoids detection. We can not get hold of it, and it seems not to meddle with the natural order unless it is to wrap a protective mantle about a lost child. It shows itself only to the innocent and to half-awake dreamers at the gates of dawn.

I incline to the view that Pan's appearance is intended by the author as an explicit statement about the supernatural. Analysis of the part played by luck in *Wind in the Willows* will support this conclusion. The story contains a number of charming coincidences such as Mole finding his old home precisely on Christmas Eve. But I find only two real srokes of fortune. The first occurs early in the book when Mole and Ratty are lost in the Wild Woods. The pair are saved from perishing in a snowstorm only because Mole has the luck to stub his toe on a buried boot scraper which marks Mr. Badger's doorstep. The second intervention of blind luck occurs late in the story when Toad, fleeing from the law, falls into the river. No one has seen him fall; no one is trying to rescue him; and he is on the point of drowning when he is swept by the current around a bend and into the grasp of his friend the River Rat.

The two instances share a in commonality: that the characters involved are near death and powerless to save themselves when luck intervenes. If we think of these interventions, not as chance occurrences, but as rescues by a guardian power, we are predicating a view consistent with the image of Pan who steps in to rescue the otter child, but who does not wish to be seen or known.

If we are dealing with the supra-natural, it is a power which tries never to tip its hand but which does so to save the lives of those who have no other recourse.

It happens that I retain a clear recollection of my own reaction to the snowstorm episode from my first reading of the story as a child. I was appalled by it. It was one of only three incidents in the story which I disliked. To think that I had come so close to losing Mole and Ratty! But for the one-in-a-million chance that Mole tripped on the boot scraper, they would have been done for. When the brave and resourceful Rat could not save them, things were serious. What if Mole's foot had missed the boot scraper by an inch even? The question did not bear thinking about.

I had no such anxious reaction to Toad's close call. Perhaps I cared less what happened to Toad. Like many children I gravely disapproved of Toad. But I think a more likely explanation for my indifference to the second close call is that I had by then recognized that in Grahame's world, special help existed for those who had exhausted their own resources. It may well have been the appearance of Pan which banished my anxiety.

We have seen that the supernatural differs from author to author in the extent to which it intervenes in their stories. In Kenneth Grahame's work it is a shy force determined to remain hidden. In Tolkien the supra-natural is obscure and difficult to fathom, but it is mighty and purposive, capable of setting intricate chains of effect in motion. The choices made by individuals to the supra-natural is unclear. Were we to examine Susan Cooper's series beginning with *The Dark Is Rising*, we would see an instance in which the supra-natural takes direct charge of events. The characters are fully controlled by the powers they serve.

By analyzing luck we find a considerable range of views and values among writers who acknowledge the supra-natural. The same kind of analysis will tell us much less about those writers who avoid challenging the odds. Yet we shall not have to look far to find profound differences within the rationalist camp. Shall we call all of the writers who abjure the supra-natural humanists?

I think it fair to do so.[1] As we have made our definition of the mythic/religious writer broad enough to cover all forms of belief in the supra-natural, I think we must balance the breadth of that definition with an equally broad definition of humanism. A humanist then may be any author whose characters exist without reference to the supra-natural.

We recognize of course that not everyone defines humanism in this way. There persists in literary criticism a tendency to associate humanism with a complex of renaissance values. It may be argued that the humanists not only reject the supra-natural, they harbor a positive faith in the power of reason and in the perfectibility of human kind.[2] If we attempt to make our definition of humanism carry that much freight, we shall need to identify a third and a fourth class of world-view before we can hope to subsume all of the good children's books.

First of all there is the view which holds that the human adventure is absurd. There may be those who would deny that the existentialist view has found expression in children's books but we have only to consider the works of Ellen Raskin. Raskin's power to snatch comedy from the jaws of banality immediately puts one in mind of the plays of Eugene Ionesco. Let us apply the test of luck to Raskin's book *The Mysterious Disappearance of Leon, I Mean Noel*.

A little reflection discloses that almost no occurrence in the story grows out of chance. Luck is in no way responsible for any of the astonishing events. The Fish family and the Carillon family force their children to marry at age five because marriage seems a practical solution to a legal and materialistic problem which the families face. The Fishes and Carillons are nothing if not materialistic and legalistic. It becomes immediately clear that, in Raskin's world, children are subject to any absurdity which their elders choose to impose upon them. What is worse, ill-considered items of adult nonsense can become the mainspring of the budding personality. Little Caroline Carillon (nee Caroline Fish) known as Mrs. Carillon from age five upwards assumes that it is her destiny to go through life with Leon.

On her twentieth birthday Mrs. Carillon is to meet Leon for the first time since their wedding day. In the first hour of their rendezvous at a seaside hotel, Leon disappears under mysterious circumstances. Then begins an astonishing odyssey in which Mrs. Carillon, sustained by a mystical faith that she will find her husband, sets out to track him down.

Back and forth across the country she goes acquiring an adoptive family on the way but never for an hour abandoning her search. Not only is she burdened by a faith in her destiny, she is handicapped by a belief in reason as well. She possesses certain clues which she has confidence will lead her to Leon if she pursues them logically. What she overlooks is the fact that she is no great shakes at logic.

While there are no lucky strokes in the story, there are a few turns of fortune which at first appear remarkable, and these are worth a moment of study.

1. After years of searching Mrs. Carillon chances to meet a friend from her childhood named Augie Kunkle. Augie has since become a middle aged maker of cross-word puzzles. He possesses a tidy, logical mind and has just the skills to help Mrs. Carillon interpret her clues.

2. Augie seems to experience a fantastic run of bad luck upon becoming reacquainted with Mrs. Carillon. He gets knocked on the head so often that his doctor orders him to wear a football helmet at all times.

3. One night Mrs. Carillon is persuaded to watch a television program she does not usually watch and there on the screen is the man she met as Leon at the seaside hotel years before.

The reader soon discovers that none of the events in question are really against the odds. Enough time has elapsed and Mrs. Carillon has toured enough places that she was almost bound to run into Augie or, if not Augie, someone of his rational temperament. Though Mrs. Carillon for a time feels responsible for Augie's head injuries, it becomes clear that he is accident prone. It seems quite likely to me that Augie's vulnerable head is a comment by the author upon the role of reason in life. He who lives by his head suffers by his head. If one insists upon being reasonable in this world, one can expect repeated bashings.

What has to be explained about Mrs. Carillon's luck in seeing the supposed Leon on television, is why it did not happen sooner. The man has by then become a well known actor. Mrs. Carillon is probably one of the last people in America to see him. This circumstance is explained by the fact that until that time Mrs. Carillon watched only certain programs which she believed would help with her search. Augie has only recently persuaded her that she had been misinterpreting her evidence, thus allowing her to change her television habits.

Of all the people in the story Augie Kunkle is the sanest, the least offensive, and possibly the most effective. This is not to say that others should attempt to emulate him. The author makes it clear that the world does not work that way. For every reasonable being, there are two who are greedy (they are best off marrying each other), one who is superstitious (her worst fears all come to pass), several who are ambitious (some make it and some do not), and a lot who are mainly nosey. There is nothing these people can do about themselves. They are what they are.

In Raskin's work there are no clear breaches in the web of cause-and-effect. There is no traffic with forces beyond nature. For this reason I would place her among the humanists, but clearly there is in her work no optimism about human perfectibility. Her faith in reason is highly qualified. The life of reason may be the best life, but few are qualified to live it. Those who do had best not expect the rest of the world to be reasonable. Perhaps I was a little hasty in saying that the supernatural does not exist in Raskin. It exists in the minds of certain characters. It is there in the form of blind articles of faith, which contribute greatly to the absurdity of our species.

Besides those writers with a vision of the absurd we have also to consider all of those for whom the question has become not humanity's perfectability, but its outlook for survival. Perhaps we can agree to consider existentialist and survivalist as varieties of the humanist tradition though they may lack some of the classic virtues.

As we have seen, the necessity to maintain a consistent policy toward luck forces all authors (except a few with the finesse to remain neutral) into taking a stand for or against the supra-natural. Thus all authors who are good enough to maintain a consistent policy can be classified as humanists or as mytho-religious writers. One can take a neutral or "maybe" position and one can scale down almost to nothing the degree to which the supra-natural interacts with the natural world. What one cannot do is write from the "yes" and the "no" position in the same work. We must remember, of course, that authors may be of divided opinion respecting the supernatural but of the same mind respecting many other things.

Authors of both camps can repose much or little confidence in the human race. From the religious perspective it is possible to view humanity either as the reference point from which all created things derive value, or as puny playthings for unfathomable powers. From the humanistic viewpoint it is possible to look upon human reason as the only seeing-eye in a blind universe; or humanity can be seen as an animal species dangerously over-developed in intellect, much as the sabre toothed tiger was over-developed in fang capacity.

It is possible to affirm or deny freedom of will from either position. Susan Cooper and Lloyd Alexander both acknowledge the supernatural. Alexander's characters make choices and live with the consequences. Cooper's characters may balk a little, but the hand of the supra-natural is upon them. They can go only where they are supposed to go.

On the humanist side we see a similar spirit. In this connection S.E. Hinton and George Seldon make an interesting contrast in that they obtain very different results, both working with the urban poor. Hinton is a hard-bitten realist. Her lifelike characters are largely determined by social forces. In her book *Rumble Fish* she explicitly describes her protagonist as being like a steel marble in a pinball machine. He is slammed from place to place and does what he is driven to do. There is an implication that he perhaps ought somehow to get hold of his destiny, but it is too late for that. Conditions have already hardened him to the point that he cannot change. Seldon writes animal fantasies about a streetwise cat and mouse who live by scrounging in Grand Central Station, New York, New York. Their lives are rich with things to do and choices to be made. Tucker Mouse is acquisitive and materialistic by nature, but he is not a slave to his passions. When his heart is touched he rises above his bent and, in the freedom of his being, he grudgingly shares what he has hoarded.

Mytho-religious writers and humanists both have expressed profound feelings about nature. These days the humanists tend to have the most to say on the subject; yet appreciation of nature is everywhere evident in Tolkien. His conservationism is probably as strong as Jean George's, for example.

In terms of philosophical perspective, children's literature as a whole differs from literature in general only in that it shows a tendency to be more positive about life and more supportive of the reader. I cannot think of any good children's work which is wholly negative. Children's books can and do present profoundly bleak and sobering views of life, but as a rule these dark penetrations are accompanied by very positive assessments in other areas.

In Jean George's *Julie of the Wolves* we get a very bleak look at humanity's destruction of wild life. The very people who best know and best love the natural wilderness are being driven to destroy it. If Julie's father can be induced to shoot wolves from an airplane, there is little hope. At the same time the reader is given the example of Julie herself. She is a stirring example of human endurance and of humanity's capacity to empathize with nature.

Children's literature is made up principally of balanced views and positive views, but it would be a mistake to conclude from this inclination that children's literature is limited with respect to the range of philosophical opinion it expresses. I cannot think of a children's book which gives positive expression to the views of Marquis de Sade, but the viewpoint of most philosophers can be found in children's literature if one knows where to look.

That we are able to divide the good children's books into two distinct categories does little to explain what makes a good book good. The fact that we are able to assign a book to one camp or the other only proves that the author has been self-consistent in his interpretation of luck. Consistency in this matter is important, but it is only one of the vital constituents of literary quality.

For the purposes of this discussion let us set aside all of the aesthetic and the informational components of children's literature and focus only upon philosophical content. We quickly discover that a good author's view of life abounds in rich observations which relate not at all to his position on the supernatural. Kenneth Grahame's world is not only a world in which the supernatural is there to intervene at the utmost pitch of need, but it is a world in which *the law* need not loom over-large in the reader's mind. Toad is not punished for escaping the law. He is not a good Toad, but he finds safety among friends. He is of Badger's community, and the community upholds him, deserving or not. This aspect of Grahame's world is no less important (and it is a good deal more individualistic) than his view of the supra-natural.

In conclusion we find that the test of luck is useful in distinguishing between the supra-natural and the alien. We have also found it helpful in pinning down an author's position with respect to the supra-natural. We have found that, indeed, most children's books can be classified as mytho-religious or as humanistic. We have also found that no consistent complex of values attaches to either classification. Many important values cut across the line and are found in both classifications. We have discovered an interesting dichotomy in literature, but it does not prove to be the key which explains literary merit.

Did we expect to find the key? No, because common sense tells us that there is no royal road to quality. It is always a pleasant experience when analysis supports common sense, is it not?

NOTES

[1]Beuet, William Rose. *The Reader's Encyclopedia.* New York: Crowell, 1955, p. 525.

[2]Abbagnano, Nicola. "Humanism" in Edwards, Paul. *The Encyclopedia Of Philosophy,* 4, 69.

BIBLIOGRAPHY

Chase, Richard. *The Jack Tales ;* Told by R.M. Ward and his kindred in the Beech Mountain Section of Western North Carolina and by other descendants of Council Harmon (1803-1876) elsewhere in the Southern Mountains with three tales from Wise County, Virginia. Boston: Houghton Mifflin, 1943.

Cooper, Susan. *The Dark Is Rising.* New York: Atheneum, 1973.

Earnshaw, Brian. *Dragonfall Five* and *The Royal Beast.* New York: Lothrop Lee, and Shepard, 1975.

George, Jean. *Julie Of The Wolves.* New York: Harper & Row, 1972.

Grahame, Kenneth. *The Wind In The Willows .* New York: Charles Scribner's Sons, 1961.Originally published, 1903.

Hinton, S.E. *Rumble Fish.* New York: Delacorte, 1975.

Keith, Donald. *Mutiny In The Time Machine* (Boy's Life Library). New York: Random House, c1963.

LeGuin, Ursula. *A Wizard Of Earthsea.* Berkeley, CA: Parnassus Press, 1968.

MacDonald, Betty. *Mrs. Piggle-Wiggle's Magic.* Philadelphia: Lippincott, 1974. Originally published, 1949.

MacLennan, Phyllis. *Turned Loose On Irdra.* New York: Doubleday, 1970.

Raskin, Ellen. *The Mysterious Disappearance Of Leon (I Mean Noel).* New York: Dutton, 1971.

Selden, George. *Cricket In Times Square.* New York: Farrar, Straus and Giroux, 1960.

Selden, George. *Happy Cat's Pet Puppy.* New York: Farrar, Straus and Giroux, 1974.

Tolkien, J.R.R. *The Hobbit.* Boston: Houghton Mifflin, 1938.

Tolkien, J.R.R. *Fellowship Of The Ring.* Boston: Houghton Mifflin, 1967.

Travers, P.L. *Mary Poppins.* New York: Harcourt Brace, 1962. Originally published, 1934.

White, T.H. "The Sword in the Stone," *The Once And Future King.* New York: Putnam's Sons, 1958.

Williams, Jay. *Danny Dunn And The Smallifying Machine.* New York: McGraw-Hill, 1969.

12

HUMANITY AND NATURE IN PATRICIA WRIGHTSON'S
THE ICE IS COMING

Millicent Lenz

Lenz's essay argues that Patricia Wrightson's Australian aborigines harken back to a time before the sacred and humanistic dichotomization. Wrightson's *The Ice Is Coming* is set in present day Australia, yet the central character, Wirrun, and the tribe from which he comes partake of an ageless, polytheistic, animistic approach to the world. The novel turns on the conflict between these two opposing positions, the magical/religious and the materialistic/secular. Wrightson celebrates the aborigines whom she sees as both spiritually in tune and morally advanced. Those people who represent contemporary secularism, the Happy Folk, are the contrasted exploiters. Lenz explores this contrast in a careful analysis of the novel. She finds in it not an indictment of contemporary Australian social and political problems, but an exploration of what is universally human in the experience of one particular aboriginal boy.

HUMANITY AND NATURE IN PATRICIA WRIGHTSON'S
THE ICE IS COMING

Patricia Wrightson's *The Ice Is Coming* incorporates a world view that predates the dichotomization of human experience into the sacred and the secular. It embodies the ageless polytheistic, animistic interpretation of reality which survives today in the beliefs of the Australian aborigines. The central character, Wirrun, sees the world as animated by spirits, alive with magic and mystery, a perspective that is religious in the broadest and deepest sense, yet has nothing in common with the Judeo-Christian religious tradition in particular, nor with institutionalized religion in general. It is a world view more accurately described as mythological, embodying primitive folk-beliefs, concretely representing a people's cosmic view. Though such a mythological interpretation of the world is characteristic of primitive peoples, Wirrun's world is not simply that of a primitive. Indeed the magical animistic beliefs of his tribe are challenged by the secular, materialistic world view of the urban white Australians and the tribe's beliefs withstand the conflict.

Much of the power of the novel derives from the conflict between these two diametrically opposed views of the world: the magical/religious and the materialistic/secular. Wrightson's dramatization of this conflict challenges a narrow sense of religion. Her tale broadens the definition of religion and sensitizes her reader to vestiges of primordial memories and primitive beliefs. Thus, Wrightson cannot easily be placed on a continuum between a religious and a humanistic world view. Rather, she challenges the two categories and in so doing expands the definition of what it means to be religious and, likewise, human. To begin with some assumptions central to the world view of the novel and then to enumerate the range of characters and their gathering conflict might illuminate this book's complex point of view.

There can be no doubt that Wrightson's sympathies lie with the ancient mythological perspective, with its appreciation of the mysterious yet threatening powers that animate nature, its poetic and dramatic richness, its strong sense of values, of taboo ("bad" magic) and mana ("good" magic). Central to this ancient Australian mythology is the belief in the magic powers of the spirits that inhabit living creatures and also dwell in earth, rock, and water -- some of them hostile, some of them indifferent, some of them capable of providing help to humans. The ancient idea that man's well-being depends upon close contact with the earth can be seen in the literature of many peoples. (The most vivid embodiment of this idea is in the Greek myth of Antaeus, who was invincible so long as his feet touched the ground, but vulnerable the moment he was lifted into the air.) Humankind longs for assurance of its close link to Mother Earth--a longing reflected in the belief observed in some primal religions that the central supporting pole of a dwelling represents a "navel," a point where the human habitation is linked to earth as by an umbilical cord. *The Ice Is Coming*, set in present-day Australia, incorporates through its human and spirit characters this consciousness of humanity's vital relationship to the land.

Also of crucial importance is man's response to the non-human natural world. More specifically, Wrightson communicates through Wirrun the critical importance of a caring attitude on the part of human beings towards the natural world. The book is built around an implicit hierarchy of human worth which corresponds directly to the degree of an individual's sensitivity to and attachment to the land and all of creation. Humanness itself is defined in terms of caring; the fully human person is first and foremost a caring creature, who cares even when he is powerless to do anything to express his concern. Interestingly, however, Ms. Wrightson's fictional world indicates no caring god; no benevolent spirit stands behind nature. Nature itself, far from being infused with grace, is amoral, unromanticized, indifferent to human judgments of good and evil, committed only to survival. Yet the perspective is not that of naturalism, for nature is in need of human caring and respect for the mystery underlying natural phenomena.

Australia provides a setting alive with ancient, magical life, where rocks "wink" and move, where shape-shifters play their pranks upon the uninitiated. Wrightson might be likened to D.H. Lawrence in her pagan sensitivity to "the spirit of the place" -- in her case, the "powerful magic" of the Australian land and landscape. It is a land of terrible and awesome mystery, knowing no compassion or kindness for the creatures it has given form, yet having the power to call forth the love and heroism and devotion of mankind to save it from its ancient enemy, the ice. Within nature dwell the spirits of anti-life, the Ninya, egotistic, greedy ice-creatures, embodiments of the inability to nurture. Symbolically the Ninya are akin to the core of ice that imprisons Satan in Dante's *Inferno*. They could also be understood as symbols of the death force, *thanatos*.

The book opens with a description of the land as significantly resembling a human hand:

> The old south land lies across the world like an open hand,
> hollowed a little at the palm. High over it tumbles the sea . . .
> Under and in this tumbling of wind and water the land lies quiet
> like a great hand at rest, all its power unknown.[1]

The image expresses unawakened potential and unrevealed personality. The land is further personified by reference to "its beautiful, terrible heart," where "something waited" (p. 15). Further, the opening chapter of the book introduces the chief characters in such a way as to establish the quality of their relationships to the land and to bring into focus the basic conflict: the struggle between the Ninya, with their deadly power of ice, and the Eldest Nargun, with its power of fire, for control of the land.

The first characters to be introduced are the human inhabitants most remote from the land, predictably lacking an appreciation of its value. These are ironically named Happy Folk, to whom appearance is all; they are the white, urban Australians who are always seeking, but never finding happiness. Superficial, trivial-minded, materialistic, they are caught up in a frantic trading in "happiness": "it is their business and their duty. They study it and teach it to their children, debate it . . ., export and import it. Most of all, they buy and sell it." Tellingly, they have no understanding for the land and no time to perceive it, but "sometimes, in their search for happiness, they make expensive little excursions into the land with cameras" (p. 11).[2]

The world of the Happy Folk is devoid of interconnectedness, continuity, or mystery--all of the things still appreciated by the People who have retained their link to earth. The Happy Folk could be said to represent secularism at its worst; they represent the denial of values, nihilism, or perhaps hedonism, rather than belief in the human spirit. When the ice threatens the land, the Happy Folk are concerned only about how to capitalize on the novelty to increase their beach tourist trade. "Some motels advertised in the papers: SWIMMING OR SKIING? EITHER WAY YOU CAN'T LOSE" (p. 149). The young scientists among the Happy Folk approach the ice as something to be measured. They tell Wirrun, the young man of the People, that their purpose is only "plotting an isotherm . . .

We're not making value judgments" (p. 153). They are not involved in the struggle against the Ninya, and this lack of commitment demonstrates their indifference to values.

Following the Happy Folk in the cast of characters are the Inlanders, who spring from the same ancestry but are not "a separate race," because "the great old silent land" has been "at work" on them (p. 12). The Inlanders are "jealous children of the land," and in this they are like the People.

The next group, the People, differ from the Inlanders in appearance, being "dark-skinned, with heavy brows and watching eyes, and they belong to the land; it flows into them through their feet" (p. 11). The image expresses the intimacy of their connection to the earth. Indeed, they are under the spell of the land: they "claim the land as theirs; but really it is the land that claims them" (p. 11). Wirrun, one of the People, is a young man who, having "gone to one of the Happy Folks' schools," now works at one of their service stations. He is thoughtful, the kind of person for whom "thinking came more easily than talking" (p. 18). He is initially unaware of his connection to the land; he does not know "that the land flowed into him through his feet. He only knew that he liked to walk on the earth in lonely places" (p. 18).

Next are the earth spirits, "the oldest race of all . . . born of the land itself: or red rock and secret waters, dust-devils and far places, green jungle and copper-blue saltbush." Among these are "the Narguns, monsters of rock poured molten from the fires in the heart of the land" (p. 12), familiar creatures to readers of Wrightson's previous book, *The Nargun and the Stars*.[3] They dwell in caves or holes in the ground, and are not friendly to humankind. The People must avoid them to escape a "quick and crushing" death. The Eldest Nargun, as old as the land itself, can summon "the red fire of its beginning," but slumbers defiantly at the edge of the sea, against which its power of fire is useless (p. 12).

The earth spirits include also the rock spirits, among whom is the Mimi, Wirrun's companion on his mission to save the land from the Ninya. The shy rock spirits live inside rocks; they are invisible to ordinary humans, although Wirrun, after he receives the power of the People, can see them. They are described as "tall and very frail, so frail that the wind might break them" (p. 13). The Mimi, nonetheless, learns how "to lie along the wind" (p. 14) when she is swept away by it, and only thus does she manage to survive, being carried to "the centre of the old south land . . . a place of waiting . . . and age." Here lie "the age and travail of the world, and the Happy Folk call it a desert" (p. 15), oblivious to its worth.

It is at this center of the Australian land that the Mimi and Wirrun are brought together by a fate that seems to emanate from the land itself. Wrightson states: "perhaps it was the old southland itself that called up the wind" (p. 14). Their meeting place is also the point where the earth opens to the caverns of the Ninya.

The Ninya, ice spirits, are portrayed as "men of ice in caverns of ice" (p. 15). They are "men like men of the People, except that they, like their caverns, are pure and sparkling white . . . They are the makers of ice and their blood is white." Green-eyed, beautiful, but cupidinous, they:

> live together as brothers, but there is no kindness between
> them. The frost goes deep. Their voices creak and grate;
> they often howl in anger; and every man of the Ninya
> wants all and wants it for himself. So the power of this
> wanting and this power of ice lie under the sun-beaten
> sand, prisoned and waiting (p. 15).

Their greed for the land is constrained only by their fear of the Eldest Nargun with whom they battled ages ago, whose "power of fire" "melted [their] bones into rivers and sent [them] under the ground." In this opening chapter, the strongest-willed among them urges them to "find the Eldest [Nargun] and catch it quickly in a fist of ice. *Then* we are free." A singer among them then chants their battle refrain: "In a mountain of ice shall the Nargun, the Eldest, be held" (pp. 16-17).

Wirrun is the last character to be introduced in chapter one. His desire to see "the great quiet centre of the land," which he had heard about from one of his friends, has brought him to "the small salt lake with its outcrop of rock" (pp. 18-19) where he camps for the night. It happens to be the very spot where the Mimi has landed and slipped inside the Ninya's rock. Wrightson views the fated character of these events from an omniscient perspective:

> So they lay that night as the old south land had ordered it:
> the young man from the east sleeping under the plum, the
> rock-spirit of the north frozen on the salt. In caverns
> beneath them the Ninya raged and fought for the
> possession of the land; and far down the world the Eldest
> Nargun crouched on its shelf of rock while the sea swirled
> over (p. 19).

Here, masterfully interwoven, are the quintessential elements of the dramatic conflicts that make up the remainder of the book.

The ensuing narrative embellishes and fleshes out the relationships of these characters to the land. These relationships can be placed in perspective by charting Wirrun's growth towards self-knowledge and awareness of his humanity.

Chapters two and three of part one show Wirrun growing in awareness of the needs of the land and crystallizing his insight into his personal responsibility to it. On his visit to Alice Springs, where he is amazed to see the country "hanging upside down and floating in the air" and to observe ice on his waterbag in near summer (p. 21), he is told by an old man, "That's them Ninya" (p. 23). Wirrun reflects:

> Somewhere deep down, perhaps in his feet, he knew that a
> loved and beautiful country should not be left alone to
> battle against age and drought, heat and ice. It shouldn't
> be left to float upside down when the wind came. Maybe it
> wasn't. For it was very likely that the old man had told
> him only part of the tale (p. 24).

Wirrun concludes that the ice is not his business, yet his thoughts continue to dwell upon it. When he returns to his rented room in the Happy Folks' town, he watches for newspaper accounts of the strange frost and confides in his friend, Ularra, his own experience of it. Significantly, Wirrun does not think of this rented room as home: "one of the things that Wirrun in his short life had never found was the place, the one spot in all the land, that was home" (p. 28). Both he and the Mimi are isolated before they meet and take up their quest, but the reasons for their isolation are different. Wirrun's isolation is psychological, stemming from his thoughtful respect for nature, as well as his own choice, whereas the Mimi is isolated physically, against her will, snatched up by the wind and deposited far from her home, "infinitely alone" (p. 26).

Chapter four, part one, portrays the Ninya, at a mountain in the north, being incited by their leader to seek the Eldest Nargun and imprison it in ice. This scene is balanced by a picture of the Nargun at the seaside, hundreds of miles away, awakening from its stupor, hungry and carnivorous:

> Nothing moved the ancient monster to love any more; only to yearning. So it hungered often, and seized what the sea brought near . . . There was shock and stillness in the water, and a mist of blood and white flesh (p. 41).

The details of the Nargun's devouring of the fish bring out its inhuman, unsympathetic character. Nonetheless, it is to the Eldest Nargun that Wirrun and the People must turn for help against the ice. This chapter brings into relief the contest between the elemental forces of ice and fire, mythologizing the conflict; also, the Nargun is identified as a deterministic force behind life, remote, aloof, a yearning maw--a pre-moral being. Though it expresses the life force, it has no fondness for life.

Part two portrays Wirrun's journey to the mountains where he deepens his awareness of nature. The mountains speak to him, and he carries on a dialogue with them. When he meets the darkness, personified in the shape of a man of the People, he undergoes a crucial test. The darkness challenges him to fight, but he wisely refuses and runs and then holds the darkness at bay by building a fire (pp. 49-50). Wirrun realizes the moral ambiguity of nature, and he reflects: "You couldn't choose to have the rocks and ferns and moss and the green shadows but reject the cliffs and the snake" (p. 50). It is his encounter with Ko-in, however, that defines Wirrun's mission and helps to make a clear demarcation between human and non-human nature. The mysterious Ko-in has his origin in human invention: he is called "hero," "larger than life; not man but of man, sharing his better self." "As the mountain had bred its shadowy creatures so man through long ages had bred Ko-in" (p. 75). In contrast to the earth-creatures, Ko-in is a moral being, and he helps Wirrun to achieve a moral awakening. When they first meet on the mountain, they speak of their ways of caring. Ko-in is a guardian of the land, and cares for it "when the ice grips it and when the fire scorches it" (p. 57). When he asks Wirrun how he cares, Wirrun replies in a passage rich with meaning:

> "There's a dung-beetle by that log. I care for that. And there's a rotten toadstool with a worm in it: I care for both of 'em. I care for that bit of fern, and the little white men by the sea, and the horse-thing in the night. I care for the ice and the fire" (p. 57).

Ko-in, as Wirrun's tutor in humanness, gives form to Wirrun's latent awareness of his humanity and also verbalizes Wirrun's need of others: "There must be the People" (p. 57). Then he directs him to a cave where he finds the power of the People--an unpromising-looking ball, "round, both soft and hard, and enclosed in coarse net . . . dark with age and damp, and with dust that the damp had darkened." Inside the netted outer bag is a ball "the size of a cricket ball: a closely wound ball of soft cord made from what he guessed was possum fur" (p. 59). Despite its unimposing appearance, this ball holds, in Ko-in's words, "a very great magic . . . that reaches across many countries and covers all the land. A magic that reaches to the sky. Wherever the ice may lead you this magic will have power!" (p.

128

61).

Ko-in not only bestows the power of the People upon Wirrun, he introduces him to the Mimi, whose aid is essential to his quest. Upon parting from Wirrun, Ko-in calls him, affectionately, "man," and promises to watch over him. Ko-in does not reappear in the book, though later Wirrun recalls their conversation on "caring." Ko-in's reappearance would be superfluous, since Wirrun has internalized the values Ko-in has helped him to shape, values that could be described as "existential" within the framework of an animistic, mythological world view.

After the Mimi and Wirrun are reunited, Wirrun's campfire incites the Wa-tha-gun-darl, small earth creatures who fear fire, to attack him, but he earns their good will and seizes the opportunity to question them about the Eldest Nargun and to warn them of the Ninya. It is the Nyols, whom Wirrun and the Mimi meet after taking leave of the Wa-tha-gun-darl, who tell him that the Eldest Nargun has "Gone into the sea" (p. 118). Wirrun feels their reluctance to help, and the Mimi explains their passivity: "They are small creatures of earth, in doubt and fear of the ice" (p. 119). The Wa-tha-gun-darl and the Nyols demonstrate the vulnerability of earth-creatures; they have no natural inclination towards heroism, nor do they care for human concerns, though later they show great courage in battling the Ninya. They represent nature's simple instinct for self-preservation.

Part four presents the bloody conflict between the Ninya and the Wa-tha-gun-darl. The carnage is starkly described in black/white imagery:

> Small black shapes darted from hiding, sticks swung and smashed. The white man toppled and the sticks beat at him. Broken ice flew in the moonlight. The man lay smashed; white blood came out of him and spread on the ground (p. 123).

The pristine whiteness of the Ninya strangely enhances their deadliness. Caught in the Ninya's ice, four of the Wa-tha-gun-darl fall victim to despair and die. The symbolic equation between ice, despair, and death seems evident. The Nyols come to the aid of the Wa-tha-gun-darl and turn back the Ninya, but the significance of the deaths of the four Wa-tha-gun-darl is underscored by the comment: "They had not before known any death among their kind" (p. 126). The initiation of the Wa-tha-gun-darl into the knowledge of death underscores the lethal power of the Ninya over nature.

Wirrun's pain on hearing the news of the deaths witnesses to his humanness. In contrast, the Mimi and the Nyol (the bearer of the bad tidings) see but do not share his grief. They

> watched him with their old spirit eyes. This, they knew, was the curious thing that men were made for: to care. Spirits might care sometimes when something could be done. If they were the right kind they might help when help was needed. They might be and know and remember and do; but men cared even when they could not do. Only the earth itself knew what good that was--some cord that the earth had twisted and used to bind its creatures together (p. 132).

The cord of caring binds humankind together, and seems to extend to the earth like an umbilicus.

The legendary Bunyip, which Wirrun encounters next, serves as a major contrast to Wirrun's humanity. Wirrun and Mimi rescue it from the ice in which the Ninya have trapped it, even though the Bunyip, like the Nargun, is no friend of humans. It is known to seize men and drag them into waterholes to kill and eat them (p. 136). In appearance the Bunyip is grotesque:

> It was a thing of many kinds that could not be truly seen,
> but its eyes were like death and its bellow was like fear. It
> was like a calf, like a seal, like a man, it was white, it was
> black. It was all these things, together and separate, in one
> fearful beast, and it had haunted the land since the land was
> young (p. 136).

The Bunyip shares the forbidding aura that surrounds the Eldest Nargun--its gaze is "spirit-old, knowing loneliness and fear" (p. 137), and Wirrun cannot look directly into its eyes. But the Mimi can, and she understands that the "Great One" is angry because the Ninya have treated it "as if it were some small thing." Freed by Wirrun and the Mimi from its icy prison, it later repays the favor by transporting Wirrun to the edge of the sea where the Eldest Nargun sleeps.

Wirrun's transport under water is, symbolically, one of the key episodes in the book. Structurally it occurs at a key point: the end of part five, where Wirrun is snatched from the company of the Mimi (p. 166). Clutching the net-enclosed ball, with its magic power for good, he passes through a dream-sequence, reminiscent of Jonah's sojourn in the belly of the whale and of countless other underwater scenes symbolic of rebirth:

> Only a few things could he ever remember about that time:
> his own helpless stillness like a chicken in its shell; the
> inescapable strength that folded itself round him and bore
> him; the flutter of the flowing water against his skin. And
> one other thing, a smell: of iodine and slime and decay,
> but mostly of age (p. 167).

The images suggest Wirrun's rebirth from the womb of time and his initiation into the secret of life's origins. Metaphorically, the imagery relates to a later passage describing the Eldest Nargun's knowledge:

> It knew the land in every grain of its rock: the molten
> pouring, the long twisting and shaping, the grinding by
> wind and water, the hammer-strokes of sun and frost. It
> knew life, that warm and secret decay that crept over the
> land. The land was in the Nargun and of it (p. 187).

In the process of his rebirth, Wirrun takes upon himself some of the wisdom of the Nargun.

Once in the vicinity of the Eldest Nargun, Wirrun finds his own resources too puny to approach it. He remembers Ko-in's words: *"There must be the People"* (p. 174). He seeks and finds the help of both humans and earth creatures. George Morrow, an inlander with special sensitivities to the "realities of the land" (p. 149), plays an important part in keeping the curious Happy Folk away from the battleground of the Ninya and the Eldest Nargun. Through Morrow, the people respond to Wirrun's call for help. The Yabon, a shape shifter who has followed Wirrun and Mimi in the guise of a dog, becomes Wirrun's "double" to deliver a message to the men of Mt. Conner, who are needed to sing the Ninya home (p. 178). It is, however, Old Johnny Wuthergull of the People who plays the key role. Old Johnny has the power of the folk-knowledge; he knows how to talk to the Eldest Nargun (p. 183), having derived this skill from his father.

At a crucial point in the battle to save the Eldest Nargun from the ice of the Ninya, Old Johnny arrives. He is

> old indeed, his face a powdery brown and deeply
> wrinkled, his hair and beard white. He had the gentle
> smile and seeing eyes that were common among old men
> of the People . . . He said nothing until he heard for
> himself what Wirrun had to ask (p. 209).

When Wirrun asks the old man to talk to the Eldest Nargun, he first requests to see the power, which he touches. Then, he seems "to go into a dream" (p. 210) and gives it back.

When Old Johnny brings the Eldest Nargun back to Wirrun, it is a mere pebble to the inexpressible disillusionment of Wirrun and the People:

> "I talked to it and I fetched it out," he said proudly. He
> held out a brown-crepe hand and opened it. On his palm
> lay a stone, a large pebble, the size of a teacup (p. 211).

Seeing the distress of the others, Old Johnny explains that the Nargun has "used itself up fighting the sea" (p. 211).

For Wirrun and the People, it is a moment of sharp pathos. They feel "foolish and betrayed," and no longer believe in the battle. Wirrun is "empty: empty with shock, and weary days and nights, and wasted work" (p. 212). It is the Mimi, who can see the Eldest Nargun in its true reality, who saves the situation. Wirrun is awestruck to see her expression as she beholds the stone; her amazement tells him that she sees something he has failed to perceive. He touches the power, and his vision clears. His faith reawakened, he takes the Eldest Nargun into his own hand, "the Great One with the power of fire" (p. 215), and carries it into battle against the Ninya.

The combined forces of the Eldest Nargun, the People, the Mimi (representing the earth and rock spirits), and the boy Wirrun triumph over the ice. Symbolically, the powers for good within nature and humanity must ally themselves in order that all may survival. The most beautiful of all earth spirits, the Yauruks (birds), have a special role: they atone for their previous betrayal of the Eldest Nargun's whereabouts by summoning the whales from the sea to shatter the ice at a decisive moment (p. 216). The Bunyip and the Nargun of the cave wreak vengeance upon the Ninya. Warmth and peace are restored to the Australian land. It remains for the Mimi to share with Wirrun a final insight before she departs for her home in the north. When Wirrun disparages "the mighty Eldest Nargun" for its small size, she admonishes him:

> "What does a man know of size? Greater than you is
> great, smaller than you is small; you know no more . . . is
> not the rock-pool a world among the stars? Life and death

are in it, and light and darkness; there are journeys and homecomings there. Is a starfish smaller than a star?" (pp. 222-223).

Wirrun is reminded of his earlier insight, temporarily forgotten:

"There's a dung-beetle by that log. I care for that. There's a rotten toadstool with a worm in it: I care for both of 'em: and Ko-in had answered: 'You are of the People'" (p. 223).

Size is no measure of significance; nothing is too small to matter. The existential world view is evident here in the belief that it is the individual's own loving, caring perspective that endows a thing with worth. The Mimi sees the fallacy of judging worth by size, but she does not demonstrate a caring concern. Caring and loving are uniquely human, but the individual needs constantly refreshed awareness to sustain these human qualities. Eyes can be opened and vision refreshed by close communion with the land and its spirits, both beautiful and terrible. Non-human nature can make us aware by contrast of our human difference, and of the mutual need of humanity and nature for one another.

Recent attention has been given to the racist treatment of Australian aborigines in children's books.[4] Yet, clearly Wrightson's story transcends the social and political issues of Australian race relationships to focus upon what is universally human in the experience of one particular boy of the People. To see in the Ninya, by reason of their whiteness, a symbolization of the destructive forces of white society in its oppression of the Blacks would seem a mistake. Nevertheless, the criticism of a particular kind of white people--the Happy Folk--is unmistakable. Wrightson's main concern is, however, with values that transcend race and class; she sees the dangers of humanity's exploitative stance towards nature, and she speaks to the condition of all human beings in their struggle to achieve and retain full humanness. She gives us the picture of humanity amidst a nature devoid of compassion, infused by a blind force which sustains life, "that warm and secret decay." In this black world, human beings invent love and heroism and value out of their own innards, out of their own suffering and imagination--an existential view of the human condition. Nature encompasses both the amoral life force (the power of fire, *eros*) and the opposed force of death (the power of ice, *thanatos*). The life force needs human help--especially human songs and the human sense of community--to win despite difficult odds over its age-old enemy, the ice.

[1]Patricia Wrightson. *The Ice Is Coming*. New York: Atheneum, 1977, p. 11. All subsequent references to the text will be given in parentheses following the quotation.

[2]Cf. Susan Sontag. *On Photography*. Farrar, Straus, Giroux, 1977, pp. 8-9: Photography, as a mass art form, is "mainly a social rite, a defense against anxiety, and a tool of power." Just as photographs "give people an imaginary possession of a past that is unreal, they also help people to take possession of a space in which they are insecure." Even more significantly, they are a way of "refusing" experience, "by limiting experience to a search for the photogenic, by converting experience into an image, a souvenir." Later she sums up the impact of the photographic image upon the interpretation of the world: "The camera makes reality atomic, manageable, and opaque. It is a view of the world which denies interconnectedness and continuity . . . " (p. 23).

[3]Patricia Wrightson. *The Nargun And The Stars*. New York: Atheneum, 1974.

[4]See *Interracial Books for Children Bulletin*, 9, 2 (1978), entire issue. The term "Australian Blacks" is preferred today over "Australian Aborigines" (p. 8, same issue).

13

EQUAL TO LIFE: TOVE JANSSON'S MOOMINTROLLS

Nancy Lyman Huse

Huse's essay on Tove Jansson's Moomin books places them beyond the religious/humanist categories. She shows that Jansson offers allegiance to neither the change and growth of the humanist perspective, nor to the higher world or the afterlife of religious belief. Her central figure, Moominmamma, stands very near to Orthodox Christian grace, yet the intentions for or uses of this quality are wholly within the context of the secular life. This sizeable central character seems a mix of Charlotte's total goodness and Mr. Grumpy's capricious acceptance as shown in his party for the undeserving animal friends. Huse shows how Jansson balances this powerful acceptance with aspects drawn from her father who represented a venturesome and demanding style. The two allow her to create at once a mystical mythology and a work celebrating human autonomy.

EQUAL TO LIFE: TOVE JANSSON'S MOOMINTROLLS

In describing Tove Jansson's Moomintroll fantasies, Eleanor Cameron states that these 1966 Andersen Award books present one of the most unusual worlds in the realm of fantasy. Jansson's characters "are all beings created wholly out of her own imagination."[1] The rounded, funny moomintrolls were originally cartoon characters developed by Jansson. They seem different from the animated toy characters of other comic, episodic fantasies, from the mythic creatures and talking beasts of spiritual or visionary fantasy, and even from such "domestic" beings as *The Borrowers* (sometimes used as a comparison for Jansson's work). Their land, Moominland, is not the kind of symbolic, coherent kingdom found in mythic fantasy, where the triumph of good over evil calls upon supra-human powers; nor does it challenge its creatures to the full use of human potential or lead them to ultimate maturation. Contrary to what we have come to expect in serious, interpretive literature, Jansson does not posit her world at conflict with the powers of the Dark, to use Susan Cooper's term, or engage in a maturation process to reach a balance between self and others, as in the stories of Wilbur the pig and Arrietty the Borrower. Nor does she set out to mock human vanity or simply spin child-toy adventures, as many fantasies which are neither spiritual quests nor humanistic searches do. Jansson's work does not fit into an easily defined position at either end of or even, perhaps, along the continuum between the ordered, mythic worlds of spiritual quest-fantasy and the progressive, rational worlds of humanistic tales.

She bases her characters in family relationships, perceived in much the same way modern psychology perceives them, but places them in a mythic world rich in strange and wonderful beings at whose center is the Moomin family. Moominland's coherence seems to rest in the theme of personal development and friendship, especially, but not exclusively, as experienced by the young Moomintroll, in the cycle of the seasons passed in a secure but stimulating menage. This fictive creation differs from tales of supra-human powers, even though Moominland is as magical as any fantasy world one can visit. Moominland is not a world which reflects a higher one, nor is it a country which demonstrates the foibles of our own. Instead, in her universally significant fantasy world Jansson celebrates the reality a child encounters with its alternating terror and joy. Her unique, comforting yet strikingly modern world view emerges somewhat randomly in the early Moomin books and with a powerful consistency in the later ones. Jansson's success in depicting a world view which is neither traditionally humanistic nor religious rests in her presentation of character, particularly the Moomin parents, and their relationships to each other and the natural world they inhabit. Two autobiographies clarify the significance of Jansson's own experience in shaping that world view and introduce questions about the relationship of her illustration and her writing.

When I began using the Moomintroll books in my children's literature classes a few years ago, this "originality" intrigued me. Jansson resisted description under the critical framework I was trying to establish with my students. Her galaxy of comic characters first caused me to focus on "originality" rather than on "convention" in describing Jansson. Moominland is inhabited by creatures of varied ages and attitudes: Snufkin, the freedom-loving wanderer; Sniff, the babyish, kangarooish companion of Moomintroll; Moomintroll himself, who looks like a comic rhinoceros with a nice long tail but feels and thinks like a young person of sensitivity and imagination; Moominmamma and Moominpappa, his indispensable parents and fellow adventurers; the Fillyjonk, a reed-like spinster who usually likes to clean her house; and, generated over more than three decades, a host of woodies, creeps, hemuelens and other newly-coined but soon familiar folk.

I was also impressed by the perceptive statement about the value and wonder of life which was evident even in the early, episodic, almost haphazard tales, *Comet in Moominland* and *Finn Family Moomintroll*.[2] World view really becomes the significant dimension in discussing Jansson's originality, for in later works such as *Tales from Moominvalley, Moominland Midwinter, Moominpappa at Sea* and *Moominvalley in November* she seems to be consciously developing an overarching thematic structure. The stories depend on continual movement between the core of physical security best represented by Moominmamma's commodious handbag, and the metaphysical risk involved in experiencing and even becoming one with cosmic phenomena like the sea, the seasons, and the sky. "Self-definition in a benevolent universe" is a possible epigrammatic description of Jansson's theme, but this fails to include the loving tension between individual and community essential to her version of self-definition, as well as the cataclysmic proportions of the floods, the storms, the alternately barren or lush topography, and the dark pools and hidden glades which the creatures love and fear.

Central to Jansson's vivified world view are the Moomin parents, particularly Moominmamma. Moominmamma is the core of security in Moominland. She is the pivotal character whose meaning and presence makes Jansson's work both distinctly personal and universal, and who enables this artist to construct narratives which neither hold up external standards of perfection nor suggest that human (troll) nature is in need of improvement. With her strong, loving mother figure, Jansson seems to defy our usual expectations that serious literature is in some way heroic, in some way about our need to improve. In Moominland, it is true, creatures do change -- especially in the later books. But the difference between Jansson and many other writers is that in her books there is no imperative for this change, either with the other characters in a tale or with the reader. The creature has a place and will be loved regardless of inner or outer change or the lack of it. Moominmamma does not view others as flawed. As nearly as I have seen it done, Jansson captures in art the notion of "mother" as it exists for the very young child. Recalling her childhood impression of growing up in a "tremendously rich and generous and problem-free home,"[3] the writer comments that she was unaware of the economic difficulties of her artist parents, as well as of other problems they faced. "Anything was possible, everything was exciting . . . My mother, especially, had an unusual capacity for mixing stern morality with an almost exhilarating tolerance, a quality I have never met with in anyone else."[4] In Jansson's fantasy world, Moominmamma does provide essential values and norms, but she will not exclude those who do not meet them. She is friend or mamma to the fussy fillyjonk, the obnoxious mymble (a round, contented, free type) and the introverted hermit-fisherman of *Moominpappa at Sea*. Existence gives one an intrinsic right to Moominmamma's love.

One of Jansson's best stories, "The Invisible Child," collected in *Tales From Moominvalley* and, fortunately, anthologized in Arbuthnot, is a clear example of the troll mamma's central role in the books.[5] Ninny, introduced to the Moomintroll household by their fuzzy-haired friend Too-ticky, is the "invisible child" who has faded away from sight because she had been "frightened the wrong way by a lady

137

who had taken care of her without really liking her,"[6] the icily ironical kind" who ridiculed instead of scolded. At first, the Moomins can see only the silver bell and ribbon the child wears around her neck. Mamma declines the suggestion to take Ninny to a doctor, and tucks her in just as she tucks in Moomintroll, leaving "the apple, the glass of juice and the three striped pieces of candy everyone in the house was given at bedtime" (p. 113). Luckily, a recipe left by Granny has a few lines for a medicine "if people start getting misty and difficult to see." Even before she starts to take the medicine, however, Ninny's paws -- "very small, with anxiously bunched toes" -- appear (p. 114). Though Ninny's paws fade each time she is frightened by bumbling family members, Moominmamma's strong affirmation of *the way she is* causes more and more of her to appear. Wearing a new pink dress and hair ribbon made from Mamma's shawl, Ninny soon lacks only a face and a sense of humor. The medicine doesn't seem to have any more power, so Moominmamma decides that "many people had managed all right before without a head, and besides, perhaps Ninny wasn't very good-looking" (p. 122).

When Ninny, terrified of the sea, notices Pappa threatening (teasingly) to push Mamma off the dock, the invisible child hisses, screams, bites Pappa's tail, and appears at last in full face -- snub-nosed, red-headed. Startled Moominpappa falls into the water himself, and Ninny shouts with laughter--now the most uninhibited child in the family. Security has given Ninny the power to act on her emotions.

Numerous examples of Moominmamma's unconditional, intuitive love and its role as the basis for action and the central value of the books appear even in the early stories. In *Comet in Moominland,* when Moomintroll rushes off into danger to rescue a pet, his mother waits quietly and alone outside of the cave which shelters the other creatures,until her son returns. In *Finn Family Moomintroll,* she alone knows her child when he has been physically transformed by the goblin's hat. She is seen at the beginning of *Moominsummer Madness* carving a bark boat for Moomintroll--the first of the season, which always goes to him. Although interrupted by an enormous flood and a summer of foreign adventure (including a hilarious interlude in the theater), she remembers, without being asked, to complete her gift by carving a dinghy for the tiny boat. She thus seals the experience of the summer within the safe and pleasant rituals of home and the now tranquil sea. When she wakes from hibernation in *Moominland Midwinter* (moomintrolls hibernate with their stomachs full of pine needles) she joins with her child in enjoying the early spring even though his winter hospitality has emptied the pantry of jam and pressed the silver tray into service as a sled. "Mother, I love you terribly," Moomintroll tells her,[7] this is his realization after a winter awake, during which he has learned, "One has to discover everything for oneself. And get over it all alone" (p. 143). In the last Moomin books, Jansson depicts Moominmamma, too, as someone who needs time to herself; yet she remains an expert at getting the family off on picnics when danger threatens.

As a literary creation, Moominmamma has as yet few peers, for as Too-Ticky remarks, very few stories are written about those who welcome heroes home. Beyond her loving tolerance and acceptance, Moominmamma exemplifies the ability to let people alone. She thus provides both absolute freedom and absolute security, essential to wholeness but not a way of shaping a *bildungsroman.*

Jansson's autobiography, *Sculptor's Daughter,* offers us much direct evidence of the experiences which forged such a unique world view. The incidents she chooses to relate from her childhood clearly demonstrate how dependent the Moomintroll books are on her own experience and on her memories of her parents.

For example, she narrates a mood-piece in which, "doing just what she wanted to do," she burns old rolls of film left from her mother's work as an illustrator, simply to enjoy the sight and smell of the burning. In *Moominland Midwinter*, this odd activity is the choice of Moominmamma in her encounter with early spring. Other physical descriptions based on her childhood memories, such as the experience of *enjoyable* ocean storms and tidal disturbances which reveal lunar landscapes, and fascination with candles deemed "interesting" because they might burn nearby walls -- all examples of the secure child venturing out into the unfamiliar with confidence and exhilaration -- are incorporated into the fantasies as very natural aspects of Moomin life.

Two episodes in *Sculptor's Daughter* give charming testimony to the origins of Moominmamma. The child-narrator describes the bohemian parties given by her colorful father, all dependent for success on being "improvised" at the last minute. "Mummy has everything ready" -- a well-stocked pantry so one can "improvise something."[8] The ideal life must include openness, freedom, spontaneity; yet the enjoyment of these things depends on the core of safety, the design and framework within which one acts. The notion of "making a whole" of things, of being equal to the task of arranging the reality one encounters as flux, and of seeking out danger in order to make yet more beautiful designs, is intrinsic to the Moomin tales. This same secure bravado and potential artistry is apparent in an early memory Jansson has of building a golden calf (taken, alas, to be a lamb by her grandmother) for the purpose of "clamoring for God's attention." Such spirit as that of the five-year-old would-be-idolator-sculptor, and of the Moomins themselves, is explained by the islands of complete security and safety in Jansson's memoir. The most notable for its relationship to her mother, and to Moominmamma, occurs when Tove and her mother are snowed in alone for several days. Her mother tells her they have gone into hibernation: "Nobody can get in any longer and no one can get out!" (p. 165). The child's delight in their underground life is complete; she laughs, shouts I LOVE YOU and throws cushions, rejoicing alone with her wonderful mother in front of the fire. The image of utter safety, repeated in various ways in the autobiography, is extended beyond the hibernation the Moomins engage in, to the light on the verandah of the blue house, a power so great that it draws all creatures to it.

The narration of *Sculptor's Daughter*, by a child whose age may be five or six, spells out the premises of life as Jansson deals with it in Moominvalley. Maturing, moving from childhood to adulthood, is not the issue. Security and the courage to live are focal. Self-affirmation, rooted in a secure love relationship and eagerness for experience, is not a goal but a reality in the stories; in some sense, the tales are metaphoric shouts of joy and love. In demonstrating the child's exhilaration, Jansson seems to be one of those writers who, according to Arthur N. Applebee, shows the implications of a familiar paradigm rather than challenges beliefs.[9] Jansson's work constitutes a series of images of a familiar paradigm rather than a conflict-centered drama. Travel and discovery are frequent in the tales, but occur as a result of the undemanding love at the center of each book; adventure is a response intrinsic to reality as much as mother's love is inherent in reality. Going forth into the unknown is a natural function, like breathing and eating. To a large extent, travel and adventure constitute the "Pappa" side of life, but they are narrated in reference to the "Mamma" source of security.

The light on the verandah has its deepest meaning when it burns for a returning voyager. The core of safety must center in a whirlpool, a raging storm, a comet's path, or its value as a refuge and haven is lost. From time to time, Moominpappa (and Moomintroll) must venture out, away from the verandah, to explore the world. For Moominpappa, this is a way of fueling his art, the writing of memoirs and the keeping of diaries. While the journey-quest device seems a more conventional element than the intuitive, accepting home-image, the *Adventure* (Moominpappa's boat) also has its origins directly in the writer's childhood. Her father, the sculptor Viktor Jansson, "gave the necessary background of excitement."[10] The autobiography reflects the wildness of his parties and music, the antics of his numerous pets, the nerve-wracking but hallowed time of casting a mold in the studio, and his Viking love for the challenge of a storm at sea. It was his choice to spend each summer with the family on an island in a fisherman's cottage, creating the sources and settings for some of Jansson's adult books as well as the Moomin tales.

While the *Sculptor's Daughter* offers a rather clear explanation of Jansson's central thematic impulse, it is *The Summer Book* which explains the intimate relationship Jansson enjoys with nature which is essential to the Moomin books. *The Summer Book* is the story of a young child and an old woman passing their summers on an island in the Gulf of Finland.[11] This work, drawn from Jansson's adult experience as well as from her childhood, recreates the strength and beauty of lives so much a part of the sea that the child is certain she has conjured up an especially fierce storm by her prayers on a too-quiet day. She needs to know the limitations of her own powers in relation to the wild, churning sea, yet her confidence in these powers must be preserved. Thus, her grandmother takes credit and blame for the terrible storm. Belief in the mind's power to interact with natural forces occurs repeatedly in the Moomin books, but without recourse to supernatural powers. It is Moominpappa's boisterous confidence which supplies the energy for the episodic adventures from which the family sometimes needs the rescue of a Moominmamma picnic.

Encounters with the natural world within and without the Happy Valley, where the round blue Moominhouse and its verandah shelter the extended family of creatures who happen along, fit neither a good-versus-evil pattern nor a nature-versus-culture one. The sea, the most pervasive and decisive force and image in the books, is the object of Moominpappa's scientific scrutiny until his child tells him that the sea "seems to do just what it likes . . . There's just no rhyme or reason in it."[12] The sea is a living thing, "a weak character you can't rely on," unpredictable as a person and just as worthy of love, respect, and tolerance. Pappa declares, "It's an enemy worth fighting, anyway," as the little trolls shout over the breakers, equal to the task of braving the ocean and making friends with it. Like other of their friends such as the ski-enthusiast hemuelen (another funny rhino-type with an elongated snout suggesting the inherent qualities of the bureaucrat who loves to arrange other people's lives), the sea is a fearsome but wonderful mix to be accepted as it is. The trolls and their companions are part of the mysterious tides, storms, and sunshine; the essence of life is experience, the unfolding experience of a child who knows the incredible terror of separation, yet knows even more fully the comfort and safety of a parent's presence.

In *The Summer Book,* a seafaring neighbor elicits the comment: "A person can find anything if he takes the time, that is, if he can afford to look. And while he's looking, he's free, and he finds things he never expected" (p. 67). Almost a summary of Jansson's work in the Moomin books, the comment especially describes her father's zest for life and Moominpappa's intrepid curiosity. With its

140

assumption that "looking" is essential to a fully realized life, the statement calls attention to the essentially visual nature of the Moomin books. As the daughter of two artists and a painter herself, Jansson has created a fantasy world in which sensory observation and stretching the limits of experience are vital, and occur as a natural part of living. Not only the themes of her books, but her illustrations of them, exhibit the cozy security in the midst of chaotic adventure Jansson offers as a child's eye view of the world.

The illustrations are full of the sweet absurdities and intense enjoyment characteristic of the Moomins. A well-educated artist, Jansson has extended her intuitive, spatial powers into her verbal constructs. This is a significant factor in her use of emotion as the real "inner logic" of her fantasies -- emotion not subject to critical evaluation, but simply presented as "being" rather than "becoming." Hers is not a linear artistry; while the early books use more loosely bound episodes and the later ones more emphasis on "states of mind" (really "states of feeling"), the pictures remain constant and show that each Moomin book is about the loving embrace of unfolding reality. Jansson says that her works are centered in love -- "I love my characters and I love my readers" -- and that she writes for the "ones easily frightened."[13]

Clearly, Jansson's own artistic sensitivity, rooted in her childhood with her loving, daring parents, has made her aware of the terrors of separation, of not belonging, of being in actual physical danger. Her childhood in Finland was upset by World War I, a fact which has caused Scandinavian critics to assert that her works are about security in catastrophe.[14] She has even been compared with Harry Martinson (Swedish winner of the Nobel prize for literature in 1974) because of her tenderness and cosmic anxiety.[15] Just as the "Mamma" core of the Moomin books sets them apart from such domestic adventure tales as those of Laura Ingalls Wilder (where the father figure is far more important to the narrative than the mother), the "Pappa" quest for danger enlarges the scope of the works and validates the security theme. The presence of fear, Jansson believes, is as strong a principle in childhood as the presence of love.[16] Thus, her books have fear as their "negative" side. The crushing waves, the burning comet, the desolate island, the enormous flood, are met in love.

Significant examples of this duality occur throughout the books; the clearest may be the "Groke," a creature who seems to represent the Nordic cold. Her name is the Swedish word for "growl," and she is the closest to a "pure evil" the Moomin books have. Wherever the Groke sits, she turns the ground to a frozen grave. Yet, Moominmamma says the Groke is lonely; it is her doom never to be liked by anyone. Moomintroll, disliking her as everyone does, nonetheless leaves a lamp burning for her at night when the family is living on an island in *Moominpappa at Sea*. He realizes that the lamp is her one comfort, even though if she comes too close to the light she will put it out forever. Characteristically, Jansson does not explain why Moomintroll is not afraid of the Groke, beyond establishing the general principle that nothing in the world need be shunned. While such plot incidents suggest a joyful response even to the most awesome natural phenomena, the illustrations do so even more effectively. The books are replete with them; the creatures tumble up and down the pages. Strategically placed full-page drawings throughout the series are deliberately used to allay the terror the printed word may cause the child reader.[17] Jansson's definition of herself as an artist by profession, her essentially nonlinear story-telling, and her dependence on illustration to mitigate the fear aroused by verbal constructs all demonstrate the existential nature of her work.

The difficulty of discussing a graphic artist in a print medium may be one reason why literary critics outside of Scandinavia have not found Jansson a rich subject for analysis; readers unfamiliar with her work need to look at it as much as they need to listen to it in the act of reading the stories or reviews of them. Discussion of a few full-page illustrations which mitigate fear through reassuring design will, I hope, make more vivid the abandon I am suggesting as the mood of the Moomin books. Unfortunately, readers of the English and American editions miss the use of color to create an "undersea" effect in the original illustrations.

In *Comet in Moominland,* one of the earliest, most catastrophic and least domestic of the books, the illustrations are especially effective in their mitigating role. At the end of the book, the creatures huddle in a cave waiting for the descent of a huge, flaming comet, pictured as a frightening spectacle (p. 187). Yet the illustrated page before this, and the one after it, show respectively the waiting animals round-eyed with fear while nonetheless safely huddled together; and Moominmamma, handbag and all, giving a solid hug to the most frightened creatures. *Finn Family Moomintroll,* also filled with the terrors of the unpredictable, has a marvelous plate showing the way the Moomin drawing room looks when it is accidentally (via the hobgoblin's hat, a device like the magic pebble which trips up Sylvester in William Steig's classic) turned into a florid jungle. Creatures swing on jungle creepers from the hurricane lamp to the drapery rods; they look afraid, but the picture is funny. In *Tales From Moominvalley,* perhaps the best of Jansson's work and as fine as any children's book I have read, a fillyjonk knows that something terrible is going to happen before a wild ocean storm shatters the knick-knacks, furniture and window-glass she spends her time fussing with. The picture (p. 57) shows her standing in the midst of her possessions as they are crashing about. Significantly, she is unharmed by the storm, and in fact freed by it to sit on the beach and know real safety there. While the picture itself could be terrifying were it not for the funny-looking fillyjonk, the illustrated storm becomes concrete and better known, more fully experienced by the reader, and thus less frightening.

In the last of the books to date, *Moominvalley in November,* an excellent tale in which an assortment of creatures travel to Moomin Valley to visit the trolls, only to find that they have gone off in the *Adventure,* the pictures convey the sense of separateness the creatures bring with them and retain despite their becoming used to one another, family-like, during their stay. One plate (p. 154), used as the cover design for the paperback edition, shows them -- each representative of various stages from infancy (Toft) to old age (Grandpa Grumble), and various modes of life (settled spinster, itinerant musician, bureaucrat) -- assembled on the verandah. Each is markedly different from the others in appearance; all are shown in the relaxed complacency of daily family life. This picture follows a more frenzied domestic scene in which the fillyjonk leads an assault known as spring cleaning before she leaves, recovered from the scare which brought her to visit Moominmamma in the first place. The fears each of the six had responded to in making their journey to the valley have been dealt with through the simple actions of keeping the household going. Only Toft, the baby-creature, waits on the dock as Moominmamma and her family return; the others, grown-ups, have gone home -- unchanged from their essential selves. Knowing they have been loved and loving, they are equal to life.

The self-affirmation and individualism which constitute Jansson's world view, with her exuberance for life and thus for human nature, cannot be dismissed as a light-hearted, truth-dodging representation of existence. Viewed as a whole, and with contemplation of the illustrations in relation to the text, the Moomin books give a needed sense of the beauty of life to the modern child. Neither the all-encompassing framework of spiritual fantasy (a type often categorized as the "highest," most valuable kind)[18] nor the witty self-criticism of the rational humanist offers the kind of celebration of new life which must ground a human being in a world which eludes totalized mythic explanations and can often seem too disappointing under the satirist's pen. Jansson's consistent joy does not omit terror, but -- and in this respect she does what other serious writers do -- enables the reader/viewer to include the terrifying among the familiar, through the process of discovery and experimentation typical of childhood.

The child-protagonist, Moomintroll, need not change. Like the sea, his life is one of flux, of unpredictability, variation and surprise. In the early books, he is more apt to be on an external odyssey, in the later (beginning with his acquaintance with winter in *Moominland Midwinter)* on an inner journey. Nonetheless, each book shows him loving and being loved, and acting in response to the natural world. As an individual, Moomintroll is exceptionally sensitive and dreamy--a presumed self-portrait of Jansson herself. Just as her funny, fussy fillyjonks and stubborn, dull hemuelens are adults who are loved as they are, and who are free to change or not to change as they determine for themselves, so Jansson's cast of child-characters demonstrates the principle of being-loved-as-one-is. Even more than Moomintroll, the other child characters tend to be artfully unchanging.

Little My, a tiny mymble or self-absorbed, uninhibited, life-celebrating creature, is the adopted sister of Moomintroll who says what only a "brat" can say. She is the one who goes sledding in Moominmamma's tea-cosy, tells more fibs even than a Whomper (who tells so many he has to go to bed at sundown in *Tales from Moominvalley*), and who asks Ninny if she wants a biff on the nose when the poor thing is still the terrified invisible child. Little My is indestructible, and glories in her own being; no one tells her, or expects her, to grow up. Toft, another baby-creature, is one of the "easily frightened," who are in danger from too much fearing, too much separation from the core of safety. He knows he belongs in Moomin Valley, knows he will be a welcome sight as the Moomins return at the end of the last tale. Though they needed to be away and alone, there is no doubt about his place with them. In fact, he has chosen to grow a little bit, to alter his idyllic conception of the Moomins to include the notion that, like him, they are all at times sad or angry; however, had he remained as unaware of others as he had been at the start of the book, his embrace from Moominmamma would have been as warm.

Speaking of her own creatures in the tone of tolerance and affirmation her mother character projects, Jansson says, "What would happen to this world of ours if a *misabel* [gloomy creature who finds a home in the theater exactly suited to her tragic sense] suddenly acted like a *mymble* ?"[19]

Although Tove Jansson has received little more than generalized praise or quick dismissal from critics outside of Scandinavia who include her because she is an Andersen medalist but rarely discuss her in detail, she is the object of a good deal of scholarship in Sweden. Moreover, she is enormously popular there, even with the dominant sociological critics, who seem to forgive her uncritical tales because she offers something "necessary" to childhood.[20] Various comparisons to fantasists such as John Bunyan and Lewis Carroll have been suggested; a French critic, Isabelle Jan, states that Jansson resembles realistic writers such as Laura

Ingalls Wilder and Louisa May Alcott more than she does fantasists.[21] Jan's comment is especially interesting, for she dramatizes the fact that our usual notion of "fantasy" assumes a significant encounter with the supernatural, or with some failing inherent in human nature or reality itself. Jansson's celebration of storms, modeled on her father but enabled by her mother, shows that certain artists evade our categories at the same time that they enlarge and clarify them. An original mythology; a dazzling image of autonomy: Jansson offers both.

NOTES

[1]Eleanor Cameron. *The Green and the Burning Tree.* New York: Little, Brown, 1969, p. 12.

[2]Moomin books have appeared in twenty-two languages, beginning in 1946. Jansson's English publisher is Ernest Benn. In the United States, most of her books have been brought out by Henry Z. Walck, Inc. In the 1970's, her books have been available in Avon paperbacks. I have used these except where indicated below. Titles and dates of U.S. publications are as follows: *Comet in Momminland,* 1959; *Finn Family Moomintroll,* 1951; *Exploits of Moominpappa,* 1966; *Moominsummer Madness,* 1961; *Tales From Moominvalley,* 1963; *Moominland Midwinter,* 1962; *Moominpappa at Sea,* 1968; and *Moominvalley in November,* 1972. At least two other titles, and comic books about the Moomins, have appeared in England but not in America.

[3]Jansson, quoted in Eva von Zweigbergk, *Barnboken i Sverige 1750-1950.* Stockholm: Raben and Sjogren, 1965, p. 468.

[4]*Ibid.*

[5]Tove Jansson. *Tales from Moominvalley,* Trans. Thomas Warburton. New York: Henry Z. Walck, Inc., 1963.

[6]*Tales,* p. 109. Subsequent references in the text are to this edition.

[7]Tove Jansson. *Moominland Midwinter,* Trans. Thomas Warburton. New York: Henry Z. Walck, 1962, p. 159. Subsequent references are to this edition.

[8]Tove Jansson. *Sculptor's Daughter,* Trans. Kingsley Hart. New York: Avon Books, 1976, p. 40. Subsequent references are to this edition.

[9]Arthur N. Applebee. *The Child's Concept of Story* . Chicago: University of Chicago Press, 1978, p. 24.

[10]Jansson, quoted in Anne Commire, ed., *Something about the Author,* v. 3. New York: Gale, 1972, p. 90.

[11]Tove Jansson. *The Summer Book,* Trans. Thomas Teal. New York: Random House, 1974. Subsequent references are to this edition.

[12]Tove Jansson. *Moominpappa at Sea,* Trans. Kingsley Hart. New York: Avon, 1977, p. 158.

[13]Tove Jansson. quoted in Stromstedt, p. 97.

[14]von Zweigbergk, p. 469.

[15]Birgitta Goteman, in *Tove Jansson pa Svenska,* ed. Birgit Antonsson.

Stockholm: Uppsala, 1976, p. 72.

[16]Jansson, in Stromstedt, p. 101.

[17]*Ibid.*

[18]Ruth Nodelman Lynn. *Fantasy for Children* . New York: Browker, 1979.

[19]Jansson, quoted in von Zweigbergk, p. 470.

[20]Lars Backstrom, in Antonsson, p. 71.

[21]Isabelle Jan. *On Children's Literature*. London: Allen Lane, 1973, p. 120.

BIBLIOGRAPHY

*Chapters in which the books are discussed are indicated at the end of each citation.

Alcott, Louisa May. *Jo's Boys, and How They Turned Out.* Boston: Roberts Brothers, 1886. Chapter 7.

Alcott, Louisa May. *Little Men.* Boston: Roberts Brothers, 1871. Chapter 7.

Alcott, Louisa May. *Little Women.* Boston: Roberts Brothers, 1869. Chapter 7.

Bates, Daisy, Collector. *Tales Told to Kabbarli* as retold by Barbara Ker Wilson. New York: Crown, 1972. Chapter 9.

Baum, Lyman Frank. *The Wizard of Oz.* New York: Macmillan, 1962. Chapter 4.

Baumann, Hans. *In the Land of Ur: The Discovery of Ancient Mesopotamia.* Trans. from the German by Stella Humphries. New York: Pantheon, 1969. Chapter 3.

Bodker, Cecil. *The Leopard.* Trans. from the Danish by Gunnar Poulsen. New York: Atheneum, 1975. Chapter 3.

Brinsmead, H.F. *Pastures of the Blue Crane.* New York: Coward-McCann, 1966. Chapter 9.

Carroll, Lewis. *Through the Looking Glass.* In *The Complete Works of Lewis Carroll,* ed. Alexander Woollcott. London: The Nonesuch Library, 1939. Chapters 4 and 8.

Carroll, Lewis. *Sylvie and Bruno.* London: Macmillan, 1890. Chapter 8.

Carroll, Lewis. *Sylvie and Bruno Concluded.* London: Macmillan, 1894. Chapter 8.

Chase, Richard. *The Jack Tales.* Told by R.M. Ward *et al.* Boston: Houghton Mifflin, 1943. Chapter 11.

Chauncy, Nan. *Half A World Away.* New York: Franklin Watts, 1962. Chapter 9.

Chauncy, Nan. *Hunted in Their Own Land.* New York: Seabury, 1967. Chapter 9.

Chauncy, Nan. *Tangara.* London: Oxford University Press, 1972. Chapter 9.

Clark, Mavis Thorpe. *The Min-Min.* New York: Macmillan, 1969. Chapter 9.

Cooper, Susan. *The Dark Is Rising.* New York: Atheneum, 1973. Chapter 11.

Cormier, Robert. *After the First Death.* New York: Pantheon, 1979. Chapter 2.

Cormier, Robert. *The Chocolate War.* New York: Dell, 1974. Chapter 2.

Cormier, Robert. *I Am the Cheese.* New York: Dell, 1977. Chapter 2.

Earnshaw, Brian. *Dragonfall Five and the Royal Beast.* New York: Lothrop, Lee, and Shepard, 1975. Chapter 11.

Friis-Baastad, Babbis. *Don't Take Teddy.* Trans. from the Norwegian by Lise Somme McKinnon. New York: Scribner, 1967. Chapter 3.

George, Jean. *Julie of the Wolves.* New York: Harper & Row, 1972. Chapters 10 and 11.

Grahame, Kenneth. *The Wind in the Willows.* New York: Charles Scribner's Sons, 1961. Chapter 11.

Hinton, S.E. *Rumble Fish.* New York: Delacorte, 1975. Chapter 11.

Hurlimann, Ruth. *The Cat and Mouse Who Shared a House.* Trans. from the German by Anthea Bell. New York: Walck, 1973. Chapter 3.

Iterson, S.R. van. *Pulga.* Trans. from the Dutch by Alexander and Alison Gode. New York: Morrow, 1971. Chapter 3.

Jansson, Tove. *Comet In Moominland.* New York: Henry Z. Walck, 1959. Chapter 13.

Jansson, Tove. *Exploits of Moominpappa.* New York: Henry Z. Walck, 1966. Chapter 13.

Jansson, Tove. *Finn Family Moomintroll.* New York: Henry Z. Walck, 1951. Chapter 13.

Jansson, Tove. *Moominland Midwinter.* Trans. by Thomas Warburton. New York: Henry Z. Walck, 1962. Chapter 13.

Jansson, Tove. *Moominpappa at Sea.* Trans. by Kingsley Hart. New York: Avon, 1977. Chapter 13.

Jansson, Tove. *Moominsummer Madness.* New York: Henry Z. Walck, 1961. Chapter 13.

Jansson, Tove. *Moominvalley in November.* New York: Avon, 1972. Chapter 13.

Jansson, Tove. *Tales from Moominvalley.* Trans. by Thomas Warburton. New

York: Henry Z. Walck, 1963. Chapter 13.

Kastner, Erich. *The Little Man.* Trans. from the German by James Kirkup. New York: Knopf, 1966. Chapter 3.

Keith, Donald. *Mutiny in the Machine* (Boy's Life Library). New York: Random House, 1963. Chapter 11.

Kingsley, Charles. *The Water Babies: A Fairy Tale for a Land Baby.* London: Macmillan, 1863. Chapter 8.

LeGuin, Ursula K. *The Farthest Shore.* New York: Atheneum, 1972. Chapter 5.

LeGuin, Ursula K. *The Left Hand of Darkness.* New York: Walker and Co., 1969. Chapter 5.

LeGuin, Ursula K. *The Tombs of Atuan.* New York: Atheneum, 1971. Chapter 5.

LeGuin, Ursula K. *A Wizard of Earthsea.* Berkeley, CA: Parnassus Press, 1968. Chapters 5 and 11.

Lewis, C.S. *The Horse and His Boy.* New York: Macmillan, 1954. Chapter 6.

Lewis, C.S. *The Last Battle.* London: The Bodley Head, 1958. Chapters 5 and 6.

Lewis, C.S. *The Lion, The Witch, and The Wardrobe.* New York: Macmillan, 1950. Chapters 1 and 6.

Lewis, C.S. *The Magician's Nephew.* New York: Macmillan, 1955. Chapter 6.

Lewis, C.S. *Prince Caspian.* New York: Macmillan, 1951. Chapter 6.

Lewis, C.S. *The Silver Chair.* New York: Macmillan, 1953. Chapter 6.

Lewis, C.S. *The Voyage of the Dawn Treader.* New York: Macmillan, 1952. Chapter 6.

Linevski, A. *An Old Tale Carved Out of Stone.* Trans. from the Russian by Maria Polushkin. New York: Crown, 1973. Chapter 3.

MacDonald, Betty. *Mrs. Piggle-Wiggle's Magic.* Philadelphia: Lippincott, 1974. Originally published, 1949. Capter 11.

MacDonald, George. *At the Back of the North Wind.* Elgin, IL: Cook, 1979 (1st ed. 1871). Chapter 8.

MacDonald, George. *Lilith.* Grand Rapids: Eerdsman, 1981 (1st ed. 1895). Chapter 8.

MacDonald, George. *The Princess and the Curdie*. New York: Penguin Books, 1966. Chapter 8.

MacDonald, George. *The Princess and the Goblin*. New York: Penguin Books, 1964. Chapter 8.

MacDonald, George. *The Wise Woman*. New York: Garland, 1976 (1st ed. 1882). Chapter 8.

MacLennan, Phyllis. *Turned Loose on Irdra*. New York: Doubleday, 1970. Chapter 11.

Marshall, James Vance. *A Walk to the Hills of the Dreamtime*. New York: William Morrow and Company, 1970. Chapter 9.

Marshall, James Vance. *Walkabout*. New York: Doubleday and Company, 1961. Chapter 9.

Molesworth, Mary Louisa. *The Tapestry Room*. London: Macmillan, 1879. Chapter 8.

Mountford, Charles P. *The Dawn of Time: Australian Aboriginal Myths*. Paintings by Ainslie Roberts. New York: Taplinger, 1969. Chapter 9.

Mountford, Charles P. *The First Sunrise: Australian Aboriginal Myths*. Paintings by Ainslie Roberts. New York: Taplinger, 1972. Chapter 9.

Mulock, Dinah. *The Little Lame Prince*. Garden City: Doubleday, 1956 (1st ed. 1874). Chapter 8.

Murphy, Shirley Rousseau. *The Castle of Hape*. New York: Atheneum, 1980. Chapter 5.

Murphy, Shirley Rousseau. *The Ring of Fire*. New York: Atheneum, 1977. Chapter 5.

Nichols, Ruth. *The Song of the Pearl*. New York: Atheneum, 1976. Chapter 5.

Nostlinger, Christine. *Konrad*. Trans. from the German by Anthea Bell. New York: Franklin Watts, 1977. Chapter 3.

Ottley, Reginald. *Boy Alone*. New York: Harcourt, Brace and World, 1965. Chapter 9.

Ottley, Reginald. *Rain Comes to Yamboorah*. New York: Harcourt, Brace and World, 1967. Chapter 9.

Phipson, Joan. *The Way Home*. New York: Atheneum, 1973. Chapter 9.

Poignant, Axel. *Piccaninny Walkabout: A Story of Two Aboriginal Children*.

Sussex: Angus and Robertson, 1957. Chapter 9.

Raskin, Ellen. *The Mysterious Disappearance of Leon (I Mean Noel)*. New York: Dutton, 1971. Chapter 11.

Renvoize, Jean. *A Wild Thing*. Boston: Little, Brown and Co., 1971. Chapter 10.

Richter, Hans Peter. *Friedrich*. Trans. from the German by Edite Kroll. New York: Holt, Rinehart and Winston, 1970. Chapter 3.

Salinger, J.D. *The Catcher in the Rye*. Boston: Little, Brown and Co., 1951. Chapter 2.

Selden, George. *Cricket in Times Square*. New York: Farrar, Straus, and Giroux, 1960. Chapter 11.

Selden, George. *Harry Cat's Pet Puppy*. New York: Farrar, Straus, and Giroux, 1974. Chapter 11.

Steiner, Jorg. *Rabbit Island*. Trans. from the German by Ann Conrad Lammers. Pictures by Jorg Muller. New York: Harcourt Brace Jovanovich, 1978. Chapter 3.

Tolkien, J.R.R. *The Fellowship of the Ring*. Boston: Houghton Mifflin, 1967. Chapter 11.

Tolkien, J.R.R. *The Hobbit*. Boston: Houghton Mifflin, 1966. Chapters 5 and 11.

Tolkien, J.R.R. *The Return of the King*. Boston: Houghton Mifflin, 1965. Chapter 5.

Travers, P.L. *Mary Poppins*. New York: Harcourt Brace, 1962. Chapter 11.

White, T.H. "The Sword in the Stone," *The Once and Future King*. New York: Putnam's Sons, 1958. Chapter 11.

Williams, Jay. *Danny Dunn and the Smallifying Machine*. New York: McGraw-Hill, 1969. Chapter 11.

Wilson, Barbara Ker, Editor. *Australian Kaleidoscope*. Sidney: Collins, 1968. Chapter 9.

Wrightson, Patricia. *The Ice Is Coming*. New York: Atheneum, 1977. Chapter 12.

Wrightson, Patricia. *The Nargun and the Stars*. New York: Atheneum, 1974. Chapter 12.

Wrightson, Patricia. *An Older Kind of Magic*. New York: Harcourt, Brace,

Jovanovich, 1972. Chapter 9.

Zei, Alki. *Petros' War*. Trans. from the Greek by Edward Fenton. New York: Dutton, 1972. Chapter 3.

Zei, Alki. *The Sound of the Dragon's Feet*. Trans. from the Greek by Edward Fenton. New York: Dutton, 1979. Chapter 3.

Zei, Alki. *Wildcat Under Glass*. Trans. from the Greek by Edward Fenton. New York: Holt, Rinehart and Winston, 1968. Chapter 3.

INDEX

154

CONTRIBUTORS

Ann Donovan is on the faculty of Central Washington University where she is Curriculum Librarian. Formerly a teacher and school librarian, her current research concerns changes in children's reading patterns. She holds a BA in Education, an MLS, and is completing an MA in English with a critical thesis on Angus Wilson.

Margaret P. Esmonde died shortly after she completed her essay. Her husband has written to say that this was her finest work. Its sensitivity suggests she created the essay as a way of dealing with her own situation at that time.

Grace R.W. Hall completed all but her dissertation for a doctorate in physics at Boston University and holds a Master's degree in English from Simmons College. She was a Teaching Fellow for three years at Boston University and has taught part-time at Simmons College, Eastern Nazarene College, and Northeastern University. With her scientific studies in astronomy, chemistry and physics she brings a unique insight to the study of literature and one buttressed by an exceptionally extensive knowledge of Biblical literature.

Abigail Ann Hamblen earned her MA at the University of Nebraska and has also studied at Boston University and Radcliffe. For some years she has studied and written in the field of American literature. Her articles and stories have appeared in such journals as *The Georgia Review, The University Review* (Kansas City), *Western Humanities Review, St. Croix Review, Yankee, DownEast,* and *The Humanist.* In addition she is the author of *The New England Art of Mary E. Wilkins Freeman* (Green Knight Press) and *Ruth Suckow* (Western Writers Series). She has also written two novels for young girls: *Agatha On Stage* and *Magic Summer.* Currently she is completing a study of William March, the Alabama writer, and of Tillie Olsen, well-known feminist and author.

Nancy Huse teaches Children's Literature and Adolescent Literature at Augustana College, Rock Island, Illinois. Her previous publications include *John Hersey and James Agee: A Reference Guide* (G.K. Hall, 1978) and articles on the teaching of English in *Arizona English Bulletin and English Quarterly.* Currently in progress is a book on the work of John Hersey (Whitson Press). Future projects in the study of children's literature will include examination of criteria used in evaluating children's books in Sweden.

Marilyn Jurich is an Assistant Professor in English at Suffolk University, Boston, Massachusetts. She teaches courses in Verse Drama, Law and Literature, Fantasy

157

and Folklore, Writing for Children, and Children's Literature. Her interest in folklore is reflected in articles published in *Children's Literature, The Lion and the Unicorn,* and other journals. She has presented papers at MLA and other professional meetings and is a published poet.

Lois Kuznets, Associate Professor of English, San Diego State University, has been teaching and writing about children's literature since 1975. Her interest is centered on the novel for the child of middle years and her analyses focus on the complex relations between form and content in these works.

Millicent Lenz, Associate Professor of Library Science, Memphis State University, did doctoral study in Old English and has worked as both an English teacher and a librarian. She is co-editor of *Young Adult Literature: Background and Criticism* (American Library Association, 1980). Her specialties in children's literature include fantasy, poetry, and traditional literature.

Rebecca Lukens, Associate Professor of English, Miami University, Oxford, Ohio, is author of *A Critical Handbook of Children's Literature* (Scott, Foresman, 1976; second edition, 1982), co-editor of *Woman: An Affirmation,* a multi-genre anthology of literature (D.C. Heath, 1979), and past-president, 1981-82, of the Children's Literature Association.

Joe Milner teaches courses in Children's Literature and Adolescent Literature at Wake Forest University where he serves as Chairman of the Department of Education. He is a member of the Board of Directors of NCTE, a past Coordinator of Curriculum for North Carolina's Governor School, Editor of the North Carolina English Teacher, and Director of the North Carolina Writing Project. He has contributed to *ALAN Review, English Journal, English Education, Kappan, Children's Literature, Wallace Stevens Journal,* and other scholarly journals directed to pedagogical and critical concerns.

Lucy Milner has been engaged in the teaching of literature as a high school English teacher, an editor, and a writer. Her recent research has been on the effect of teaching theories of literary criticism to gifted high school English students. She holds a BA in Philosophy and an MAEd in English Education.

Anita Moss, Assistant Professor of English, teaches Children's Literature at the University of North Carolina at Charlotte. She has taught experimental classes in literature and writing in elementary school and conducted numerous workshops for public school teachers. Currently, she is a member of the Awards Committee of the Children's Literature Association, a member of the Board of Directors of the Children's Literature Association, and a member of the executive board of the Division on Children's Literature, Modern Language Association. She has published articles and review essays in such periodicals as *South Atlantic Bulletin, Children's Literature Association Quarterly, Mythlore, Phaedrus,* and *Children's Literature.*

Joan Nist's study includes a research grant to the International Youth Library, Munich, and participation in Loughborough Conferences in the U.S., Stirling, and Dublin. Recipient of a Read Scholarship to the USSR, Nist developed multicultural interests during residence in Hawaii and Brasil.

Bruce Vogel says of himself that he was a theatre bum until age 30. In 1962 he accepted a position as a library assistant in a small public library with the understanding that he was to re-establish the library's dormant puppetry program. Subsequently he enrolled in library school and since 1968 has worked as a children's librarian. Since 1974 he has been Coordinator of Children's Services for the Alameda County Public Library.

Milner, Joseph O'Beirne

Webs and wardrobes: humanist and religious world views in children's literature